11th Edition

Divorce & Money

How to Make the Best Financial Decisions During Divorce

Attorney Violet Woodhouse, CFLS, CFP™
with Matthew J Perry

This one's for Karen
and Karen alone

Acknowledgments

Writing has been described as a lonely business, and I suppose it is. But this book is not mine alone, nor is it only from me. Along the way I have had such support, encouragement, and outright help in the writing of *Wit & Wisdom of the Great Outdoors* as to be immeasurable. I must gratefully acknowledge and thank with all my heart my mother and father. My brothers and sisters, too numerous to mention. The Amann family who helped me along the way. Marge and Joe Pascale. The editors and station managers who liked my work enough to share it with their readers and listeners and those readers and listeners who made the lonely hours worth the effort. My students, colleagues, and friends who have done likewise. Jim Stahl, Bob Klaznich, Jim Pellman, and especially Jeff Sonstegard who so often provided illustrations for my work, usually at a moment's notice. Lorne Persons, Ted Garceau, Beaver Zawacki, Stan Skelton, Mark Anderson, and Pat Abrahamzon. Jack Pezze who first tried to make sense out of this nonsense. Joyce Kowalik who learned to read my handwriting and translate it through a typewriter. Susan Gustafson and the folks at Pfeifer-Hamilton who shared a vision and made it into a reality. Karen and Katie Wilber without whom there'd be no Jerry Wilber. And Jim Weinandt without whom there'd be no *Wit & Wisdom of the Great Outdoors.* Or of anyplace else.

Introduction

Are you busy? Got a minute? I thought we might go outside. Into the great outdoors. We might hear a loon's call or the yip-yipping of lonely old coyotes. We might ride on a gentle roll of water, or hike into the pines, or go into a winter's night with the moon shining on our backs like a pack. We might stumble onto a rainbow or try for a falling star. We might find a goose or a trout. We might trail a dream of a twelve-pointer, though we'll settle for a dream of a less-pointer. We'll go find the smell of woodsmoke in quiet places. We'll find something, that's for sure.

This book is not meant to be an almanac (exactly) nor a calendar (precisely) nor a journal (specifically). But come along anyway. Come along with us on this too long, too short trail of life, one day at a time, one page at a turn, for a year or so. Come fish with us, hunt with us, build a snowman, smell the smoke of campfires and wildflowers. Smile with us. Frown, if that's your disposition.

And, oh yes, bring a pencil. Because *Wit & Wisdom of the Great Outdoors* is not finished. It still needs you—to log your comments about the great out-of-doors, to record the comings and goings, the clouds and the shining sun, the weather or lack of it, the good luck and the bad. A good idea will do. And a good joke. So, please make your own notes.

Then, if our trails should cross and you have the book in your pack and you'd like to share those notes, I'd consider it an honor to read what you've written. That would be only fair.

January

January

And so we've come around for another go at it. This is January, the month of the Moon of the Great Spirit, the month of the Wolf Moon. And as January settles in, curls about itself, and tweaks our noses with melancholy days and long nights, the anglers look to their tackle, hunters to their guns, campers to their gear; and once again we settle our bones onto toboggans for mad, delirious rides into the new year.

1 It's January already. Time to go fishing in the Caribbean. Time to go camping in Southern California. Time to win the lottery. Time to face reality.

So, I guess it's time to face the New Year. Time to thank our lucky stars. Time to take down the Christmas tree and time to stick it in a snow bank. Time to fill it with food for the birds—seeds and leftover fruitcakes. Poor birds. Time to shovel snow. Time to clean the guns again. Time to exchange those Christmas neckties for fishing tackle. Time to take the kids ice fishing.

Time to read a good book. Time to study seed catalogs. Time to eat the deer liver. Time to walk the dog. Time to clean the chimney. Time to put a cold-weather kit in the trunk. Time to split some kindling. Time to check the antifreeze. Time to fix the snowblower. Time to go skiing with the kids and grandma. Time to shovel snow again. Time to fill the bird feeder.

Tax time coming! Coming time to pay the piper. Time to take a nap.

Notes

2 Gladys, my ice-fishing neighbor, is forced to hole up. The flu, she says, and I stay mum, because I know she celebrates the holidays pretty heavy with her fishing buddies.

Anyway, I go out alone, and to my surprise and semidismay, I find some guy, a stranger, already working the best northern-fishing spot in the lake. Ours. Naturally, I cozy up to him, the way we ice fishermen do, to admire the brace of four-pounders already on the ice. I ask him how he knows about this spot. Seems he got a map of our lake that shows exactly what the shoreline is like, what type of bottom lies where, the weed lines, sandbars, drop-offs, deep holes, and depth lines. With that piece of paper, the son-of-a-gun knows more about our lake than I do. With the map and his knowledge of northerns—oops, here comes another one—he sets up right along the edge of our drop-off, five feet down in ten feet of water, where the northerns cruise the edges.

I hurry back to tell Gladys of the interloper. She jumps out of bed, mixes herself a medicinal hot "lemonade," grabs her gear, and beats me out by 150 yards.

January is the time to tie flies, to reload shotgun shells, to plot springtime, ice-free adventures. Now crappies are firmly sandwiched between bitter layers of new ice and muddy lake bottoms, where snapping turtles lie buried in mass graves, breathing for the season through gill-like tissues just under the skin at the base of their tails. Hummingbirds whoop it up in Mexico, and badgers hibernate in tunnels below the frostline.

Notes

January

Figure this. We are actually closer to the sun now, by about two million miles, than we'll be in June. Deep snows have come to purify the earth, and our own waters become clean once more beneath blankets of ice. Great horned owls with no respect for the calendar get all heated up pretty soon with elaborate courtship rites and ghoulish in-the-night howls and shrieks.

3 Bannock has been the bread of travelers since people first hit the trail—improving campside suppers, shoreline lunches, and foul dispositions. But if it's been a while since you've tried the stuff, or you never really got into the bannock habit, let's take care of that right now. (Okay, so it's January; we can do this on the fireplace. And if this was the real thing, we would've made it in advance and toted it in plastic bags, where it'll keep for weeks.)

I'm giving you a one-person recipe, so multiply accordingly. Put together one cup flour, one teaspoon baking powder, one-half teaspoon salt and two tablespoons powdered milk. At mealtime, grease a skillet and warm it on the fire (place). Add enough cold water to the mixture (in the plastic bag) to form a soft dough. Mold it into inch-thick cakes and fry until a crust forms. Then turn it (like a pancake) and drop the skillet at a steep angle before the fire a few minutes to bake. Butter and eat it. You might want to open the patio doors for an outdoorsy effect.

Or is that too much?

Notes

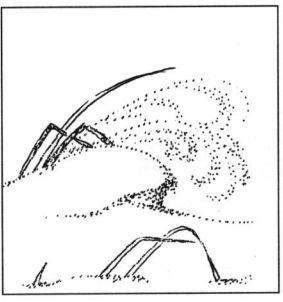

4 Gladys says that everybody who has ever fished for northerns in the summer and caught some, has at one time or another done so with a red and white spoon. And that anybody who's done likewise in the winter did it with smelt. She figures everybody but me knew about using the two together when the ice gets real thick and the fish don't want to go to the bother of biting. Then she shows me how to do it without mangling the minnow the way I usually do. Just in case you didn't know that secret either, here's how she does it. She clips a medium-sized red and white spoon to her leader and lays a semithawed smelt crosswise on two of the hooks and slips a rubber band around the hooks and the smelt without tearing it one bit. Then she drops the thing into one of my holes, down about seven feet, and jigs every once in a great while. Sure enough, after around twenty minutes, the line starts moving out and then stops. When it starts moving again, she sets the hook hard and pulls up a nice northern. Naturally, she won't give me my hole back.

Upsik, the Eskimos call it, this snow that's picked up and carried by the muttering winds of January. White-tailed deer begin to shed their antlers now. Frogs lie buried at the bottoms of lakes and ponds. Mink and otters, under a brittle Big Dipper, are afoot tonight in never-ceasing supper safaris.

Notes

January

Goshawks hunt for unsuspecting suppers. Newts are alive and well under the ice. Efts—newts that lose their gills and grow lungs—sleep snugly under snow-covered logs and leaves. Worry-free woodchucks (we call them groundhogs) lie in deep, deep sleep, their temperatures only slightly higher than that of their frozen bedrooms, their breathing and pulse nearly suspended.

5 Anglers, skiers, tobogganers, skaters, mushers, and snowman-makers dress in layers to guard their outsides from snow and cold. And to keep their insides heated, these outdoor doers eat right, and they eat often—on the trail if they can, because everything tastes better on the trail. To do this, in the warm cocoons of their kitchens they might take two cups (for four patties) of supper's leftover baked fish and combine it with two eggs, two tablespoons (at least) of chopped onions, one-quarter cup milk or water, and salt and pepper. They goop all this together and add enough cracker crumbs to create a cohesive thickness that'll form into patties and hold together. They half-fry four strips of bacon, take it out, and brown the patties on both sides in the grease. They loop a piece of bacon around each, wrap the units individually in aluminum foil, and freeze.

Sometime later, during a break in some outside action, they pull the stuff out of a pack, nest it in a half-dozen glowing coals till it's steaming hot, tuck it in a bun, sit back, open their mouths, close their eyes, and thank the Lord for the good, simple things in life.

Notes

6 Programmed to automatically regulate warmth for survival, our bodies, when cold, adjust heat production and circulation to maintain life.

When the core temperature drops, the brain and central nervous systems receive the highest priority. To keep them warm, the body shuts off circulation, to some extent at least, to the extremities.

Toes, being farthest from the core and being given no vote in the matter, are the first to feel the reduced flow of warming blood and to suffer.

"When your feet are cold," our grandmothers always told us, "put your cap on."

Grandma, as usual, knew what she was talking about.

Our head, for one thing, is full of holes (something else Grandma told us more than once), and making it a principal point of heat loss. So it figures that when these holes are properly capped, the heat stays corralled in the body, where it'll do some good.

Winter campers wear caps while sleeping for the same obvious reason.

Beneath the lifeless frosting of ice, lakes and ponds teem with life. Here at the bottom, midges, mayflies, and dragonflies spend the winter as eggs or young-sters. Meanwhile, evening grosbeaks visit sunflower-seeded feeders. Evening light begins to lengthen ever so slightly, and these days end with a hint of dusk just before the curtain of night slams down.

Notes

January

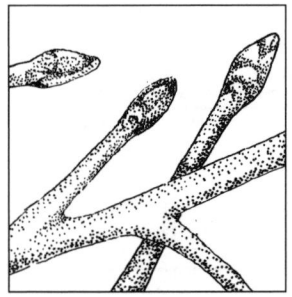

As we welcome sleep at day's end, so do the trees around us welcome wintry days of rest. Their leaves fallen, their sap drained to the cellar, they nap, setting tightly their buds, waiting patiently, as only trees can wait, for their days in the sun. River otters make long snow slides, just like the neighborhood kids, in celebrations of winter. And billions of frozen-solid mosquitoes lie beneath the snow.

7 The weasel is a traveler who does most of its hunting at night. It has good eyesight, a keen sense of smell, and a curiosity that causes it to investigate anything and everything.

It knows no fear and refuses to admit that anything could possibly harm it—and with the exception of an occasional owl, it's probably right.

Weighing only a few ounces, this little bundle of fury takes on animals many, many times its own size, usually coming out the winner.

With a shrill scream of rage that throws an opponent off guard, the weasel strikes like a snake; and every time it strikes, fur or feathers fly. Scared half out of its wits by such buzz-saw tactics, the opponent forgets about being brave and remembers an important appointment far, far away.

Fortunately for human or beast who ventures out-of-doors, this critter is small. If it were the size, say, of a rabbit or raccoon, I for one would be content to throw another log on the fire and take up knitting.

Notes

8 Snow's the boss. And every form of life that lives within her realm bows to the pressure of her power as she makes her way into winter and settles in for the long haul.

Robins and ducks and hummingbirds flee when snow comes rattling at their doors, rather than suffer her company. Frogs and snakes and bears hide in hibernation. Chickadees and deer and grouse, given no choice, make do, living from day to hungry day, changing their diets, until the snow lifts a cold finger to give them temporary respite. Weasels and snowshoe hares and ptarmigan change colors at her coming, escaping detection in the whiteness of her cloak. Cottontails climb upon her coattails to reach wintry buds of sapling trees. Meadow voles and insects hide under her blankets. From red fox and pheasants she hides suppers. In icy snares she traps deer—the very old and the very young. Trees and bushes in her way, she knocks down.

Not even the two-legged in snow's kingdom are spared her influence. To leave their warm nests they must wrap themselves in heavy cocoons, and she snags as many as she can as they rush about in four-wheeled frenzy.

It's hard to believe, but the "whi-whi-whi" of white-breasted nuthatches and the clear "fee-bee" of chickadees are actually songs of spring. Usually chipmunks are slugabeds in winter, but if January takes a break and briefly lets March in for a spell, they might sneak out for a quick peek. And each track in the snow has a story of its own to tell—some good and some not so.

Notes

January

Reptiles, their thin bodies near freezing, lie stiff and unmoving in ant hills and hollow logs and on lake bottoms. Sundogs, rainbowlike bright spots on either side of a reluctantly rising, coldly glowing sun, are born from sunlight shining through ice crystals in the air. Lynx hunt for snowshoe hares, beating us out of hasenpfeffer suppers. Chickadees come to the feeder like so many windblown leaves.

9 How often we rush to and fro, skitter hither and yon, plotting and planning and praying for happiness, expecting it to come magically, wrapped and beribboned—not realizing, or not remembering, that happiness cannot be found. It must be created, homemade if you will, from the bits and pieces, the stuff and nonsense of each day's life and living.

Poets and folks who love the out-of-doors are luckier than most, I think. For us life is a huge reservoir, a smorgasbord of such bits and pieces, stuff and nonsense, to be tasted, touched, felt, seen. Savored. A mayfly hatch can send us a-singing. An east wind holds out a promise. A snowflake is a lone thing of beauty and a raindrop reflects the world. Streams talk to us. So do geese V-ing against a sunset. Trout, shining in the morning light, are rainbows of rejoicing. Redwing blackbirds on reedy thrones sing to us alone. To each of us, each new season unfolds with promise, and we hang on to dreams with a vengeance. And, once in a while, each of us, poet and you and me, has a natural tendency to exaggerate just a touch, if you know what I mean.

Notes

10 My Uncle Jake runs out of things to do, what with the lakes frozen over and all. (He doesn't like ice fishing. Hard to believe.) So he comes over here to bug me.

The other day he's reminding me one more time of the fish I lost last summer because my drag wasn't set right. He says real fishermen don't go by a it-feels-right guess when they're setting the drag, but set the tension at a level of one-quarter to one-third of the line's breaking point. Of course he demonstrated.

Now, I share my den with the furnace and the hot water heater, so he hands me my rod and reel, attaches a de-liar to the line, heads out the door, and hooks it to the washing machine a dozen feet away. I have ten-pound test on. He yells at me to start reeling. When the de-liar reads about three pounds, he yells again to set the drag, and I do. "There," he says, "that oughta do it."

And because he can't help himself, he reminds me for the fiftieth time that only a dunderhead fiddles with his drag at the same time he's fighting a fish.

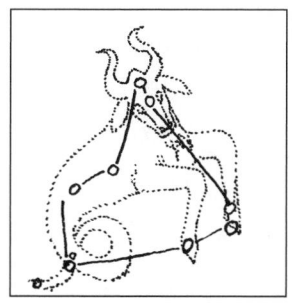

Birds and animals, reptiles and people born these days are born under Capricorn. You'd have to be standing in the Tropic of that name to see the sun shining directly overhead at noon. Raccoons, if the weather's okay, might venture for a short time from their dens of tree cavities or abandoned woodchuck or skunk holes for a whiff of winter. Shrews tunnel snugly in the grass and leaves under the snow.

Notes

January

Snowfleas, looking like so much spilled pepper, dot snowbanks. Ruffed grouse fly headlong into those same snowbanks to warmly spend the night, hidden from foxes and owls, and the bitter cold. Fox squirrels might visit feeders, and flying squirrels leave "sitzmarks," landing spots, in the snow where they set themselves down.

11 It is difficult to believe that a faithful old dog that romps with the kids, or a coiffed and pampered poodle that keeps grandma company, has another side to its character. In domesticating the wild critters that have become our pets and pals, we haven't eliminated their hunting instincts. Under the right circumstances, Spot, Fido, and Rex, those slipper-carrying, hearth-napping companions, become some of the most serious of all predators of wildlife—especially deer.

Dogs—large and small, terrier and spaniel, Lassie and Toto—when left to themselves, outside, for any length of time, chase deer. They don't eat what they kill. They do it for the fun of it—especially in the deep-snow conditions of late winter and early spring, when dogs can travel atop the snow crust and deer cannot. Pregnant does and fawns make particularly easy prey. It is an unnecessary loss. The situation is not the dog's fault, but rather that of an unknowing or uncaring owner who has never come across a hamstrung deer starving, freezing, or bleeding to death while Rover, back home, snoozes before the fireplace.

Notes

12 Though for most of us the snow has piled up to here, and the temperatures have plummeted down to there, somewhere to the south the bluebirds are beginning to get the itch to move back home. That means that we, as a lot of good folks do, ought to make sure they have homes to come back home to.

Their old homes—hollow trees and wooden fence posts—have about all disappeared, and with them the bluebirds. Indeed, it's been so long since some of us have seen one, we've wondered whether such animals still exist.

Well, they do. And some good folks throughout the country are helping them in their fight for a comeback. These good folks build and maintain bluebird houses with plans they get at libraries, conservation agencies, and bluebird restoration agencies located in states throughout the nation.

For about half a dozen dollars and that many minutes of their time, these good folks are giving us back the bluebird—us and our kids and our grandkids—and good folks like us ought to be lending a hand—starting now.

Caddis fly larvae, in tube-shaped cases of tiny pebbles, ride out January glued to bottom stones of streams near water striders buried in mud. Mink, like otters and kids, make snow slides. Gangs of short-eared owls spend their free time rousting near open fields in pines and balsams if they can. Whining snow creaks and complains underfoot as the gang tromps and stomps from school buses to warm kitchens.

Notes

January

That's probably Mercury lying low in the eastern sky just before sunrise. Chickadees, nuthatches and blue jays are fond of suet in the bird feeders, and woodpeckers insist on it. Red crossbills feed on spruce seeds. Sperm whales migrate northward off the California and New England coasts. Whitetails continue to shed antlers; and in the brittle night, great horned owls sail on broad, silent wings, as quiet as the cold.

13 Down the road lives a kid you have to admire. He's the kind of kid who takes his hunting and fishing pretty serious, and he doesn't like to waste one iota of anything he catches or shoots. And he had a problem. It seems even he couldn't find a decent thing to do with those small hides of squirrels and rabbits. So he got to studying, and in an old magazine he came on a recipe for tanning the hides with the hair firmly in place and the pelt as soft as a baby's cheek.

He mixes a gallon of soft water, one ounce of sulfuric acid and a quart of salt and soaks the clean hides in it for three days. Then he wrings them dry and soaks them overnight in a bucket of water and one-half cup of sodium carbonate. Then he wrings and rubs and pulls and stretches them again until they're dry again. And that's it (unless they dry hard, in which case he repeats the operation). The kid did a bunch of hides and conned his ma into making a vest out of them. And he's so proud of it he wants to wear it to the prom.

Though his mom and his girlfriend are trying to talk him out of it.

Notes

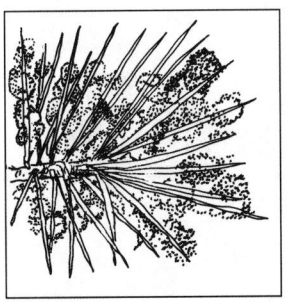

14 Winter camping holds many delights. Always has; always will. But nothing drains the entertainment from back country nights more completely than a lousy night's sleep. And if the tent's good and the sleeping bag suited to conditions, nothing is more unnecessary. For getting as snug as a bug in a sleeping bag is as simple as doing a few sit-ups and push-ups (though not enough to work up a sweat) before wriggling into the sack.

And pulling a wool cap over the head and clean, dry socks over the other end (but never wearing a full set of clothes). And eating a steaming plateful of chow before putting the lanterns out (or a chocolate bar, which isn't as much fun). And once you're all zipped up and in, doing some isometric exercises (pushing one hand hard against the other and foot against foot).

And, of course, if you've got a bag that zips onto another one and someone in it to snuggle up with, you're the warmest, wisest, luckiest camper of all. But, then, you knew that.

According to the Inuit, that feathery snow clinging to the trees and mailboxes and fence posts, creating the stuff of Christmas and postcards, is qali. Star-nosed moles rest and forage in snow-covered tiny mountain molehills; and moose, with yard-long legs, move in small groups to yarding areas of heavy cover. The cold winter's moon hurries the sun to bed.

Notes

_____

_____

_____

_____

_____

_____

_____

January

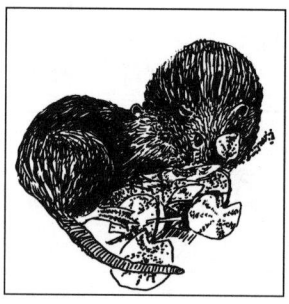

Muskrats venture out of cozy huts to feed on root stocks, like cattails below the freeze line. If they can't, if it's a hard-frost winter, for supper they must settle for the cattail insulation of their homes. Because they stay green all year, evergreen trees continue to make food on sunny days, though I doubt if it's much.

15 Let's face it. All too often when we're ice fishing for crappies or blue gills, we catch the little bitty ones that probably should not be released even if we could get them back down the hole. They're hardly worth filleting, yet wasting them is out of the question. So we eat them as Scandinavian fish cakes.

We put one cup milk, one egg, two tablespoons potato flour (or dehydrated flakes), one teaspoon salt, one-quarter teaspoon nutmeg, and one tablespoon minced onion in a blender and blend well. Then we scrape the meat off the vertebrae of these small fish, add one cup to the mixture, and blend it into a smooth mashed potato consistency. We shape this batter into silver-dollar-sized cakes about one-half inch thick or into balls about one inch in diameter and fry them in butter or shortening until brown, serving hot.

These cakes refrigerate well and can be easily reheated. The kids in our house like them because they're bite-sized and they taste great. Their mother likes them because they have no bones to worry about. And their dad likes them because they use up those little fish, which are about all he's catching these days.

Notes

16 For the many people whose idea of having a good time includes getting from here to there on snowmobiles, putting away tents in the wintertime can be a thing of the past, for their machines can take them and their gear wherever they'd like to go (except downtown New York City and the French Riviera, which is okay because snowmobiles don't like those places anyway).

Summertime camping gear, except for maybe sleeping bags, serves well on the snowbound trail, which makes this such an economical way to go for a couple of pals, a couple of couples, or a couple of families.

Kids and extra gear can always be carried in the sleds towed so easily by snowmobiles.

This truly is an ideal way to camp—stopping occasionally to fish, ducking into the timber to set up camp, building small cooking fires that can later be enlarged into social-council blazes, taking a last look at the glittering heavens, crawling into the tent and then a soft sleeping bag, and sleeping the sleep of the blessed.

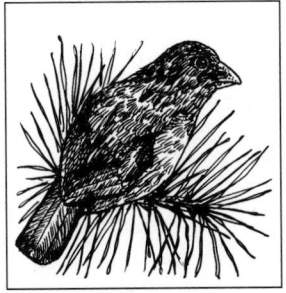

Rosy-breasted pine grosbeaks pipe their clear, rolling whistles from the upper limbs of lifeless trees. From the first day of winter, that oh-so-short day, we've gained about twenty-four minutes of daylight so far, at around two whole minutes a day. Against the snow, blue jays have never looked so blue, pines never so green, and ravens never so black.

Notes

January

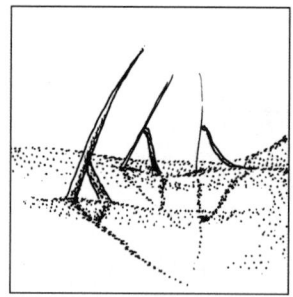

Golden grassy stems poke holes through pearly white, seemingly soft snows of intricate, ever-changing patterns. Ground squirrels sleep, curled in tight little balls in their dens. Their normal heart rate of 350 beats per minute drops to but 5. Their breathing slows from 50 breaths a minute to 4. Living off fat stored last fall, raccoons might awaken from long naps now to snack on a mouse or a squirrel's cache of acorns.

17 Animal-rights activists number in the millions. Many hold that animals, domestic and wild, have certain rights, one of which is a right to life—a life that cannot be taken.

These are not necessarily wild-eyed fanatics, but an articulate, well-financed, well-orchestrated movement with a membership that is growing. Obviously against hunting, these activists would eventually prevent us from owning leather wallets and would have us holding up our pants with something other than leather belts. T-bone steaks would be out of the question.

This vigorous, crusading lot wins battles daily. One battle they have apparently won is the battle against trappers, whom they have convincingly portrayed as sadistic monsters deriving pleasure from torturing innocent teddy-bear-like critters. If those of us who hunt, fish, enjoy a salami sandwich now and then, and mostly keep our pants up, sit idly by while our trapping brothers and sisters take the heat on this one in this round, we ought to apologize to them for it and prepare to stand in line for our turn.

Notes

18 It is not so important, I think, to catch fish, to actually haul them aboard, in the daisy days of spring, in the rosy days of summer, or even in the ragweed days of autumn. Such days have blessings of their own, and the catching of fish is merely the icing on the joy of being up and about and close enough to water to wet a line.

But in the bitter, dark days of winter, when the wind gouges and the cold slashes, when teeth chatter and toes ache and fingers become Popsicle-frozen, then we want to catch something. Fry it. And eat it. Just rewards for our courage and stamina. A "can't (or at least, can't almost never) miss" method of finding crappies under the ice starts with understanding, for one thing, that they are usually suspended, generally off rocky bars, humps, and points that drop steeply into deeper water. The depth of this suspension depends on a number of factors, and some experimentation is called for. Often when anglers are crappie fishing side by side and only one is catching anything, that one has found the correct depth. The other is probably fishing above or below the suspended fish and should watch the successful one closely.

Woodpeckers drum to establish territories and attract goodlooking mates. American goldfinches begin to show bright yellow feathers—springtime stuff, and in the middle of January. The once-brown coat of weasels is now white, blending in perfectly with the snow. Indeed, if it weren't for their shadows, we might not see them at all. Pileated woodpeckers peck holes in trees for dinners of carpenter ants.

Notes

January

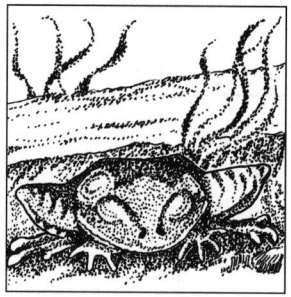

Nearly frozen solid, wood frogs lie under snow-covered dead leaves, awaiting the warm thawing days of spring. Salamanders hibernate in decaying roots of trees. Red squirrels chew on pinecones, mushrooms, and nuts, which they gathered and hid last fall, often following tunnels they dug in the snow. Wind, the voice of winter, bickers with rattling leaves on oaks. Up in the trees, sluggish porcupines feast on the sweet inner bark of maples.

19 Not so long ago, the prairie chicken supplied the greatest upland shooting ever known to hunters. There was nothing to compare with it anywhere. They were so abundant that they seemed without limit. The boom, boom, boom of their mating dances echoed the drumming of the Plains Indian and the beating hooves of a million buffalo.

Market hunters often killed as many as fifty to seventy-five per hunter, every day; thousands were trapped, though it was the plow that finally did them in.

Civilization has given us much to be grateful for, but I'd rather have the wide, unbroken prairies back and the bird that went with them. The prairie chicken—also called square-tail, yellowlegs, prairie hen, prairie grouse, and pinnated grouse—is much like, and sometimes mistaken for, the sharptail grouse. Prairie chickens today are found in limited numbers in a dozen or so states, half of which offer some shooting.

Prairie chickens contributed a tremendous chapter to American sporting life and history. I'm sorry I missed it.

Notes

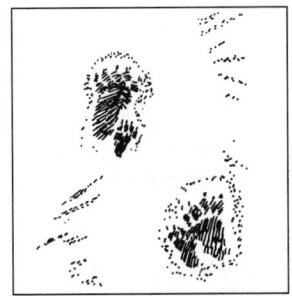

20 By the very nature of our activities, we outdoors-people often find ourselves in unexpected, thought-provoking situations. As such, our very success or failure often depends upon our ability to be flexible, to improvise, to make do.

For instance: by design, the basic function of the basic handkerchief is to blow noses. For most folks, it has no other uses. Not so, however, for folks who spend a lot of time outdoors. Your hanky may well be your most important piece of equipment. You might use it as a potholder when removing boiling beans from roaring fires. You might use it as a washcloth or towel. You might tie it, cowboy fashion, around your neck to keep the sun off it, or around your nose, outlawlike, to keep dust out of that, or around your forehead as a sweatband. You can soak it with bug dope and fasten it to your collar. You might use it as a tie for a splint on a broken arm, as a sling to keep that arm in place, as a cover for cuts and sores, or as a cushion between blister and toe. You can shore up a broken paddle with the hanky or plug up a mosquito hole in your tent, or use it as a patch on the seat of your pants.

Weather doesn't matter too much to porcupines. In howling blizzards or twenty-below-zero temperatures, they poke along, food hunting, leaving their tracks as signs of solitary shopping sprees. And on all but the coldest days, fishers hunt snowshoe rabbits, their favorite meals, leaving, if they're rushed, paired tracks up to sixteen feet apart.

Notes

January

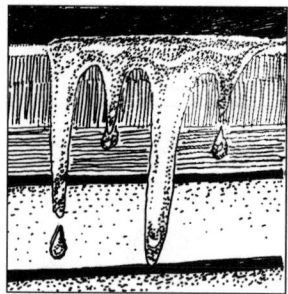

January thaws beckon to our cabin-fevered melancholy. But we know. We can wait. Ursa Major, the Big Bear, slowly climbs the northern sky tonight, perhaps under the camouflage of clouds. Optimistic chickadees continue their two-noted "spring-soon" calls. Rabbits gnaw at the bark of saplings, unaware of the fox moving in, shadowlike, from the east and the stalking weasel coming in from the west.

21 He borrows my good knife once and has to use a sawing motion to cut the butter, so a friend of mine gives me a knife-sharpening stone for Christmas—an unkind cut, for now no longer can I hide my pointed lack of honing skills behind a lack of equipment. So I read. I study. And I come to the conclusion that cutting through the rigamarole of this knife-sharpening business takes a keen mind. For one thing, half the experts tell me to use oil on the stone, half say water, and half say the heck with using anything. I dunno. Most do agree, however, that I am to draw the blade toward me, as if I'm trying to cut a thin slice off the stone. I'm to do this with the blade at maybe a twenty-degree angle (let's see, up and down is ninety degrees, half that is forty-five degrees, and half of that isn't quite enough). One guy says to take five swipes on one side and five on the other, then four on the first and four on the second, then three and three, two and two, one and one, zero and zero. Now I think I've got it. But say, you're a sharp fellow, have you got a minute? My place. My stone. My knife. BYOB.

Notes

22 Keeping minnows alive has always posed a problem for fishing folks. In the summer they get too hot and die. In the winter they get too cold and die. What to do?

My neighbor, Gladys, summer or winter, uses a flat pint whiskey bottle to keep her minnows in fighting form. I've seen her carry a couple of dozen at one time—minnows, that is—without losing one. When she gets to the stream or lake she transfers the minnows from the bucket to the bottle.

She changes the water occasionally, but as she keeps moving and the jug keeps jiggling, she has no trouble keeping the little fish alive.

When she sits, she merely gives the bottle a vigorous shaking every once in a while.

The flat shape and small size of the bottle allow her to carry it in her hip pocket or creel in the summer and in her warm parka pocket in ice-fishing season.

In anticipation of the question of just how Gladys comes by so many empty whiskey bottles: well, that, we figure, is her business.

Great horned owls silently search the nighttime snows for rabbits and grouse, their noisy, plaintive, tremulous hooting marking the continuation of Saturday night carryings-on in the middle of the week. And though the sights and sounds and smells of winter lie hidden now beneath the snows of January, the chickadees and grosbeaks and blue jays are recharging the sluggish batteries of our souls.

Notes

January

Great snowy owls, pushed from the Arctic by lack of lemming-food, sit perched on fence posts in the daylight, watching, waiting on the bog to set up "today's specials" of small birds, food-hunting themselves. They watch and wait, too, for mice and moles venturing to the surface to catch a spot of daylight and to fulfill the other needs of mice and moles. Baby deer develop in winter-empty bellies of their mothers.

23 This is the way the kids' grandmother does it—duck, goose, partridge, quail, woodcock, white meat, dark, skinned or plucked—it doesn't matter. The birds are shaken in a bag of (or lightly rubbed with) salted-and-peppered flour while the pot (dutch oven, deep iron skillet, crockpot, electric frying pan, or roaster) gets smoking hot, but not so hot as to burn the butter she's put in to melt.

The birds are browned well all over (not enough to cook them but to sear in all the juices). Then the heat's turned way down and enough water is added to almost half-cover the meat (for those so inclined, a cup or two of good, gentle red wine for dark-meat birds, or white for white, added to the water does no damage whatsoever).

Now the covered pot is kept just simmering low and the water at near the half way mark until the meat tears easily from the bones.

At that point she lifts the birds with slotted spoons from the pot to the platter, fighting off as best she can her grandkids and son-in-law until grace is said. No meal deserves it more.

Notes

24 Old Gladys, she takes her ice fishing serious, and for one thing, none of her lines (except when she's hauling a fish on another one) is ever at ease. None sits still for long.

She'll pick up a line, raise it a couple of feet, dance the bobber around a little, and let it flutter back down. Watching that one like a hungry panther ready to spring, she reaches for the other one. Back and forth. All the time.

See, she figures that under-the-ice fish are lazier than the dickens, and if she lets her bait just lie there like a wet mitten they won't gather the ambition to bite. So she teases them with a wiggle and shake every little bit, until the lazy buggers, bowing to their predatory instincts, can't help themselves any longer. She even gives the minnows at the business end of tip-ups a jolt now and then, to keep them on the job. Because it's been a while since she's fed the fire back at her cabin, and she doesn't like going home to a cold house without supper in the pickle pail.

On the frozen banks of tiny, trout-toting streams, now caught in January's grasp, stilled more or less into whispering silence, sphagnum moss quite contentedly carries on, growing away like crazy. The deadly sweeping talons of a nearby great horned owl interrupt a rabbit fleeing from a fox. This same owl is beginning to lay eggs. And fishers cautiously hunt porcupines, morel mushrooms of the fisher world.

Notes

January

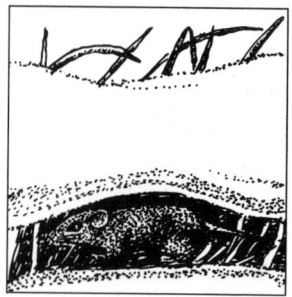

Under the bottom layer of snow—pukak to the Inuit—hidden beneath the thick white quilt of coldness, teems an arena of resting, sleeping, tunneling, snuggling, eating, breathing, and dying creatures—a thriving community of shrews and voles and mice and their kind. Bobcats sleep away today's daylight hours in shrub swamps, but hunt for rabbits, mice, squirrels, and foxes and opposite-sex bobcats tonight.

25 Add to the reasons that the disappearance of family farms makes us sad that it's bad for hunters, too. Little farms get swallowed up and turned into mega-operations by huge corporations with absentee owners whose idea of a good time centers on taking the advice of efficiency experts.

They don't want and won't tolerate strangers, armed strangers, on their places of business. They post the land, and given today's world, who can blame them?

Other sellers divide their farms into smaller parcels, which are bought by people who move from urban areas, who have worked hard to buy their little places in the country to get away from crowds. The last thing they want is armed strangers intruding on their privacy. They post the land, and who can blame them?

If the day ever comes that all private land is posted, most hunters will be forced to hang up their guns for good and settle for memories of the good old days—memories their sons and daughters will never share. If there's a whiz out there with a computer who can help us figure a way out of this one, now's the time to step forward.

Notes

26 In winter, northern pike cruise the forests of water weeds beneath the ice, often remaining near their summertime feeding beds until forced by diminishing oxygen levels into deeper waters. Constantly on the move, northerns actively hunt these weedy hiding places of smaller fish and minnows, even now feeding in water temperatures too cold to trigger similar activity in panfish or walleyes.

The normal feeding pattern of northerns is hit, run, pause (to turn the side-grabbed bait fish head first), and gobble. In winter they use the same pattern but do it all in a slower motion. So we have to counter that by waiting for a slower count after the "pause" before setting the hook.

Artificial lures, of course, must be jigged in order to attract hungry northerns. A friend of mine drops a favorite lure to the weed bed bottom, counts to six, pulls straight up a couple of inches or so for another six count, and then goes back down for six. Repeats the process as often as necessary. Because it's Gladys, of course she catches fish.

Starlings begin to show yellow beaks and to exchange drab coats for their midnight black of spring. And garter snakes lie in hibernation in rock piles, building foundations, and decaying roots of trees. Any time a hint of a thaw comes now, maple syrupers think of pancakes and waffles and snowshoes.

Notes

January

Ragged cattails rattle in these icy north winds that sweep over the countryside, spreading fluffy seeds across the snow—except for the few that stay quite intact, because the caterpillar of the cattail moth has bound them tightly together with silky strands and crawled inside for a long winter's nap.

27 Golfers have their usual partners, and bowlers bowl with the same bowlers every week, and it's common practice for regular committees of poker players to extract nickels and dimes from one another.

But those who love the outdoors have the advantage over the others. For some reason friendships forged in canoes, in tents, in duck blinds, in fishing boats, on deer drives, and along ski and hiking trails are special, unique. They last lifetimes and beyond, made of the magical stuff of shared confidences and trust and camaraderie.

Such friendships know no age limits—grandpas and kids feel quite at home together on fishing docks; no race limits—white and red and black become equal under yokes of canoes, at the tough ends of long portages; and no sex limits—the hearts of men and women alike skip beats at loons calling or trout tail-dancing on waters.

And just about anybody who will sit or lie real close to me when a nighttime thunderstorm's shaking the dickens out of the tent or a wolf's cry splits the moon a half-dozen steps from the flap is a pal of mine—now and forever—especially if he's willing to get up first and start the coffee.

Notes

28 In wetland areas—marshes, swamps, bogs, fens, muskegs, potholes, and sloughs—you will find, at one time or another, such life as spring peepers, bullfrogs, northern water snakes, painted turtles, wood frogs, spotted salamanders, wood turtles, redbelly snakes, snails, Blanding's turtles, and garter snakes. And such life as milkweed beetles, dragonflies, viceroy butterflies, brown-eyed butterflies, sulfur butterflies, Baltimore checker-spot butterflies, mulberry wing skipper butterflies, and purple- and red-bodied damselflies. And such life as masked shrews, meadow voles, muskrats, mink, beavers, white-tailed deer, star-nosed moles, black bears, snowshoe rabbits, bobcats, otters, lemmings, raccoons, and cottontails.

In a wetland turned parking lot or shopping mall or subdivision, you will find none of the above.

Wetlands provide cradles for countless fish and wildlife species. They absorb and disperse water falling on or flowing through them, providing natural flood control. And they act as buffers, keeping soil and pollutants from lakes and rivers. You never see a parking lot doing that.

Beneath the cloak of snow and ice, thousands of tiny creeks, apparently void of life, but actually very much alive with tiny minnows, roam through countless thousands of fields and woodlands. Frogs and turtles lie beneath the ice in near deathlike sleeps. Low, moaning winds trace erratic lines of rabbit tracks and shake spindly birches.

Notes

January

Downy woodpeckers leave the woods, briefly, to feed on tiny grubs in goldenrods. Usually solitary creatures, red foxes begin pairing up. Cedar waxwings feed on leftover highbush cranberries. Folks checking woodpiles ought to have at least half their wood left now. Oak leaves, or a few of them at least, give up tenuous holds on brittle branches to do their tuk-tuking toe dances across January's dancehall floor of snow and ice.

29 I was out ice fishing with Gladys. During a lull in the action (actually lulls were all I was having), Gladys mentioned that one of the women on her bowling team had come across a "Wit & Wisdom of the Great Outdoors" in which I referred to people who catch fish as *fishermen* and used words like *he, him,* and *his* when whoever I was writing about could just as easily have been a *she, her,* or *hers,* and where did I get off being so uppity.

Well, I figured I could do some educating of her for a change. I informed *her* that the word fisher*man* was a universal one, like *man*kind, referring to members of either sex, and that the use of *he* and *him* and *his* was equally generic, and that I am allowed only so many words and couldn't be writing fisher*man* or *woman* and *he* or *she* because it was too cumbersome and anyway fisher*woman* sounded funny and furthermore I wasn't trying to put down anybody just because they were members of the weaker sex.

"Well, that clears that up," *she* huffed as she put all *her* fish in one pile and all my none in another. "I'll see ya tomorrow, *Sis,*" she said, and walked home by *her*self.

Notes

30 Midwinter tackle box cleaner-outers might consider gutting dried-up ballpoint pens and fillkng them with split shot. Keeps them orderly and handy and dispenses them nicely—one at a time.

And nighttime anglers have it easier finding tackle boxes and assorted gear if they've affixed to them reflector tape, like the kids use on bicycles.

Plastic worms stored in sealable lunch bags won't stick together or to other tackle and won't absorb smells of sunscreen, reel oil, bug dope, and peanut butter sandwiches that find their way to the bottoms of all tackle boxes. These same baits stored in small jars with a little water stay fresh and firm. Add a drop of anise oil.

Along with a small screwdriver, a safety-wrapped single-edged razor blade is a perfect "just what I need" tool when it's just what you need.

And though the tackle box is crowded, a small roll of plastic tape is handy for mending rain gear, winding loose rod guides, preventing treble-hook hang-ups, and sealing the mouths of fishing partners out-fishing you and reminding you of it with disgusting regularity.

Stuffed into crevices and hollow trees and under blow-downs, their metabolism at less than half speed, just barely breathing, slowly dissolving up to a hundred pounds or more of insulating fat, female black bears rouse themselves just enough to give birth to two or maybe three seven- or eight-inch cubs weighing maybe four or five ounces each. Those bully blue jays are back in the feeders again.

Notes

January

Many raccoons, tired of the wait of winter, begin to get on with mating. Red crossbills may nest in January, while there's still time, or they may not; they do it all the time. White-tailed deer yard up where deep snows limit their ranges. Moose browse on willows, birch, ash, and aspen. And while January hasn't exactly been a fiesta of frivolity, an unfolding of a butterfly, we've made some progress.

31 When asked why he hunts and fishes, a fellow mumbles something about being a part of the great out-of-doors, about the call of the wild and the wish to put meat on his table.

"Aha!" comes a finger-pointing retort. "Notice the price of this pork chop, the cost of this chicken, of this batch of bologna, of this fish stick compared to what you spend for licenses, for rods and reels, boats and motors, guns and bullets and night crawlers—all for a paltry partridge, all for a trout."

Whatever other reasons we have for doing what we do, putting meat on the table is one of them. And a good one it is too—the economics of it be hanged.

A Sunday-roasting pheasant, a Christmas goose, a shore lunch of a walleye so fresh there's a wiggle in its tail—this is the food of life, above nickel-and-dime considerations. One might as well put his heart up for bids. For sale: one heart. Though 'tis broken once or twice, is still in working order. Best offer.

Notes

February

February

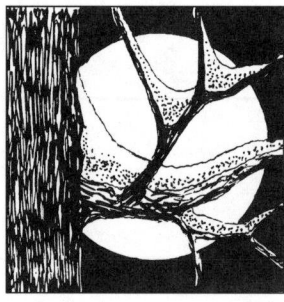

February on the calendar looks like such a short month, but in our hearts, it seems so, so long. February teases—holding out the carrot stick of March while refusing to let go of January. February is the month of the Snow Moon, or the Hunger Moon. On these days when February holds us hostage, we tie flies, sort tackle, and page through catalogs, planning for a spring that sits somewhere out there on the edge of a hazy tomorrow.

1 It's February already. It's time to look out for the groundhog. Time to tie some flies. Time to build some bluebird houses and a couple for wood ducks, too. Time to take the kids skating. Down on the pond. With hot dogs and chocolate. Time to pot some pepper seeds. Time to catch a walleye for lunch. Or half a dozen for dinner. Time to run the scales on the duck call. And the goose call. And what the heck, the turkey call.

Time to watch the chickadees at the feeder. Time to sip hot cider before the fireplace. Time to laugh in the moonlight. Time to paint a picture. Time to take the time to take the kids on a winter campout. A one-nighter will do. Time to strap on the snowshoes for a hike through the woods.

Time to think about cleaning the tackle box. Time to put that thought away. Time to go to boat and camping shows. Time to write the farmer and the landowner "thank you" and "howyadoin" notes. Time to make every day an earth day. Time to take grandpa jigging for bluegills. Time to dream of spring. Foolish dream. Time to get a valentine and time to be one.

Notes

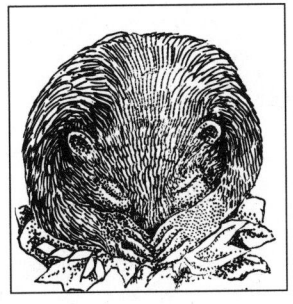

2 An ice-fishing shack offers much more than a refuge from the cold winds of winter. Much more than mere shelter against the elements. An ice-fishing shack is one of the great inventions of the world, providing us with as glorious a pastime as we will experience this side of eternal glory, allowing us to fish, no matter the weather, when we really need to.

But more happens in an ice-fishing shack than catching fish. Husbands and wives get reacquainted with no more distraction between them than jigging waxworms. Fathers and sons and daughters talk softly, one-on-one, and discover they still like each other. A couple of buddies can untangle the Mideast situation in an ice-fishing shack and straighten out the tax mess and ease world food shortages—by catching a couple of bluegills. Not just a little bit of good missionary work has been accomplished in an ice-fishing shack.

And gourmet peanut butter and jelly sandwiches have been prepared in ice-fishing shacks and hot chocolate brewed and hot soup stewed—all good for the heart and soul. And ice-fishing shacks have saved the sanity of millions of cabin-fevered gentlemen and ladies.

When the walls can hold us no longer, we get out the snowshoes or skis to wade or crunch or glide our way over icy fields and snow-filled forests. I'm betting the groundhog's afraid of its own shadow. The cold forces rabbits and mice into the open in search of food—seeds poking through the snow—where they themselves become food for owls. More quarter-pound baby bears are being born, and coyotes and bobcats continue to look for mates.

Notes

February

Don't look now, but we've gained an hour of daylight since that short day back in December. Everything born these days is born under Aquarius, the water carrier, which we can't see right now. Over coffee this morning someone says that a hawk can see light eight times farther than we can. At 1200 feet a flying hawk can spot a dime. At that height we can pick out a grapefruit—well, with our glasses on, we can.

3 What do you do when the preacher drops by unexpectedly, and he's peeved that maybe you're always fishing on Sunday mornings, and you've got nothing in the house to go with a cup of coffee? Well, one of you takes him into the living room, making small talk about the weather, the sinful nature of the world situation, and which fish are biting where.

Meanwhile, the other of you races to the kitchen, to find nothing but the remains of the nice salmon you had for supper last night (with you, it might be a nice northern or trout, or sucker even). Fast as a flash, the kitchen partner heats up the fish, flakes it with a fork, roots out all the bones, mixes it with a glob of ketchup, a dash of horseradish, and a healthy squirt of lemon, spreads it on crackers left over from Christmas, puts them on a plate, and sends the kids in with it, while stopping to catch a breath, all in the time it takes the living room partner to explain the effects of the solunar tables on bluegills and clarify the second coming.

Notes

4 It's interesting, isn't it, how carefully we monitor our children's growth and development, how fretfully we watch over them, how fearfully we react to a cough or fever, and how thoroughly we prepare them to be strong, honest, and true—and how completely we devastate the planet on which they must live and on which they must survive.

Each day we expose our kids to ozone levels above standards intended to protect their health. Each day they are pelted by acid rain that destroys aquatic life, buildings, forests, and crops—irreversibly. Billions of gallons of untreated sewage, industrial pollution, pesticides, leaking landfills, and illegal waste dumps poison their drinking water, and we just shrug it off.

Topsoil from farmlands blows or washes away, never to be replaced. We use up underground water supplies faster than nature can replenish them. And on, and on, and on.

And we keep right on electing politicians who do nothing to bring the catastrophe to a halt, though it lies within their power to do so.

Sleep well, little one, Daddy's here.

Some goldfinches begin to take on the brighter colors that will be their Easter outfits. Chickadees fluff up their feathers to keep warm, using the trapped air as insulation. Thick lake ice booms, though sometimes it "boi-i-ings," raising the neck hairs of thick-coated folks ice fishing and skating, though we try to act as if it didn't. It takes as many as half a million snow crystals to cover one square foot ten inches deep.

Notes

February

Eager to be about it, great horned owls are nesting. Grosbeaks and finches scavenge in trees and shrubs. The metabolism of white-tailed deer has slowed tremendously, allowing them to survive on smaller rations. Aldo Leopold wrote, "We shall never achieve harmony with the land any more than we shall achieve justice and liberty for people. In these higher aspirations, the important thing is not to achieve, but to strive."

5 To many anglers, ice and otherwise, fishing means walleye fishing, and any other fishing is only passing time until walleyes can be found—for often the finding of these glass-eyed, gold-flecked beauties is the hard part.

Walleyes enjoy such a wide variety of habitats. They can be found in clear, moderately deep, clean-bottomed lakes and in large, windswept, shallow, fertile lakes with reefs and drop-offs. They're at home in rivers, too. In bigger lakes they can be twenty to twenty-five feet down, in shallower ones, five to fifteen. They're a cool-water, clean-water fish when they can be.

Walleyes are also a school fish, though, so once you find them, you find them in numbers. But, since they are also a fish on the move, they're not found for long, and the hunt must begin again. Walleyes, however, often maintain the same daily travel routes—routines that can bring them back to the same spot each day. So the angler who can't drill holes fast enough to keep up with the wandering fish can return the next day, set up an ambush, and head them off at the pass.

Notes

6 As the late afternoon sun sinks into the pines, and most of the world calls it a day, from a roost in black cover a great horned owl blinks awake, stretches a wing or two, shakes the sleep from a leg, lifts itself on soft, silent wings, and goes hunting.

A well-equipped hunter, the owl can hear the squeak of a mouse at one hundred yards, see (with eyes mounted on a swiveling head) thirty-five times better than we. Its large and powerful feet have a long, needle-sharp meat hook at the end of each toe.

The great horned owl is ruthless in pursuit. From a stand atop a telephone pole, it sits to wait, to watch, to listen. Swiftly, whisper quiet, it drops from a frost-bitten moon, striking. Head thrown back, legs stretched forward, it sinks lethal talons into a rabbit, a porcupine, an aromatic favorite—a skunk.

And then, as the moon and stars dim and the sun begins to rise in the sky, the lord of the night melts again into concealing camouflage for a day's sleep.

Some timber wolves mate about now. And in the darkness of tonight (and there's plenty of that), a red fox travels over the snow, snacking on frozen berries. But the fox is really after the heartier stuff of meat and potatoes, without the potatoes, and the rabbit just around the corner knows it and pricks up its ears at the thought of it. And nervously checks its back trail.

Notes

February

Ravens perform awesome aerial acrobatics in February's skies preparatory to courtship. A silently flying screech owl drops through the darkness, plunging its talons into a white-footed mouse that has climbed atop the snow seeking buds and seeds and bark—a last meal for the rodent, one more for the bird. Gray squirrels dig in the snow for caches buried last fall and now lying under a foot and a half of the white stuff.

7 Probably like you, I read all I can about the great outdoors, though I'm not always so certain it's a good idea. Book and magazine writers are well-meaning folks, but it seems they too often leave me feeling inadequate. Inept. Poor.

In a periodical before me, for example, I read a tale of an adventurer who flies to remote regions to catch fish. At the rate things are going, I will never do that. Another story tells of a shooter who can put out the eyes of a flea at four hundred yards. In fading light. With a BB gun, more or less.

Other stories depict fly casters with the accuracy of William Tell, anglers with tackle boxes the size of Rhode Island, and shotgunners with the history of the world etched on their double barrels. Centerfolds show sportsmen in royal attire.

I don't know. Those of us who can only get out when we can and can't go far when we do, who wear slouch hats and patched waders, and whose lives are a basic backlash must be content to do our best, dream of tomorrows, and pour ourselves another one as snow piles up on the windowsill.

Notes

8 A fellow I know who knows about catching perch through the ice believes that they never quit biting, but merely move on. He also believes that it's up to the person who plans to catch some to be prepared to fish fast and efficiently when parked over a school—taking full advantage of the fish before they decide to check out the shade of green on the other side of the lake.

He keeps at least one extra line on standby, baited and ready, with the impaled bait fish on top in the holding cell of the minnow bucket. Whenever one line comes up, this one goes down. Right now.

He uses a good-sized split shot to take the bait down quickly, without fuss. And only on the crucial last four feet does he use monofilament. From there up it's braided line, clearly visible against the ice and relatively tangle free.

He jigs, even minnows, once in a while, to keep them on the job, and he watches his bobber with a vengeance, aware that what appears to be the wind blowing it from side to side is often the wind blowing it from side to side. But it's sometimes a nibbling perch, too.

Barred owls carry on hooted conversations with each other. Crane flies, looking like large, long-legged mosquitoes, emerge from the snow to mate; they do so quickly and then the female slips back under the blanket of snow to lay her eggs in dead leaves. Tiny springtails, snowfleas, yo-yo about the snow. Ruffed grouse leave snowbank shelters to shop, on web-footed snowshoes, for buds and dried berries. Pheasants hunt for sumac berries.

Notes

February

Mudpuppies are fairly active under the ice. Bears sleep without too much change in vital functions—their breathing slow and measured, their pulse rates around a beat a second, and their body temperatures only slightly below normal. White-tailed deer, of course, have long traded the red-brown color that blended into autumn's dry leaves for a salt-and-pepper gray to match the frosty landscape.

9 Little George finally grows up enough to call Grandpa's old shotgun his own. The kid's excited. He and his dad head out to Grandpa's pasture to shoot at some clay pigeons and to give George a chance to learn his way around a shotgun.

The problem is, George can't hit a thing. He wants to. He's trying. But the darn BB's never get to where they're supposed to be. Poor George. But then Grandpa moseys along.

"Well, I'll be," says Grandpa, drowning a grasshopper in a shot of tobacco juice. "That gun fits me alright, but it shore don't fit you. Looky here. Lay the butt stock next to the inside of your forearm, wrap your hand around the grip, and put your finger on the trigger. If the gun'd lay natural-like, the stock would be fitting you. If it was too short, you'd have to add spaces between this recoil pad and the butt plate. If it's too long, like with you here, we'll just have to take all these spaces out or have a gunsmith shorten the stock.

Later, he hands the gun back to the kid. George slaps it to his shoulder, eyes the trap with a calculating eye, and "Pull," he sneers with cold confidence.

Notes

10 What is it, that magic kind of something, that calls a man or woman into the great out-of-doors, that calls people from warm beds and fires or shady trees to buck wind, heat, cold?

It might be the North Star winking at a quarter moon. Or the south wind rearranging flocks of wildflowers feeding in a meadow. It could be the northern lights in a busy sky and wolves howling for encores. Or a campfire warm enough to thaw a cold heart. Or a bubbling spring coming from nowhere and liking it like that. Or a light line pulled jumpy snug by the scornful bluster of a rainbow trout with a mind of its own.

Or a soaring eagle's call, a loon's cry, a hoot owl's hoot, a chickadee. Or the splash of a paddle or the bounce of a pebble, skip-skipping across a looking-glass lake. Or a blueberry or a single wild rose. Or the shadow movement of a white-tailed deer. Or a pinecone.

Or it could be, when the wild calls, that you find you've misplaced a piece of yourself and you need to go where you'll find it.

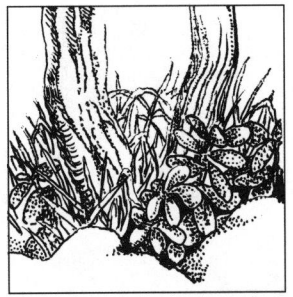

In the woods, on small bare-of-snow spots, or even almost-bare-of-snow spots, wintergreen, also called checkberry or teaberry, grows. Stone fly nymphs emerge from icy water habitats as adults to feed on algae, to mate, and to crawl back to the water to die. The squirrels haven't grown thicker coats, but they have grown heftier, fluffier tails, which they wrap as snugly about themselves as we do a down quilt.

Notes

February

Red squirrels move freely about. Their tracks tell tales in today's snow, and telling an altogether different story are the empty ribs next to them. We go fishing. Ever-active, ever-hungry shrews gallop between the snow and the bog floor in near frenzy, hunting worms, snails, and centipedes. Female mosquitoes shelter in caves, or in hollow trees, or in basement laundry rooms, or under kitchen sinks. Waiting. Waiting.

11 I envy my neighbor across the road. He's got it all together. He's the kind of guy who changes the oil right on schedule. His lawn mower blade is never dull—for long. And his fishing poles—rods and reels—never get all tangled up, never get leaned in corners to fall over and get stepped on or run over, and dogs never get his jigs caught in their hides and run, goofy, all over the place. How he manages the oil and the mower blades, I don't know, but here's how he keeps his fishing gear in order.

In his garage (and in his basement, too, of course) he solidly screwed a couple of hefty eye screws, about five feet apart, into an overhead beam. To these screws he securely fastened a length of decently heavy wire. From one of my many junk drawers (he doesn't have any) he captured a tangle of drapery hooks that I was saving for something important, though I don't remember what. Anyway, he hung these hooks over the wire at various intervals; and from them hang, safe and straight, his rods, and reels, and landing nets, and, and, and.

It's a good idea, and I'm going to do that same thing. Someday.

Notes

12 There's no bad time to do so, but late winter's a particularly good time to combine two of the things we love most—kids and fishing. If some people out there have no kids of their own to take along, well, the streets are full of them, and for the kids who have no one to take them, the frozen lakes of winter are covered with men and women who know their way around an ice auger and wouldn't mind at all a breath of fresh air.

With kids we'll pick a nice day—without being too fussy, and dress them in layers, so they stay comfortable as the weather changes, which it will. And go where panfish are plentiful, making the day a holiday, keeping a kettle of hot chocolate or stew simmering. And hot dogs and marshmallows.

We'll take a deck of cards or a checkerboard in case the action slows. Which it will. We'll make it a shorter day rather than longer, so the kids will come back for more. And we'll not do much fishing ourselves; it takes a lot of time to keep fishing kids squared away.

Of course we'll spoil them absolutely. We're talking partners here.

It might be early, but horned larks are early, and will flock to open areas in bare fields that have kicked off at least some of their blanket of snow. Stripped and naked, trees in February are fundamentalists, strapped to the frozen earth, eternally reaching for the stars, waiting for better days. While the green hornet has nestled in the warm cracks in the side of the house, she's the only one of her hive to make it. Her paper summer home is a ghost town.

Notes

February

Red squirrels mate in earnest now. Great gray owls, perched high, listen intently to movement under the snow. When they're quite satisfied, they silently drop, reach below the surface with needle-sharp talons, and hook on to a rodent. Snowshoe hares climb atop snowbanks, stretching on hind feet, reaching for bark and buds. Jumping spiders await spring tightly woven in individual silken cocoons about the size of a dime.

13 Nearly every camping-out experience includes at least one breakfast of scrambled eggs. Individual, small globs of soggy, slippery, greasy scrambled eggs. Next time you make breakfast add one-quarter teaspoon of baking powder to every four eggs as you beat in milk, for eggs so fluffy and light you'll have to weigh them down with rocks to keep them from floating away.

And when it's your turn to do dishes, don't needlessly scrub the fire-blackened bottoms of cooking pots. Such charcoaled surfaces conduct heat better and more evenly than shiny ones. Just keep a right-sized plastic bag for each pot to keep its mess to itself.

You already freeze water in various containers to keep coolers cool and to provide fresh drinking water around camp. Remember, though, that frozen orange juice, apple cider, or tea provides a refreshing change of pace.

And another very important point for the camp cook to remember is that if you frequently oversalt the main course or burn it to a crisp, somebody else will then take over, and you can get in some extra fishing time.

Notes

14 For the record. Part one. It's a bevy of quail, a crash of rhinoceroses, a bouquet of pheasants, a school of fish, a bunch of widgeon, a charm of finches, a plague of locusts, a chevron and a skein of geese . . .

A leap of leopards, a pod of seals, a sloth of bears, a congregation of plovers, a convocation of eagles, a rafter of turkeys, a covert of coots, a walk of snipe . . .

A gam of whales, a gang of elk, a fall of woodcocks, a dule of doves, a skulk of foxes, a bale of turtles, a business of ferrets, a deceit of lapwings, a descent of woodpeckers, a pitying of turtledoves, a gang or paddling or pack or party of ducks, a spring of teal, a tiding of magpies . . .

A murder of crows, a chattering and a murmuration of starlings, a mutation of thrush, a shoal of bass, an exaltation of larks, an unkindness of ravens, a hover of trout, a cete of badgers, a covey of partridge, a knot of toads, and a labor of moles.

In case you didn't know.

Raccoons are pretty much gone for good. Woolly bear caterpillars hibernate, frozen solid, in barns or under bark. Soon they will thaw and come back to life, pupate, become moths, and lay eggs, which hatch again into caterpillars. Round and round they go. Grouse have grown small, fluffy, heat-hold feathers at the base of each big feather for insulating winter underwear, and like my Uncle Jake, they won't change them till spring.

Notes

February

Still-hanging leaves of otherwise bare poplar and aspen trees probably still hang there because they were tied to the brittle branch with a silken thread by a butterfly larva, so that it could roll the leaf around itself as a winter hibernation home. Collapsed meadow vole runways show up in the snow. Rose hips reach above the snow to provide food for February-hungry birds.

15 The symptoms are unmistakable. Vague feelings of discomfort and uneasiness that (like a wood tick feeding on a dog's ear) thicken and grow to the verge, the edge, of eruption.

The unexplained restlessness, an unreachable, unscratchable itch, spreads. The victim's eyes become vacant, unfocused. Sounds cease to reach him. Thoughtless thoughts wander aimlessly through his mind. Claustrophobia rears its ugly head. His conversations sink to monosyllabic questions: "Huh?" He unconsciously caresses his decoys, rods and reels, shotguns, fish mounted above fireplace, pheasant on nightstand. He gets grumpy.

The affliction strikes without mercy here in February with the regularity of a turn at the flu trough. It is cabin fever, and there is no chicken soup antidote for it.

No. For cabin fever responds to no cure but time, a sun that rises earlier and sets later, a galloping force of grass turning green, and tender loving care till it all happens.

Notes

16 I'd like to tell you about a piece of knowledge I acquired the other day. I'm out bluegill fishing, and they're having none of it. But across the bay Gladys slaps a fish on the ice every couple of minutes. And since pride is one sin I'm hardly ever guilty of, I mosey over for a look-see.

Gladys reminds me that winter bluegills and crappies don't really bite, but gently, slowly inhale the bait, and she figures I'm getting nibbles like she is but don't know it, they're so soft. Anyway, she's using yellow, four-pound test mono with a two-foot, two-pound leader of clear, a tiny ice fly or teardrop, and no bobber whatsoever.

And now for the lesson. When she's got her hook down to where she wants it, she takes the foot or so of line between the end of the pole and the ice and winds it around a finger. She slides off the loop and pinches and twists it, making a series of kinks, I guess you'd call it. It's when those kinks shake a bit or quiver or start to straighten that Gladys's arm flashes smartly upward, and she sets another bluegill dancing on the ice.

Some pussy willow twigs begin to show signs of fuzzy catkins. Great horned owls continue nesting. Plants stiffly sticking from snow banks provide seeds for juncos, tree sparrows, and snow buntings. Maple sap begins to work its way up and up, in no great hurry. Twigs of apple trees and oaks wear velvet fuzzy coatings, which protect them from wind and cold and from drying out.

Notes

February

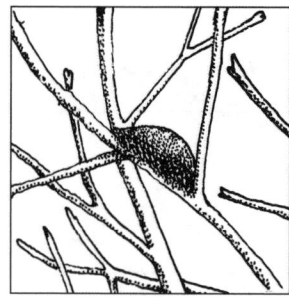

Eggs of the praying mantis, lying insulated in Styrofoam-like coffins, begin to feel the strengthening rays of the sun—when it's shining. Cardinals sing their spring love songs of "let's cheer, cheer, cheer." Damselflies, dragonflies, bloodworms, and dobsonflies lie on stream bottoms as larvae or nymphs. Many birds feed on ragweed seeds. Tadpoles have sunk to the bottoms of lakes and ponds, hardly moving for days at a time.

17 Now is the time, as snow still clutches the earth with grasping claws, to plan for the duty-free days of vacation time. For there is much to plan, enough for a year's worth of memories, and all must go perfectly. Not only that, but the planning lifts you from the icy sidewalks of inactivity and gives ballast on the desperate seas of February.

Early planning gives you the lake or river you want when the boss finally frees you from the grindstone. It saves you the campsite, the cabin, of your dreams. A favorite guide will be yours.

Now you have time to contact fish and game departments of a dozen states and the luxury of picking and choosing at your leisure. It lets you ponder the questions that should be asked, and asked, and ask them. It gets you maps of your lakes, so you might fish them in your planning. It lets you find something for the whole family.

Yes, when you have so little time to use, early planning helps you use it to its utmost; and if it's in the plans to waste some time, good planning lets you waste it well.

Notes

18 Rarely is a family unit more solidly intact than when the family shares a campsite. Rarely will a family face fewer outside obstructions. Rarely will its individual members need to rely so completely upon one another. Rarely will the contributions of each individual be so obviously necessary, so uncommonly appreciated.

The world of camping holds many wonderful mysteries for children of all ages raised in the cacophony of urban life, raised in today's tug-of-war world. To teenagers, reluctant to leave friends and the familiar goings on of their societies, a family camping experience (by all means leaving the friends out of it) can be a reuniting of the family, a rekindling of a closeness once so dear, a reminding of values perhaps taken for granted or stored somewhere in the back of our hearts.

To little ones it can be a rebirth, a baptizing into the magic of a whole new world, where father and mother are not, for a little while at least, harried briefcase-carrying, homemaking, laundry-doing chauffeurs, but the strong, close-by stuff of pioneers.

Red-tailed hawks return now, or will soon. That chickadee on the feeder is one of our smallest overwintering birds, weighing little more than a first-class letter—half of which is feathers. Does that mean we could send it across country to a warmer spot for one first-class stamp? It's the mating season for flying squirrels.

Notes

February

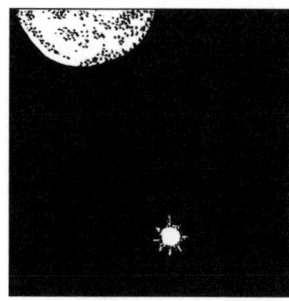

That's Jupiter, the boss of the evening sky. Great horned owls break the silence, calling "Whooooooo-whooo, who," in low resonant tones. Ice storms deal double whammies to birds; not only do they seal up buds and seeds, they also ice up feathers. Some folks see American kestrels, and some see and smell skunks. Honeybees balled up deep within hives keep themselves warm with their beating, beating wings.

19 Maybe at one time the camping experience may have been associated with adversity, hardship, calamity, and grief. But not now.

Setting up temporary quarters along a water's edge or in the midst of a pine forest or on a mountain top, as a guest of nature, without the frivolities of telephones and televisions, seems to many to be the exemplification of elegance. Hard work? Phooey.

Look, for instance, how easy it is to make this inspiration of a hot apple pie for dessert. We take some prepared pie filling, or better yet, parboil a handful of sliced apples, and add some brown sugar and cinnamon. Then we lightly toast a couple slices of bread. All around the perimeters of one slice, leaving no gaps, we lay strips of cheese. Into the center of that slice we dump the pie filling, and sandwichlike, top it off with the other slice. On a camp stove or over hot coals, in a buttered skillet, we fry the thing until the cheese melts, sealing the good stuff in the middle.

It warms the insides when we're ice fishing, too.

Notes

20 The gang got together at the Professor's the other night, and among other things, someone reckoned that he'd just bet that nine out of every ten deer rifles were .30-06s. Well, we thought that was a good and interesting observation, but high. And the Professor, as is his way, figured the old aught six might be a topic that could use expanding on, so we laid a log on the fire, poured another hot one, and settled in for the lesson.

He said the .30-06 was first a military round, developed by the army in 1906 (hence the -06), and adapted to the U.S. rifle, caliber 30 (therefore the .30-). He further informed us that the aught six was used by soldiers in world wars I and II. And it's available in lever, pump, auto, and single-shot actions. That in factory loads it comes in bullet weights of 55, 125, 150, 165, 168, 180, 200, and 220 grains. And, for instance, a 150-grain bullet has a muzzle velocity of 2910 feet per second with 2820 foot-pounds of energy.

He went on and on, but I ducked into the bathroom and got into some reading. When I got back everybody was gone.

Endangered peregrine falcons return to nesting sites. Blue jays in noisy flocks sing, or do what passes for singing, their "pump handle" spring songs. Chickadees follow suit with their own "fee-fee" whistles, and woodpeckers beat their heads against fence posts—a sure sign of love. As browse becomes scarce in deer yards, deer stand on hind legs, stretching as high as they can reach for food. Shorter, smaller animals will starve.

Notes

February

Courageous or foolhardy shoots of crocuses and daffodils poke through places where the sun shines the warmest—a sun we hope and fully expect to stick around two minutes longer today than it did yesterday. And with good reason, for May Day is only seventy or so days away. Orion, our great winter constellation, glitters above our snow. A great horned owl picks up a bunny rabbit to feed her hungry offspring.

21 There's more to bass than meets the eye—even in February, when there are none to meet the eye. For now, under thick ice, these fish put new meaning to "sluggish." They exist, alive, but apparently not too excited about it. Yet, as we sit here, females develop eggs, months before the spawn, which when it comes will be triggered by double whammies of springtime good luck—rising water temperatures and increasing sunlight.

When the water temperature reaches fifty-eight degrees to sixty degrees, males begin to harbor cottage-and-picket-fence fantasies, fanning out pan-shaped nests. And when it heats up to sixty-five, watch out! Males feverishly lure females to their beds. It's a stressful time for the fish. Never are their senses of sight, feel, and smell, their awareness, greater. No other time are their strike zones so long and wide.

Never are they so much bass as when they're making baby bass.

Notes

22 A fish house springs up on a lake, and in the time it takes to say, "How they biting?" there's another next to it, and then another, until a whole shantytown takes root. It's the way of those who love ice fishing. When one of us is catching fish, and when none of us is—well, it's only fair.

But last Saturday we're all bunched as usual, and none of us is having much luck, when a couple of hotshot college kids come out, sniff at our togetherness and lack of success, and embark on a plan whereby one of them goes ahead and drills holes along the way.

The other follows with a jig and minnows, working each hole five minutes; and, if nothing happens, he moves on to the next.

Oh, sure, they cover a lot of ice and catch some nice fish, and it's an okay way to do it, I suppose. But with us all jumping up and running to each hole they pulled a fish out of and trying our luck next to it, it plumb wore us out, and we had to go home early to take a nap.

Wild tom turkeys begin gobbling and practice strutting their stuff. And in the bogs, skunk cabbages poke their smelly heads to the surface. Back to that chickadee again. That little critter's heart beats five hundred times a minute when she's sleeping, twice that when she's awake. Male and female nuthatches begin to lose their look-alike colors of winter.

Notes

February

Crows return, which is okay, I guess. Shrews madly hunt underground tunnels for enough insects in a day to equal their own body weight. A true blizzard is a snow-driving wind of forty miles an hour or more, accompanied by zero cold. Put on your hat, button your coat, and wear your overshoes. Or better yet, throw another log on the fire and pop some popcorn.

23 Winter fishing for most folks means fishing on hard, frozen lakes, drilling holes, and dropping lines therein. It is a natural thing to do. Reasonable.

But it's not everybody's cup of iced tea. No. Some folks fish in the wintertime as they fish in the summertime (where it's legal), on little streams, running open, cutting through fields and forests. They are, of course, fishing for trout. They basically believe that 100 percent of the trout are in 1 or 2 percent of the trout waters—usually gathered at the head of deep holes, sheltered, but in position to feed.

These folks fish deep, and accurately, for they understand that winter trout expect to be waited on, and won't reach half a foot for lunch. And, where bait's concerned, they think small, and when they fish, they fish desperately slow. And they don't expect big days every day, or hardly any day.

So? Sound crazy? Not to these folks, who figure why else, after all, was long underwear invented?

Notes

24 A dyed-in-the-wool hunter had had it with winter. He had read the words off his hunting magazines and thumbed thin the pages of his books. But he longed to, had to, hunt. He couldn't eat, couldn't sleep, and shook all over.

He went to a doctor—also a hunter—in the same condition. Oh, doctor, heal thyself. He went to a pastor, who had exhibited the same tendencies as the parishioner. He went to a psychiatrist, who was on an African safari. Nothing eased the great need he had developed.

Developed? Laughing as a mad man laughs, he raced to his closet for his hunting paraphernalia, and, season or not, began the great hunt of his life. He sneaked a good sneak through unpicked corn fields and shot three pheasants—two hens and a rooster. Picking his way through scrub oak and stunted pines, he came upon a bedded doe and last year's fawn and shot them both. His appetite whetted, he went on to shoot squirrels, partridge, and blue jays and chickadees.

He's having them all mounted and framed—five-by-sevens, eight-by-tens, a couple of eleven-by-fourteens.

Minks, too, are spring thinking. Always on the prowl, always hungry, they hunt, mostly at night, for fish, mice, rabbits, birds, and when in season, frogs, salamanders, crayfish, clams, and insects. Among their favorites are muskrats, whose dens they commandeer as homes for themselves. Grouse get a taste of apple buds, where they can find them, weather permitting.

Notes

February

White oak leaves, twig-clinging all winter, rustling at each breezy blast like so many chattering teeth, must now let go, like it or not, to make room for new spring buds. There's a big difference between January snow-storms and those that come in late February. We're stuck with those of January, but February's, no matter how bad, are only temporary, and we rejoice at the difference.

25 Acid rain. Smog. Sewage-filled rivers. Filled-in wetlands. Paved roads through wildlife sanctuaries—each and all of it starts in somebody's neighborhood, somebody's town, somebody's backyard. That would be in your neighborhood and mine; in your township and mine; in your county and mine; in your backyard and mine.

We expect somebody else to do something about it—maybe Congress, the president, some all-knowing, all-powerful somebody to stop acid rain from originating from smokestacks in our town, to stop factories in our county from draining sewage into rivers where our kids fish and swim and into streams from which they drink, to stop major holes from being punched, from our backyard, in our protective ozone layer, to stop bulldozers from filling in our oh-so-delicately-balanced wetlands.

Almost every conservation problem starts at the local level. That makes every conservation problem your problem and mine. If we expect someone else to solve our problems, then we'll have a long, long, wait. Well, maybe not so long.

Notes

26 How'd the boat and motor run the last time you had it out last fall? For me, it's hard to remember. I think I was going to fix it all up before I put it away for the winter. I don't suppose I did—hunting season was about to start, and I got busy.

I think I had some trouble starting it and it ran kind of funny. I'm not sure if its transom was real solid or if the motor hookup was as good as it might be. I wonder if it'll still float if it fills up with water. I think its steering controls were wearing out and binding here and there. It's possible the registration has expired. The life jackets won't float a flea. The oars are warped. I probably used up the last shear pin, and the anchor rope is shot. Water oozes in from somewhere, and the drain plug does not fit too snugly. The carpet's frayed. The tires on the trailer were on their last mile many miles ago. The pull rope is ragged and the oarlocks squeak.

Oh, I know there's a pile of ice on the lake and the boat looks like a snowbank on wheels, but are you getting the same kind of itches I am?

Black bear cubs, just about a month old now, nestle close to sleeping mothers, nursing. Seed-eating birds migrate by day and rest at night, usually, and insect-eaters, such as robins, do it the other way around, flying at night and resting by day. Each to its own—as long as they get here. Great horned owls—we call them hoot owls—are still the lords of the night.

Notes

February

Do the fish feel their icy cover losing its thickness, do they wait as we do, for the sun to pop it off? Brown and purple butterflies—mourning cloaks—having slept most of the winter away in hollow trees, unfold and spread their wings, while some snow still lies on the ground, for a little touch of an early spring. Barred owls ask in the still darkness who is doing the cooking at your house and mine.

27 My cantankerous Great Uncle Jake doesn't like ice fishing—not at all; so from late fall till spring, he does nothing but stare evil-eyed out the window, rearrange his tackle box, and grumble. Jake is, however, about the best non-ice fisherman around—something he freely admits—and he's a great ice-out fisherman, especially for bluegills.

As soon as the ice starts to give a little, Old Jake lets out a whoop, breaks out his ultralight gear, gets out the boat, and he's gone.

Though he sometimes fishes right over the side, with tiny jigs, he usually poles the little boat through the open water between the ice and shore to a little bay that gives up its ice early. He softly drops the anchor, close to the ice, and because bluegills (with so little cover in the lake) are super spooky right now, he's cat-quiet and casts long—using wee creations with sponge rubber bodies and rubber band legs and crickets and jigs on #12, 14, or 16 hooks.

Fish-hungry folks who haven't for quite a while been able to get out to do what they were born to do can get out right about now and do it.

Notes

28 For the record. Part two. It's a pride of lions, a colony of ants, a parliament of owls, a route of wolves, a host of sparrows, a herd of elephants and curlews and wrens, a husk and a kindle and a drove of hares. A cast of hawks, a plump of grouse, a puddling or a sord of mallards, a siege of herons and of bitterns, a trip of widgeon, a wedge or drift or sounder or herd or game or bevy of swans. It's a wisp of snipe, a watch of nightingales, a colony of frogs, an ostentation or muster of peacocks, a smack of jellyfish, a building of rooks, a shrewdness of apes, a troop of kangaroos, a flight of swallows, an army of caterpillars, a nest of rabbits, a richness of martens, a grist of bees, a bale of roebucks— and a set of three deer is a leash.

It's also a litter of pups, a kindle of kittens, a pace of asses, a peep of chickens, a trip of goats, a drift of hogs, a singular of boars, a sounder of swine, a drove of cattle, a clowder of cats, a rag of colts, a barren of mules, and a harass of horses—but you knew that.

Most red foxes have mated. Those who haven't gotten around to it yet had best get to it pretty quick. And that chickadee again? With a body temperature of 108 degrees, she must eat her weight in food each day. Better fill that feeder. We'll say, "Good-bye, February, and thanks." Now, that wasn't so bad, was it?

Notes

March

March

March—jittery, nervous, fickle—threatens spring one day with sunshine and warm breezes, then turns cheat and liar, dumping hubcap-high snow on a pessimistic populace biding its time. March is the month of the Worm Moon, for surely worms follow the frost up and out, and the month of the Moon of Crust-on-the-Snow. February is done and gone, and sunrise came a minute earlier today than it did yesterday.

1 Uffda! It's March already. It's time to look out for springtime. Time for clouds, white clouds full of moonlight. Time for turning-green pastures and turning-tail snowbanks. Time for walking alone between rainy mornings and snow-maybe afternoons. Time to feel the true warmth of growing days, blue and familiar as the skies, breathing softly to the pines old, old stories new to the telling.

Time to read a good book at a March-bright lighted window. Time to look down, at dusk, into a river ridding itself of ice. It's time to watch the sky for geese coming home, and for ducks. Time to set out bluebird houses and a few more for wood ducks. Time to watch for wee pasqueflowers and crocuses and even, what the heck, for dandelions, too. Time to wash the windows. Maple syrup time. Time to talk turkey. Time to take a walk with the kids and older folks into a sun warm with March promises, shining with March hope.

Time to snuggle, to light a fire to this springtime and go with the flow.

Notes

2 A lot of neighborhoods these days are going to the dogs. Not ours—ours and plenty like ours are going to the ducks, wood ducks to be precise, and we like that. Once thought to be extinct, wood ducks are now one of the most abundant waterfowl species in some states. Much of the credit for that goes to folks, big and little, who have put together specially designed wood duck nesting boxes. That work goes on. And we can use your help. Wood ducks are early returners and early nesters, so you'll have to hurry to be ready this year.

Libraries and DNR offices can provide plans. Houses can be placed on poles or trees next to or in the water or up to half a mile away. Woodies don't mind apartment living, so you can attach several boxes to the same pole, and they don't seem to find living next to two-legged people too much of an inconvenience either. They often return to the same nest every year, and since they pick up after themselves and don't throw wild parties, they're a fine and welcome addition to this or any neck of the woods.

Rooster pheasants crow, showing off to each other and to pretty hens who've been waiting for such she-nanigans. March offers magic, for those who watch and wait. Snow mysteriously becomes tiny trickles of water, which balloon into streams and explode into roaring rivers and boil into salty, surfy oceans. Just like that.

Notes

March

In huge platforms of sticks and debris, bald eagles nest after breathtaking courtship flights. This March is an itchy month for those of us with a lust for open waters and hooks and reels and waders, with only the memories of last season and the promises of a new one to get us by. In the meantime, it would be nice to go fishing. Somewhere, south of us, let's say on the ten-yard line of life, the spring parade of birds masses.

3 Owls—where to start? Let's start with the kinds of owls: saw-whet, boreal, burrowing, screech, long- and short-eared, barn, hawk, barred great gray, great horned, and snowy.

Owls generally eat their entire prey, head first or all at once, and regurgitate, in little pellets, the indigestible stuff of fur, bones, and feathers.

Owls don't make, nor do they remodel, nests, but settle for what they can find. And as with all raptors, female owls are larger and stouter than males.

With owls, the eyes have it. Owls rely heavily on sight to locate prey. In bright light their pupils shrink to the size of a pinhead, but at night they can dilate to nearly as large as the eye itself—though even owls can't see in total darkness, of course. Their hearing is as good as anybody's.

They can turn their heads 270 degrees in either direction without breaking their necks.

And taxonomically speaking, owls are rather closely related to whippoorwills.

Notes

4 What Amos Smythe doesn't know about trout and the catching thereof isn't worth knowing. Which brings us here to the "trout pond." (That's a protective alias for this after-work stopover for a few of us fishers of trout, hungry to talk fishing.) It's where Amos hangs out, dispensing the whereats and the howtos to anyone who'll treat him to his own particular brand of poison.

The trouble is he's such a slow cuss. He takes his straight, in a squatty glass, and does more with a swig of it than any ten men on earth. While we're watch-checking, eager for him to get on with it, he rolls the stuff from one cheek to the other a half dozen times. Then he throws his head back; his trained Adam's apple leaps aside to let the liquid fire roar down, and his eyes pop like he's seen a three-pounder napping at the riffle end of Good Grief pool. He does this more than once, and by the time he's ready to begin the lesson we've got to get home to suppers and kids with homework. None of us will press his luck so close to the opener. I'll get some dope from Amos next time and pass it on to you.

Soon other birds will be moved to mating rituals, building nests, incubating eggs, and feeding hungry nestlings, but not goldfinches. They can't begin to get serious about such things until thistledown, their favorite nesting material, becomes available, which is a long, long time away. Now they're partying it up at the feeder in groups of a dozen or more. And the sun noticeably swings north.

Notes

March

Aspen (we call it popple) buds wait to explode into leaves. The sun rose this morning almost directly east in a goodwill gesture that speaks of spring. The raucous, squeaking-gate rasps of the blue jays have gotten softer, mellower, unless it's just my imagination. And March winds still have a heckuva bite. Unless that too is my imagination.

5 Up here where we live, winter still very much controls, and the only open water we see is in the bathtub and the toilet. But it's not so for all of you. For some of you, little coves and bays on the north corners of your lakes have rid themselves of ice, and you wait for that bit of open water to heat up to fifty-some degrees. And then from shore, where you find good cover of sunken brush and timber, or an inflow of water over a gravelly bottom, you are going crappie fishing.

I can see it all. You might leave the rod and reel home and borrow the kids' cane pole, or maybe not. But you'll use four-pound mono to which you'll tie a #8 hook, and above that a small split shot, and well above that a very small bobber or pencil-type float to control the depth and to telegraph bites. To the hook you'll stick a one- or two-inch minnow through the back, just ahead of the dorsal fin. You'll experiment with the depth till you find fish. Yes, I can see it, and I envy you your very good fortune.

Notes

6 Migration in the fall seems mostly an exodus of leisure, a staggered departure of convenience. But not this one of spring. This is a hurried-up, get-with-it affair, quick and crowded, done in half the time.

The eagerness, the need to reproduce sparks this great rush north for ducks and geese (and all gone birds of a feather, for that matter). They have nests to build, eggs to lay, babies to raise in this short, short time before the call comes to slip it in reverse for the too-soon return trip. Among the first to come, Canada geese knife northward at the cutting edge of the thirty-two-degree isotherm—their travels often squelched to a standstill by blizzards and ice storms. Pintails and mallards follow close behind.

Vanguards, they are, leading the feathered flood that makes up this grand parade of color and song.

Strike up the band! Mother Nature's springtime, thumbs-up, four-star spectacular spectacle is showing now in the great outdoors near you.

Dark-eyed juncos come north. Early starlings return, fooling us sometimes with their imitations of other birds in less of a hurry to brave a chancy spring. Catkins of alder bushes open, to the delight of early pollen-needing bees and to the rest of us in need of good news. Each warm day brings that parade of migrating birds a little bit closer. Maybe they're now on, say, the twelve- or thirteen-yard line.

Notes

March

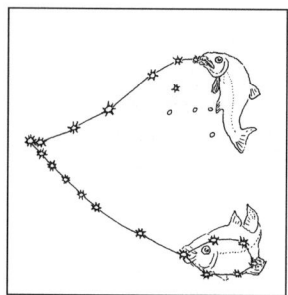

7 Though we agree that walleyes they are not, nor bass, or trout, or crappie, suckers are victims of terminology. If suckers had been given a flashy moniker like Dolly Bottom Feeder or Silver Whatchamacallit we would rise early to fish for them and lie about the catch. But for anglers longing to splash a hook into open water and feel the tug and jerk and pull of a strong fish at the end of a line, the spring spawning run of suckers moving into streams and rivers can really get the heart a-pumping.

An ideal rig is a small slip-sinker and swivel combination. Place the sinker above the swivel so it can't slip down onto the hook; attach a twelve-to-eighteen-inch leader to the swivel and a hook to that. Suckers congregate in deep-stream holes and along undercut banks and log jams. It's usually best to let the bait, a big night crawler waving seductively in the current, sit on the bottom. Pretend you're trout fishing and then let the games begin.

Notes

8 Canoeists, as in those who love the narrow craft and the feel of its paddle, are probably born, not made. But good canoeists, as in those who bring the canoe to do what they want when they want, are definitely made.

Good canoeists are made by reading some, but mostly they are made on the water, experience again proving to be the unforgiving headmaster. They have learned to hang on to the canoe when they tip. (A good canoe floats, and a shore is always farther away than it looks.) In fast water they hang on to the upstream end, so as not to get caught between the canoe and a hard place.

They do not drift in fast water, but stay in control by paddling faster than the current, forward or backward, as necessary. They have learned to read rapids, heading for instance, to the middle of a V pointing downstream—this is a chute—and avoiding a V pointing upstream. That's a rock. Good canoeists have nothing to prove. If the current becomes too much for them, they portage.

In other words, good canoeists are not all wet—in the figurative sense.

Gray jays are among the first to start nesting. Screech owls settle for an early frog or two while waiting for the first mouse crop to come creeping through the meadows. Some of the first fox kits are born. Meadowlarks arrive at my folks' place—a couple or three hours south of us. White winter hair falls off the backs of weasels and the brown stuff comes on.

Notes

March

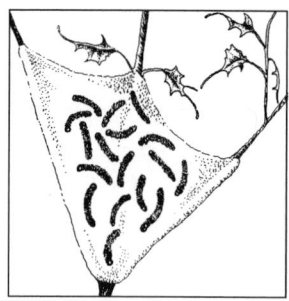

The egg masses of tent caterpillars, moth larvae, laid like scabs on branches of apple and cherry trees, hatch, loosing hundreds of tiny caterpillars that right away begin building a communal tent that'll grow as they do—until they leave it for good this summer—unless you or I get ahold of it first. Sandhill cranes and killdeer make good their promise to come home.

9 In a technical, scientific, plastic-worm world, you'd think something as commonplace ordinary as the pork rind would have gone the way of other less sophisticated gadgets. But for the last fifty years or so, nearly every type of fish in the water has been lured to the frying pan with the magic of a piece of pork.

Pork rind gives a fish the taste and smell, the texture of real meat. It's tough enough to be used and reused. Though it's effective as a bait by itself, most anglers prefer to attach it to the hooks of other lures as a trailer, often improving the action of the original. Speared to the business end of a wobbling spoon, for instance, or the tail of a wiggling crank bait, a chunk of rind increases the wobble and adds to the wiggle.

Pork rind comes in sizes small enough for fly-casting to bluegills and lunker enough for trolling muskies. With a sharp knife it can be altered to fit any fish's idea of a good time. It comes in colors, too, to add some dash to the flash of a lure. Surely a tackle box that is lacking the familiar little jars is a tackle box unfulfilled.

Notes

10 Spring woods are turkey woods and turkey-hunter woods. But spring woods are perilous woods to hunters, camouflaged from the tops of themselves to the very bottoms, who creep through the woods sounding of turkey sounds, being ever so much of a turkey.

And spring woods are perilous woods to turkey hunters wearing red like the red of a gobbler's head, or white like a topknot, or blue like the blue of a hen.

And perilous to those well hidden who wave unexpectedly or nod to a passing hunter, or talk to a hunter in a turkey's voice. And perilous to those who call so gobblelike that they themselves become the hunted of a hunter.

And perilous to those who sit hidden before a tree not wide enough to cover their shoulders nor high enough to cover their heads. For some who call themselves hunters shoot at sound and movement. They do not assume that each sound they hear and movement they see comes not from a turkey at all, but from you or me.

Some early-bird first robins have come back, to eke out a meager living in dirty snow-studded yards. We worry about the bird, even though we know it can backtrack 250 miles a day, if it has to, to warmer places. In my woods and probably yours, gossiping in the afternoon breezes of the goings-on in woody societies with the oak, the pine, the popple, and the maple stands the birch tree—slim, graceful, milky white.

Notes

March

Though they've been out before, on sunny days, thaw butterflies, perfectly disguised as dead leaves, flutter about in warm protected areas as if it were summer, a nice thought. Down the length of a tiny struggling stream wings a lone male cardinal, pivoting from branch to branch, his color against the snow like a promise of things to come.

11 Remember the hot sun shining on your shoulders, and the tossing of a plug way out there, and the sound of the pleasant kerplunk it makes as it hits the water, sending out little worry lines of waves? Remember the couple of weeks at the cabin, maybe, or morning coffee cooked on a campfire? Remember the beach and the singular pleasure of wet sand squishing through city-soft toes? Remember?

Well, my friend, forget it. For right around the corner, though spring and the ensuing summer be light years off, you'll find the pleasant stuff of the here and now. It's the boating and camping and fishing shows that I'm talking of. Guides, lodge owners, tackle manufacturers, outfitters, tent makers, and boat builders line up in row after wonderful row to talk such sweet talk to us, to bring us the promises of the promised land, the songs of loons and the smell of woodsmoke in quiet places, and enough hope to get us past the groundhog's prediction and well into dandelions and mosquitoes.

Notes

12 The coming of spring means the coming of steelheading, when the gates of heaven rest ajar, admitting some of us who might otherwise be denied a ticket.

With heaven, though, we all too often get a little purgatory, too. Ninety-something percent of all steelheaders fish the same crowded elbow-to-elbow waters at more or less the same time.

If misery loves company, then steelheading deserves some solitude.

Is it not possible for a steelheading person to have a cake and eat it too? It is. The big rivers do attract the heaviest runs of fish, but between those name-dropping waters run dozens of nearly nameless streams with their proportionate share of these beautiful rainbows.

This is deliciously lonely steelheading, intimate, in fishable waters measured not by the mile but by the foot, where we hopscotch from pool to pool and where, using yarn and spawn bags, we every so often take a very nice fish.

More red-winged blackbirds return. These males come back a couple of weeks before the females to stake out territories in cattail marshes. Houseflies lured from winter quarters eagerly mate for the first of many times—unless my equally eager, stalking, swatter-swinging spouse can lay them flat first. Willow twigs are getting yellowish. The sun has some real oomph to it, and day's end brings a nice, though short, glow of twilight.

Notes

March

13 It has no jaws, nor even a mouth really, but rather a long vacuum-cleaner hose of an opening into which it sucks up most anything in the water to digest. About this opening grow four sensory whiskers, called barbels. Its hide is a scaleless mottled gray, and on each of its sides diamond-shaped, armorlike shields provide its only defense. Toothless, it has no offense.

Its long, thick body, maybe six feet of it, maybe more, tapers near the back fin to a slender shark's tail. H. Longfellow writes of one big enough to have swallowed Hiawatha. Canoe and all. It's possible. It swam the waters when the soaring lizard pterodactyl cast its shadow over the plodding giant, *Tyrannosaurus rex*. Some living today could have been alive when your grandfather was born. Males mature and spawn at fifteen years and do so every other year; females must wait to lay their eggs until they're ten years older, then do so only every five years. The sturgeon—*mishe-nahma* to the Ojibwa, who speared them and smoked them on great feasts—have been around for around eighty million years.

And that's a long time, my friend, a long, long time.

Notes

14 "The world is so full of a number of things," wrote Robert Louis Stevenson, "I'm sure we should all be happy as kings." And one of those "things" old R. L. was writing of just had to be jerky, which offers about everything anyone can ask for in a trail food. Jerky is lightweight, easy to carry, energy high, and needs no refrigeration. It is, however, too expensive for us to use on a regular basis, unless, of course, we make our own. Which we do by cutting meat—beef, venison, raccoon, beaver, most any meat—into slices one-quarter inch thick. We soak it overnight in barbecue sauce, or one tablespoon of brown sugar to each cup of soy sauce, or any of the dozens of recipes around. In the morning we wipe the slices off a bit, put them into the oven on a greased rack with a drip pan under it. We turn the oven to as low as it goes, leave the door slightly ajar, and go away for eight to eleven hours. We eat some right away, when we come back, and then we pack our royal snack.

Venus shines in the western twilight sky. Sharptail grouse dance on "booming" grounds. Mallards and goldeneyes swim in defrosted ponds. Goldfinches become more spring-golden. Popsicle-frozen frogs begin to thaw. Red osier dogwood shrubs display reddish twigs. Wood-chucks, or groundhogs, bask in the sun.

Notes

March

The first bluebirds arrive, lured by weather that may turn against them. Brown creeper numbers are steadily increasing. More skunks are about. Trumpeter swans are trumpeting. Crows are all over the place. Flocks of horned larks gather at roadsides and in meadows. Wild strawberries poke their heads out. Mourning doves "coo-coo" magnificent sounds.

15 The philosophy of catch-and-release fishing—the returning of a caught fish to the water, so it might live to be caught another day—is a good one, I guess. An honorable one, I suppose. And probably a necessary one these days. But I'm not so certain that's the only way to go.

Let's say, for instance, that I float atop the water in a craft fitted with the very latest in everything ever devised to catch fish. At the flip of a switch, I spot, on a three-color TV screen, a big one, floating directly below me. I quickly release a chemically treated scented lure, scientifically designed to dance a schottische, throw a kiss, and wink an eye, to the preprogrammed depth, dead center on the fish's nose.

Well, I should probably put that fish back, and a few more besides.

But if you go out smartly, but not so gadget-equipped, and experience the joy of fishing as an art, and happen to catch a few fish for supper, well, I say eat them. And if you should latch on to a really big one, I say eat the insides and hang the rest of it on the wall; you've earned it.

Notes

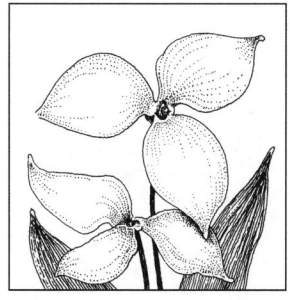

16 The thrill of experiencing the unexpected draws many to the canoe—traveling the same rushing rivers that pulled the Indians downstream, rivers where foam spins and bobs in the same eddies that wetted the missionaries, rivers where the water splashes still bright on the rocks that poked holes in the crafts of the fur traders. While the river has many good lessons to teach us, untrained canoeists should not begin their education there.

They should begin on still water, on quiet lakes, keeping one eye on the weather, for those placid ponds can become boiling cauldrons, often in minutes. Canoeists must learn to respect rough water, staying off it if they can, or if not, staying close to the lee shore. If they find themselves on rough, open water they must quarter against the waves or head into them. They must not let waves hit them broadside. Going into the wind, they should keep the bow low; going with it, they should keep the stern low.

Canoeing is as safe as Saturday night bowling, and dangerous only when foolish people take foolish risks.

Snow trilliums are up. Maple buds swell with anticipation. Barred owls go nest-hunting. White-tailed deer shed winter coats. Great blue herons come back. The same with sandhill cranes. And meadowlarks. And kingfishers. The songs of robins just flow all over the place, and earthworms ever so slowly work their way topside. Alder brush dangles catkins from twig tips. We really should go fishing or canoeing.

Notes

March

Having set their clocks by the sun, saps flow in maple trees. Flocks of Bohemian waxwings pick at maple buds. The junco migration is on again. Big brown bats take wing. At least I think that's what that was. Eagles feed on winter-killed deer until better stuff comes along. Nothing goes to waste out in the woods.

17 People must be served. Highways must be constructed, parking lots paved, malls built and subdivisions developed, for we must travel, purchase supplies for our existence, we must have somewhere to call home. Yet with it all goes more open space, green space, wild space; with it all goes wildlife—everything from ladybugs to blue jays, horny toads to tadpoles. Each of us, however, can ensure a place for wildlife in our lives. We can recreate, where we can, green space, wild space—small oases—potential homes for Mother Nature's own. This space may be no bigger than a balcony garden or window box; it may be a big backyard or a cluttered city eyesore. By adding trees, shrubs, flowers, and birdhouses, feeders and baths, by planting plants that provide food and cover, by allowing vegetation to grow into a natural state, we realize a commitment to replace some of what we've taken. We create small chunks of habitat that attract, shelter, feed, and protect—backyard bonanzas for wildlife and for us.

Notes

18 No matter the calendar, it's the warming nights and days that truly signal the coming home of spring. Those bring the robins back and the rototillers out of hibernation. And those warm shallow, protected bays to temperatures in the forties, attracting flocks of crappies and anglers anxious for open-water fishing and fine cold-water suppertime fillets.

Crappies are among the first to move into shallow waters in the spring, but to suggest they're eager to enter into a frying pan is exaggeration of the highest order. No, it takes some experimentation and close attention to detail. Line must be light, four pound monofilament; hooks, small, long-shanked, #6s and #8s; bobbers, about the size of a hefty olive—with enough split shot tucked under them to float them flush with the surface. We'll use two-inch shiners, which we might hook through the lips, because crappies often enjoy a slowly retrieved bait. We'll not set the hook very hard at a bite, or we'll tear it out of a crappie's papery mouth, have to do without fish dinner and be forced to stop on the way home for hot dogs.

Approximately the difference between heaven and hell.

Though some skunk cabbages have melted their way up through the ice some time ago, more and more do so, attracting more and more bees. There's not much heat to it, but the March sun bounces off the water, dances in the trees, and begins to melt the gum that seals the poplar buds. Partridge pick buds on apple trees.

Notes

March

The miracle is upon us. The Big Dipper. The Great Bear has swung to the east, enroute to its trip overhead. The little one walks across the sky, the pole star getting a free ride at the tip of its tail. Forest mosses begin to turn green. Early sea gulls snoop around. Jupiter rises in the east as the sun sets.

19 Smell it, feel it, stick out your tongue and taste it. Spring is busting out all over. Put away the snowshoes. Put away the skis. Build another wood duck nest, quick, they're back! And a bluebird house, they're here! Sharpen your knives and take a walk, spring is busting out all over. Replace last year's catalogs with this year's. Wipe off the guns, repair the waders, hear the partridge drumming and the pheasants crowing, blow the dust out of the turkey call. Spring is busting out all over. Fix up the bow target, give it a couple of pokes and feel how good it feels. Shoot the twelve-gauge. Shoot it again. Take the dog out, let her run, hard, over the fields and through the woods you hunted last fall. Skip a rock over the waters you fished. Snip off a bouquet of pussy willows and put 'em in a fruit jar full of water on the kitchen table. Spring is busting out all over. Call the guys out to the hunting shack. Take a couple of practice casts in the backyard, hunt up the boat plug. Take a nap. Spring is here, busting out all over.

Notes

20 By the time we actually see a wild turkey, it's often gone. We scout for turkeys, but not so much as to spook them. We concentrate on beating the eye of the bird—its ace in the hole—so we cover our hands, face, body, and boots to camouflage, to naturalize our intrusion into the realm of this big bird.

We know, too well, that any movement will give us away, so we sit with our backs to a tree wider than we are wide. We want to pile a pile of brush before us, but do not, for as we call with a call, any turkey knows no turkey calls from brush piles—only trickster coyotes.

We sit statue-still, ignore nose itches and cricks in the back. We wait until a bird coming in moves behind a tree before we aim. As we sit and wait, we forget the lighthouse warning white of socks between boot and highwater pant leg.

In a rush of wings, it is time to go home, though we have nothing to do when we get there.

In March, miracles are a dime a dozen. English sparrows have lost the grayish fuzz at the tip of each feather, revealing their true colors. The differences between nuthatches, male and female, become very obvious. The male, in his spring finery, picks up a sunflower seed and chases the female around a tree with it. Love. Ice groans in the rivers that still have ice.

Notes

March

Canada geese fly high by, looking for nesting sites. The vernal equinox—some would call it spring—moves northward at fifteen miles a day, more or less, and climbs a mountain, also more or less, at one hundred feet a day. Does fall push back summer at the same pace? If you could get them to hold still long enough, you could hold twenty peepers in your hand at one time, yet those twenty can fill up a whole night with sounds.

21 I've called them many things, but only rarely have I called them in. But that's okay, because a Canada goose is just about as pretty going as it is coming. And the sound it makes!

Geese, I know, are supposed to honk. The bullying web-footed creatures roaming my grandmother's farmyard honked—ugly, rasping, barking honks. Truck drivers honk. Rush-hour-traffic drivers honk. A guy who works with me honks when he blows his nose.

No, Canada geese call. They call. Heard from the back porch of a far-from-town farmhouse against a backdrop of a setting sun, the call is enough to make a lonely child's heart ache. Heard now in springtime, it is the symbol call of coming home. In the fall it is a call to arms and a call of farewell.

A Canada's call is the call of the wilderness, matched only perhaps by a wolf's cry or an eagle's scream. It is a call of unfettered freedom and a call of romance. A wail, a chuckle, the call of the Canada goose somewhere above a hunter, who dares not look up to find it, first melts his heart, then sends it to a million beats per second.

Notes

22 As the waters in rivers and streams that feed into the Great Lakes begin to warm and the runoff calms down, steelhead, buried within the big lakes, become active and begin to move toward them. And anglers, clothed in insulated everything, braced to brave cold, high waters and slippery banks, shake off winter blues of their own and prepare to meet them.

Steelhead, big water rainbows, gear up for the first of two annual up-river treks. The fish that traveled these same waters last fall return now as very different fish. Then they merely followed the spawning run of other fish to gorge themselves on the spawn. But now it's their turn to reproduce, and they must travel upstream to do so.

Spring steelheading usually begins in earnest after river ice breaks up—the fish holding off, stacking up in the big lakes, until the water reaches a temperature that signals the time has come to move. And move they do, slowly at first, and then more and more, up to anxious anglers in dire need.

Red squirrels bounce all over the place, chasing each other through hesitantly retreating splotches of snow or bare spots where the white stuff has given up the ghost, perhaps temporarily. That chickadee again? Some say it can change directions in midair in 1/3000th of a second. Those beggar ticks we shook off our pants legs last fall look for places to settle down and take root.

Notes

March

In an exultant expression of spring, the woodcocks come home, the male flying in a grand display of lovemaking, punctuating his antics with a triumphant "Peeent!" And the sun, what sun March skies allow, has a different feel to it, a real sun feel to it.

23 So many of us buy a lure because of what it looks like on the top, when the only part of it a fish sees is the bottom. We want the ideal: one that looks good on the shelf, in our tackle box, on the end of our line, and in the water and catches all kinds of fish, in all kinds of water, in all kinds of weather, day or night. It flutters, floats, flops, and dives on command.

Now most of us have been around long enough to know that the ideal of anything doesn't exist, at least to the extent we'd like it. What keeps us going is hope. "Hope that springs eternal," like Casey's standing up to bat.

"What are they biting on?" we ask hopefully.

"Well," shrugs the grizzled clerk who hasn't been on the water in 150 years, "innyone who's ketchin' innything is usin' this here thing with the purty little yellow thing onit." And he'll be right. Because he's told that to everyone who's been in, and that's all anyone is using—including the folks who aren't catching a thing and are too embarrassed to come in and brag about it.

But maybe this time he's right, though. Maybe, just maybe, that pretty little thing will do the trick. I sure hope so, and I'll give it a try if you will.

Notes

24 In the vast outdoor catalog of very fine sounds, the steady drip of sugar maple sap spilling out a spile to the bottom of a bucket ranks high. It is a spring symphony of the highest order. If you've never made maple syrup, you really ought to give it a try. Start small—with that one tree.

When the nighttime temps drop below freezing and the daytime temps don't, drill a slanting-up hole, three-quarter inch in diameter and a couple of inches deep, on the south side of the tree. It won't hurt it. Tap in a spile and hang the basket. From that one tree you might get twenty gallons of sap—enough for a half gallon of syrup. Sap sours, so keep it cool. When you've got what you want, boil it—outside first, on a campstove maybe for this little bit. When it's all boiled away but about a gallon, finish it on the kitchen stove until a candy thermometer reads about 219 degrees and no more.

Call then, quickly, for pancakes and ice cream; syrup's up and all's right with the world.

Killdeer are back, and none too soon. Did March come in like a lion or a lamb? No matter. The south sides, bare sides, of hills show definite signs of green. The table that will hold the feasts of April and May is being set here near the end of March. And again, none too soon. Spiders crawl out from wherever they spent the winter.

Notes

March

Chipmunks, very hungry chipmunks, climb above ground for a look-see and a stay. The larvae of the mosquitoes flex their larvae-muscles and drift to the surfaces of puddles and ponds. Early-arriving purple grackles turn over each and every leaf on the ground to find earthworms and groggy spiders—the macaroni and cheese of grackles. Black-birds, up from marshlands down south, harmonize with March wind songs.

25 Lots of folks, when the chips are down and they have to have a fish or two, go fishing with a worm or two, confident that when fish are biting on anything, they'll bite on worms also, and when fish aren't biting on anything, they'll probably bite on worms anyway.

Maybe so. It seems if there's a bait around that never lets you down, or lets you down the least, worms are it. It's so in the spring, when the water is bank-high and coffee colored and it's raining nickel drops or snowing great big springtime flakes.

Why, worms even work for us dunkers when the water is clear as glass and cold enough to freeze a whatnot. We're talking real worms—top-drawer characters in their prime—all fresh and lively and looking for a fight, properly strung and properly placed.

A worm's got to be hooked lightly—through the nose or somewhere between either end. Just once, not twice. Not thrice. Hooks and leaders must be kept as small as practical and sinkers left out of the picture whenever possible, allowing the worm to do its own thing in its own way. It knows the ropes.

Notes

26 Let us say that this is the end of the first day of a campout. And though you have repeatedly pointed out what a wonderful person you are and how terribly hard you have labored to make this an efficient, orderly camp, you have after all drawn the short straw, and you will prepare supper for the crew or suffer, they say, severe though unspecified penalties.

So you, long a drawer of short straws, have come prepared and do not shirk your camply duties.

On a long rock, table, upturned boat, tailgate, or series of canoe paddles, place first one large square of heavy-duty foil for each ungrateful campmate. Then, in a row, align plastic bags (prepared at home for just such an emergency) of bite-size pieces of lean sirloin steak, thinly sliced carrots, corn, diced potatoes, chopped onions, and chunks of tomatoes. At the end of the row put salt, pepper, butter, and strips of bacon. Have the eaters pile their foils high with whatever they like and top it all with spices, butter, and bacon. Tell them to seal the stew tightly with double folds and put it on hot coals for about forty-five minutes, turning once. They will eat right off the foil.

In a grand gesture, offer to do the dishes, too.

Baby otters get born in dens along lakeshores and streams. Balls of wood frog eggs must be getting anxious; in a race against time, they must hatch into pollywogs and turn into frogs before their pool homes dry up in a summer's sun. So much to do, so little time. Crocuses deliberately reassure us that it's really spring.

Notes

March

Crawling from under wintering moss and leaves, inch-long spring peepers hunt insects and call in great choruses that sound like so many of Santa's sleigh bells. Have these cold March winds blown themselves out? Probably not. Will they be but a dim memory in April? Yep. Late April, maybe. Tundra swans fly over. Wood ducks have come home. March's sun fans the fires of romance in bug and bird and bee. And you and me.

27 Much thought goes into getting youngsters a first gun (Horrors!), a first bow (Yipes!), a first automobile (Over my dead body!), which is all well and good as far as it goes, but we might be missing the boat somewhere along the line—a pity because a youngster's very own first boat (Oh, dear!) can be as challenging, as exciting, as rewarding, as good-kid producing as any of the many major steps a child takes in an early life of steep, narrow stair climbing.

A child's boundless energy and great and wonderful enthusiasm must be directed, or it will find its own direction. Directing a kid to the water can teach him or her self-reliance, appreciation and respect for the out-of-doors, good judgment, and the responsibilities and pride of ownership. Using Dad's boat is okay, but not the same. Using a toy thingamabob is worse.

No, it should be the real thing, but not too big nor too bulky—just right for the waters to be floated. There must be a whole lot of education.

Hazardous? It's a good possibility these days that there are more hazards ashore than there are afloat, don't you think?

Notes

28 Now it happens in these spring days, at unguarded intervals (with such infrequency as not to be numbered), that there is nowhere we have to be and nothing we have to do when we get there.

So we go to the country, hike into the hollow and deep woods to wild brooks and streams and rivers to fish for trout.

But in this fishing, we do not use our far-out casting skills. We sneak on hands and knees (like a kid slipping in after curfew), or belly even, to where trout lie bank-tight under tangled brush and branches (where we couldn't cast if we wanted to).

And once within a rod's reach of this bank, we softly push that rod forward to the water, dangling from the tip of that rod a three-to-eight-foot leader and flylike ant, beetle, cricket, hopper, or caterpillar (that often fall to hungry trout with tiny splooshes and splashes) or mayfly or caddis fly—to fish that relish them so—keeping as much of the tippet as possible out of the water in fishing for a fish that we relish so.

Red-tailed hawks come home scream-whistling, performing unbelievable 120-mile-per-hour dive-bombing drops to the earth in show-off mating rites. Salamanders move from building foundations, old pocket gopher mounds, or logs to wherever they spend the spring and summer months. Fox sparrows come in. Brooks are babbling, the garden peas look nice, the lettuce lovely, the strawberries tempting—within the pages of newly arrived seed catalogs.

Notes

March

29 "C'mon, you wimp," yells a brother-in-law you could do without, but your wife's okay, so you put up with him. And it's his canoe.

You are poised above the kind of rapids that tear big chunks out of canoes, the kind of rapids that drop like run-away escalators.

Anyway, the current makes up your mind for you, and you prove Columbus incorrect by dropping off the edge of the world. And then you tip over, as you knew your would, and you continue on down without benefit of boat.

But this has happened to you before, so you know enough not to get in front of the canoe on its solo trip through the tricky currents, so it will not, can not, pin you painfully again and again against big hard rocks. You, therefore, quickly get out of the way of the bouncing battering ram and follow it downstream where it will at some time, in some place, slow down and wait for you.

And you cannot help but notice that this apparently has not happened before to your brother-in-law, and he is not nearly as well prepared, and you take some satisfaction in that.

Notes

30 I hate bugs. It doesn't matter to me whether or not all insects are classified as bugs or if it's the other way around. I hate them all. Horseflies, deerflies, blackflies, houseflies. I don't like them. Mosquitoes, wood ticks, chiggers, wasps, hornets. They're all bugs to me and I don't like them.

And I don't like spiders or ants, either. Even as winter leaks out of March, and we're quite satisfied that spring is just around the corner, the fly in the ointment—if you'll excuse the expression—is that so are bugs. All kinds of bugs. Bugs as eggs, larvae, pupae, or adults seek out any sheltered, safe retreat to spend the winter months, but you know as well as I that they're there—waiting . . . waiting.

Okay. Maybe I've overstated the case. Maybe I don't exactly hate all bugs, for one snugly fixed to a small hook, floating vigorously down a trout stream, is a most pleasant bug indeed.

Snowshoe hares begin to lose their white coats as the snow melts, not wanting to look unfashionably white against a brown ground, easy targets of winged hunters. We can hear peepers a half mile away, but we can't see one three feet in front of our noses. Most bald eagles have nested by now.

Notes

March

Dawn comes almost an hour earlier than it did way back on the first. Coltsfoot, one of the earliest blooming wildflowers, blooms on sheltered hillsides in full sun or nearly so. Wood frogs begin calling, if that's what they do. "Croaking" doesn't do it justice. And that's March. Paid in full. It wasn't May or even April, which is upon us, but it wasn't February either. At least not too much of the time.

31 Probably none of us defines well that illusive will-o-the-wisp word—happiness. Yet how often do we rush through life, plotting and planning and working for that magical moment when we've finally arrived, really got it made? And once it has been achieved, does anyone know it, fully—even if it hits us over the head with a rainbow?

Those who love the out-of-doors do, I think. We're a lot alike in that way. We find happiness in the bits and pieces, the stuff and nonsense of each day's life and living.

Happiness, for us, is a springtime full moon (though a half will do) wrapped in early morning mist and ribboned with an owl's hoot. Happiness, for us, is Mariah, the wind, arranging gray and white clouds above needled pines, long peaceful nights lit with heartbreak half-moons, symphonies of loons riding low on the water, and the rumble of thunder on a hot summer's night. Happiness, for us, is sassy streams somersaulting through forests deep, dancing wild flowers, and wandering tribes of butterflies. For us life is tasted, touched, smelled, felt, seen, and savored, and that, my friend, is honest-to-God, downright happiness.

Notes

April

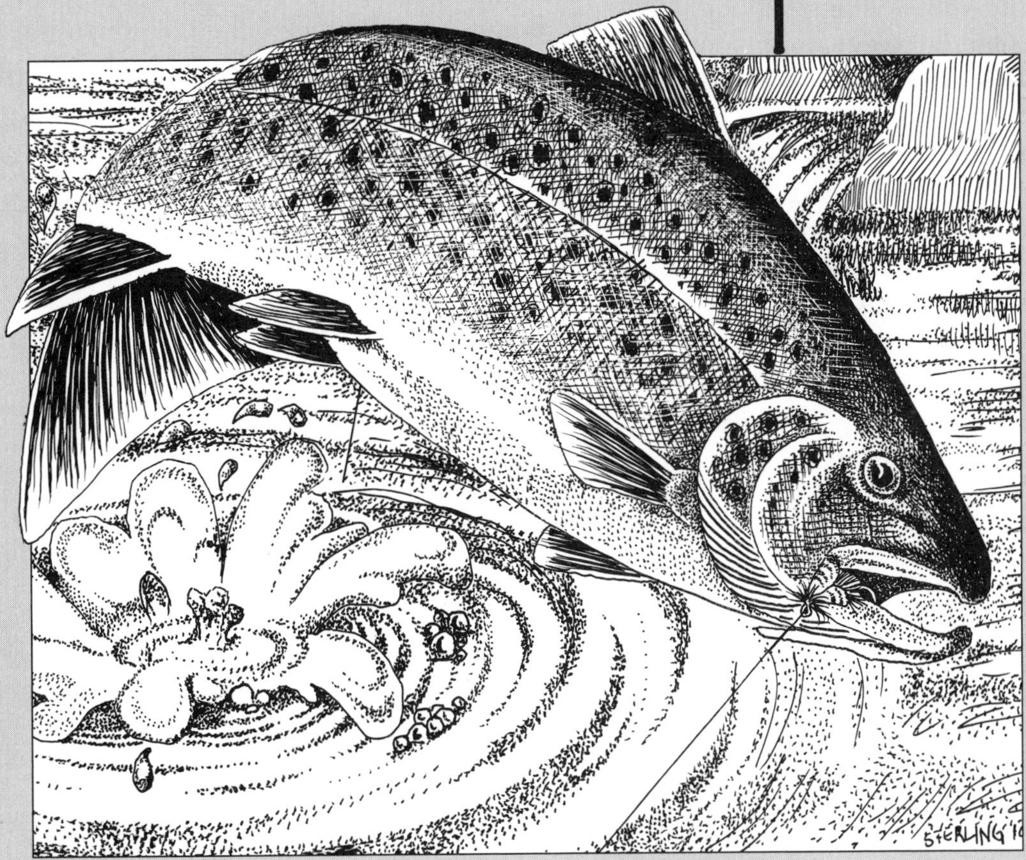

April

Ah, April. At last April. We want April to be so-o-o perfect. We expect the cold of January, we live with the bitterness of February, and we're more than willing to put up with the madness of March. But April had better behave. It is, after all, the month of the Moon of Maple Syrup Running and the Grass Growing Moon.

1 April. April has finally arrived. You know what that means. It's time to clean and fix, to mend. Time to get fit for the rigors of the outdoor life. Time to shed winter fat with a push-up. And a pull-up. Time to touch the toes a time or two. Time to take a nap.

It's time to fish for smoking suckers. Time for pussy willows and duck nesting and robin singing.

It's time to paint the lucky lures and to sharpen hooks. Time to float atop a river with an anxious canoe and thirsty paddle.

It's planting time and turkey time and time to give the bunny a hand, filling baskets with Easter eggs and fishing tackle. Time to visit old folks and expose them to this April sun. And time to put out the dock again.

Or is that rushing it a bit?

Notes

2   When we speak of wetlands, we might be speaking of a marsh. If so, we speak of something wonderful indeed, for a marsh makes up an entire universe unto itself. It is most often a shallow basin with from one-half foot to three feet of standing water at its core.

A marsh is alive with plants. Cattails grow here, elbow to elbow with bulrushes, head to toe with water lilies, side by side with arrowheads. Some plants live entirely under water, some float atop it, some hang halfway between, some stand beside it.

It is alive with birds. Some stop to rest, to refuel, some stay to breed and raise their young, returning year after year, for generations. Hovering, diving, perching, nesting, and feeding atop and within a marsh are yellow-headed and red-winged blackbirds, swamp sparrows, wood ducks, orioles, yellow throats, bitterns, herons, grebes, coots, mallards, terns, and wrens.

A marsh is alive with frogs, turtles, snakes, salamanders, tadpoles, mink, and muskrat.

When we speak of filling in wetlands, we might be speaking of filling in a marsh and all that it includes. Forever.

We can smell the changes of April more surely, more completely than we can see them: one whiff being worth a thousand . . . well, you know. Returning wood ducks check out nesting boxes. Mother ducks make the final selection in this month so full of beginnings. No matter the brief interruptions, the Ice Age, for all intents and purposes, has passed for another season. So come on, April, do your stuff.

Notes

April

Purple martins, back from winter in South America, go house hunting. Cottontails mate, as usual. Peregrine falcons return. Pussy willows bloom. Basements begin leaking. Night crawlers, well, crawl around at night. Swans return. Otters slide and glide where there's still ice and sunbathe where there isn't. Otters are versatile. Mops and brooms and scrub buckets appear from dark closets for annual rites of spring cleaning.

3 Folks for a long time have been capturing their wild moments on film—to enjoy at those in-house times when they're sofa-stuck in foul weather or bedridden in worse. Try sometime, if you're of a mind to, to add sound tracks to your treasury of the great outdoors.

You create them by propping up a battery-operated tape recorder out in the middle of nowhere where you like to spend your time—especially in the early mornings or late afternoons when things are at their busiest, their noisiest.

Trap the sounds of a loon strutting his stuff or the slap of a beaver's tail or a cocky pheasant doing some bragging. Catch a bob white repeating itself or a gobbler gobbling. And the chirps and grunts and whistles and snorts and squeals and honks and quacks and kerplunks and the winds soughing through pines and drummings and peeps and sighs and screechings and falling rains and waves scraping shores and waterfallings and hoots and bleats and gurgles and yips and yowls and buglings and buzzings and take it all home and arrange a beautiful bouquet of sounds.

It's better than bringing back a handful of wildflowers, and it lasts a lifetime.

Notes

4 Ben and I are trout fishing here in early spring when the trout are many and the anglers few. For me, I'm fishing like I always do—like I do in the summer—but Ben chuckles at that and calls me names.

For one thing, he says, this water's springtime cold and the fish aren't quite awake yet, so you've got to fish them in slow-poke motion.

And, another thing, he adds, the water's springtime cloudy, so they can't see all that well either. So, he continues, you've got to fish the fish through its nose, appeal to its sense of smell, about the most sophisticated in the animal kingdom, and to its sense of hearing, almost as good.

So what he does is to take a bit of a worm, which smells like a worm, and string it on a little spinner, which makes pretty underwater music. He fishes it as natural as he can, getting down to the deep holes and under undercut banks, and he retrieves it so-o-o-o slow. And so do I.

How many we catch, I forget, but we let a lot go and save a couple of beauties for breakfast.

Bees buzz nearly everywhere in search of any pollen they can get their behinds to. Dandelions march steadily, relentlessly, recurringly across lawns and fields and back again. Though many have been here for awhile, robins don't usually get serious about coming back until the average twenty-four-hour temperature is thirty-five degrees. Those early voices of those first few most-welcomed peepers swell in mass chorus of pop concerts.

Notes

April

Stocky, short-legged, long-billed, solitary, and secretive common snipes, also called Wilson's snipes, return to breeding grounds in marshes and bogs. Chipmunks stuff themselves with sunflower seeds spilt from feeders. The harsh, scolding "chee-chee" of the blue jay has mellowed into a springtime come-and-get-me "linnet-linnet," though you have to listen carefully for it and give the bird the benefit of the doubt.

5 For some of us spring means the coming home of robins and meadowlarks. Others of us see it in the blooming of wildflowers, and yet others of us find it in warm breezes stirring newly washed kitchen curtains. But for a good many of us, spring means bullheads—or fishing for bullheads, to be precise.

On cold spring nights, armed with lanterns, we venture forth to fish deep, black waters for these handsome (not to be confused with pretty) whiskered fish—among the first to get serious about taking baited hooks after ice-out. Though bullheads can be caught most anytime, it's in early springtime they go on extended feeding binges—in preparation for an early spawning season.

Folks who fish for bullhead are hardly a snobbish lot. We're kind, helpful, and considerate, we wear old clothes and buy our tackle at hardware stores, we find bait in flower beds. There are few better-eating anythings than firm and tasty springtime bullheads, and no fish is easier to clean. My mother is from the "You caught it; you clean it" school, but she could clean a washtub full of bullheads before a houseful of hungry kids could wash up and set the table. I bet she still can. Hey, Ma!

Notes

6 Probably none of us are so dumb we'd suck a thumb good and wet and stick it in a light socket to see if it's plugged in. Yet some of us aren't clever enough not to play the same kind of roulette with a loaded bolt of lightning.

That's what we do when the fishing's so good we ignore darkened skies and picking-up winds. Lightning should scare the dickens out of us. It stuns, shocks, blinds. It kills. With lightning, it is hard to be too careful. Fishing in a boat on a lake makes us the tallest object around and a prime target for a once-in-a-lifetime experience. If we haven't got a good forecast, or, understandably, have no faith in the one we have got, we've got to be able to read clouds and interpret changing conditions.

We've got to get to cover well before a storm hits. It we can't get to the landing, we've got to beach wherever we can. If even that's not possible, we've got to get as low in the boat as we can, pulling in antennas and fishing poles.

Lightning bolts are made up of millions of volts that travel one hundred yards or more in water, killing in a heartbeat.

All born these days are born under the first sign of the zodiac, Aries, the ram, a five-starred constellation. The spring duck migration reaches its peak about now. Bald eagles continue nesting chores, building or adding to huge platforms of sticks and debris, near but not at the top of the tallest live tree around. Robins strut at curbsides, singing loud and clear. Robins think they own April, and that's okay; though if I could, I'd sign the lease over to woodcocks.

Notes

April

Ospreys return to build nests, around three feet across and about half that deep, at the tops of dead trees. Their call, a sort of "kyew-kyew-kyew," seems kind of weak for such a tough bird. Aspen and alders are full of bee-welcoming pollen. Though the calendar lists the first day of spring on a specific day, we know it comes in stages, and whenever it finally gets here, it will seem this new spring is the first one that ever was.

7 Most of us call all little fish minnows, and though we're wrong about it, we're probably close enough to get by.

Actually minnows have their own scientific family name, which is longer than most of the little fishes themselves. This family is the largest in the fish kingdom—fortunate because minnows are among anglers' favorite choice of bait.

Almost all game fish eat minnows, thrive on minnows, must have minnows to survive. So it's doubly fortunate that minnows live in virtually every body of water in the country, which makes it easy for minnow trappers to capture, net, and otherwise secure them by themselves, without having to buy them, though bait dealers are fine people and have a right to make a living too.

Inexpensive minnow traps are available everywhere. To catch the little fish, anglers sprinkle bread crumbs, crackers, or oatmeal in and around the traps, which are anchored near weeds, stumps, or rocks in a couple feet of water. Minnow trappers must be alert though—thieves often steal the traps, which is unfortunate.

Notes

8 You never realize how much you use your big toe until in the darkness of the middle of the night, you slam it hard against an attacking nightstand, driving the little piggie that went to market well into your foot—from whence it sprouts to a glowing, growling mass of hurt. And you must walk on it.

It's a bit of a reach, but such is it, too, with rope—or the lack thereof—on a camping trip. You just never realize how much you miss rope until you are forced to do without it—far, far from home.

Without rope, packs cannot be lashed to canoes. Canoes cannot be tied to shorelines, or anchored. Without rope, foodstuffs cannot be hoisted out of the reach of marauding bully bears or thieving porcupines. Without rope, tents cannot be tethered to stakes, wet clothing cannot be hung to dry.

Without rope, those that came beltless stay beltless; the broken stuff that would have been mended with a length of rope goes unmended.

Though we are at the end of our rope, without rope we can do nothing about it. Indeed, without rope, we can't even string up the dope who forgot to pack it.

To the joy of male red-winged blackbirds, who've been waiting a couple of weeks at least, the females finally arrive at staked-out cattail marshes. Let the nest building begin. Gardeners flock to waiting hardware stores, which sprout the wonderful tools of the gardener's trade. Canvasbacks, ring-necks, and buffleheads swing by on their way elsewhere. I wish they would stay. We can see March in the willows, but we see April in the birches.

Notes

April

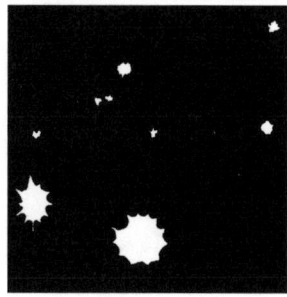

9 It's no news to anybody that bluegills fall into two distinct categories—big ones and little ones. It can be news to some, though, that they don't behave anything alike. Runt bluegills come easy much of the time, but catching the slab-sided, plate-sized bulls, well, that can take some doing. Knowing the differences in the habits, the habitats, and the temperaments of these fiery big/little scrappers makes the task of hooking them more consistently pleasant.

Big bluegills are gypsies. Here today, there tomorrow—not at all like those hang-around, nip-at-anything little pests that swarm to worm-hooked kids' lines at the end of docks. Few fish are more choosy than big bull bluegills. They might prefer floating bugs in the morning, insist upon particular sinking lures at midday, and sneer at anything but tiny black gnats at sundown.

Anglers who want the ultimate delight of big bluegills bathed in cornmeal and quick-fried in hot grease come well-armed with arsenals that include all of it and more, and they keep trying until they get it right.

Notes

10 The only thing disagreeable about wood ducks is that they leave us so early in the fall. Everything else about them is wildly wonderful. By now, the female, accompanied by her mate, has already checked the closet space and bathroom size of each tree cavity or nesting box near the spot where she was raised, and has laid, in one of them, around a dozen beautiful eggs. At this very moment, she is probably sitting on those eggs—for what will amount to a thirty-day incubation period (with two short lunch breaks a day)—if, that is, raccoons or snakes or fox squirrels or mink or red-headed woodpeckers or flickers don't make a meal of them first.

And once hatched, if hatched, the little puffballs drop from their high nest, bounce once or twice, and scoot past hunting hawks and crows and foxes and cats and dogs in a race-for-life dash for open water. Where snapping turtles and bass and herons wait with wide open appetites.

Who can doubt the ways of nature? So, I suppose, it's only fitting that those little woodies who successfully weave their way through fate into adulthood are so beautiful. They become to the bird world what a rose is to the world of flowers.

Solitary except now in mating season, belted kingfishers, with their loud, dry rattles of a call, return to woodland streams and ponds to catch fish and dig long nest burrows in sandy banks. Cowbirds come to lay eggs in the nests of other birds, the dirty rats. The male's call is a squeaky gurgling. From wood, paper wasps make paper nests, insulated against the heat and the cold and waterproof, too.

Notes

April

So secretive we hardly ever see them, saw-whet owls match up in dense forests and wooded swamps. Sometimes after the ten o'clock news and often after my bedtime, they start their monotonously repeated single-note whistles, which sound like a cross between a saw being sharpened and the landing beep of a spaceship.

11 Reading a river provides the key to consistently catching fish from it. Reading take-it-easy streams is one thing, but the broken-water rivers, with fast, smooth-flowing stretches, whitewater riffles, deep holes, fast runs, and underwater obstructions of log and rock pose more of a challenge.

In these waters fish rest and feed where they don't have to fight the full powers of the current. For instance, the current along both sides of a boulder jutting from the water leaves a pocket of quiet water just behind it. Here a fish can lie in comfort without having to fight the current and can, at the same time, dart out to feed on worms or insects washing down—maybe at the end of a hook. Or maybe not.

And fast water washes over and around underwater stumps and pilings, forming bulges on the surface—below and behind which fish rest and lie in wait for something filling to wash by. They hold at the edges of eddies and fast water, where the water shelves up before spilling into the next riffle, funnels between boulders and logs. Sounds like the river's full of fish, doesn't it? Or maybe not.

Notes

12 Perhaps too often, those of us who fish for trout depend for our luck on tackle shops or tying benches. Now there's no doubt that without some good-looking something at the end of a leader, we might as well spend our fishing time going to garage sales or pushing grocery carts. And surely anglers with a head full of entomology and a hat full of flies do catch some fish. But, besides that, it's knowing what to do once on the stream, and when to do it and why, that generally separates the be's from the wannabe's.

Consistently successful folks restrict their fishing to a few select streams, so they can learn their waters well. Very well. And, since a trout's normal position is with its nose pointing upstream, these knowing anglers will, whenever they can, make their approach, their stalk, from downstream, or as the situation demands, from the angle that offers the least chance of detection. And they try to cast relatively short lines—giving them more control over lures, which results in fewer misses and greater authority over fish once hooked.

Yes, all this do fine anglers do, which is why they're always so darn lucky.

White or blue-violet pasque-flowers have been blooming for awhile and continue to do so. They can afford to be early—their flowers come before their leaves. Mars is a morning star, and Venus takes over right after a sundown that's taking a little longer to get here each and every night. Hepatica blooms on rocky hillsides. It's a nice flower and a heckuva word.

Notes

April

Song sparrows establish territories and build nests on the ground in thick, bushy areas near streams. Red maples bloom. Bobwhite quail begin to call the sweetest call ever called. The first beaver kits are born. Bitterns arrive. More baby rabbits are born, putting valuable food sources in circulation. In the moonlight courting dance of woodcocks, males whirl and spiral straight up and then down again, complete with song.

13 Too many parents of small children make the mistake of putting off camping until the kids are "old enough." Too late, they discover that by the time the kids get old enough, they'd rather be doing something else.

No, the time to take kids out is now. We're not talking, here, of wilderness, over mountains, through rivers, and over glaciers, but we are also most certainly not talking of setting up camp in the living room in front of the TV either. Though that might be good practice, since all good camping requires good planning, and good camping with kids requires the best possible planning.

Kids don't need much to keep them happy. All they really want and need is to be comfortable, safe, and well fed. Start with short, easygoing outings, with plenty of games, books, crayons, and favorite teddy bears. Spoil them rotten on such trips. Double desserts and triple attention. Listen together to loons, tell each other great stories.

For what playpen could be better, and safer, than a tent? Pitched in the pines. Under the stars.

Notes

14 Just thinking: baby skunks are called kittens; baby otters have to be taught to catch fish; badgers are fairly close relatives to the skunk; female red-winged blackbirds don't have red wings, which doesn't seem fair; both male and female bighorn sheep have horns, though, which does; of course beavers don't use their tails as trowels to pack mud; brush wolves are really coyotes; beavers are rodents; though pretty good swimmers, mink do not have webbed feet like otters do; in late fall ruffed grouse develop growths of pectin on their feet as aids to walking on snow and gripping icy branches; elk, mule, and whitetail fawns have spots, but baby moose do not; in California, a compass points east of true north; a grilse is a young salmon; a bird dog that leaves its hunter to hunt on its own is called a bolter—among other things; what some of us call mud hens are professionally known as American coot; greenwing teal are our smallest surface-feeding ducks; and nighthawks aren't hawks at all, but goatsuckers, of all things.

Though they've been frosted into silence a couple of times and snowed over once or twice, the peepers have broken, once and for all, the backbone of winter, and they know it, and they show it, with riotous celebrations driven by automatic trans-missions. Packages of garden seeds bloom in every drug, grocery, and hardware store. Mr. and Mrs. Flicker critically inspect hollow trees for nesting sites.

Notes

April

Inside their dens baby porcupines are born—understandably—one to a mother. Triggered by the temperature, solidly packed balls of snakes disentangle themselves and poke their heads tentatively into the sun before they glide into spring. And April showers bring snails and slugs from under wintering logs and stones for a look-see. More and more birds pair up, two by two by two by two.

15 In all probability, newborn fawns were conceived under fire, carried to term through a freezing, snow-high, near-starvation winter, and born shelterless into a springtime of wet snow and cold rain.

As they take their first wobbly, hesitant steps to begin yet another generation, we cannot help but be reminded of the millions of years of natural selection that have resulted in the speed, grace, beauty, hardiness, and intelligence packaged in these little ones.

Ancient relatives of these fawns' families began roaming the earth millions of years ago, but the whitetail, as we know it, evolved only in the last twenty thousand years or so, making it a relative newcomer among the animals of the world, and native only to North America.

So, armed with the histories of their ancestors and blessed with a heritage of survival, these little critters can step with careful confidence into the future and pass it all along.

Notes

16 What a pickle! This guy goes fishing, intending to release what he catches. He has no need of live box or stringer, and has none. Suddenly, he latches on to a big one. A real big one. He lands it. He has no witnesses. Nor does he have a ruler or measuring tape. Unfortunately, though he has no need to exaggerate this beauty's size, he also has no reputation as a strict man-of-his-word where fish are concerned. But he must know, for personal reasons, how big it truly is.

Desperate, he remembers that a one-dollar bill is six inches long and two and a half wide (so is a twenty, but being a father, he doesn't see those often). He takes a half dozen ones out of his wallet and lays four of them lengthwise and two crossways alongside the fish to determine its size, plus change.

He further remembers the old formula for estimating its heaviness: length plus the girth squared divided by eight hundred. Now he knows.

Though the devil tempts him to keep his prize, he releases it, smug with the answer, in case some should ask how his day went.

Or in case they don't.

Box elder trees bloom. And flocks of grackles, sounding like so many rusty swinging gates, stop by for lunch and a gab session. Shiny black whirligig beetles, looking like watermelon seeds with feet, muck about in still-chilly waters. Birds come and come and each—or most at least—is more than wonderfully welcome, but it's the wild goose who comes north to us with freedom in its cry and adventure in its heart that plants the seeds of each in us.

Notes

April

Garter snakes awake to find themselves hungry and move to ponds to dine on singing, breeding frogs. Buds on weeping willows begin to open. Gooseberry bushes decorate themselves with tiny leaves. Woodcocks parent like crazy and snipe "winnow" like mad. Canada geese lay eggs and pocket gophers dig out new pockets. Grass grows and deep within the bowels of garages and storage sheds, lawn mowers lick their lips.

17 They will come. They will come to farmyard and backyard, to window sill and balcony, to patio and porch, to uptown and downtown, to front door and back. Chickadees will come for bacon drippings, peanut butter, suet, and sunflower seeds. Pine siskins will come for thistle seeds and milo. Goldfinches will come for thistle and sunflower seeds. White- and red-breasted nuthatches will come for peanut butter, suet, and sunflower seeds. Evening grosbeaks will come for sunflower seeds. Downey, and hairy, and pileated woodpeckers will come for peanut butter and suet. Dark-eyed juncos will come for millet, peanut butter, and cracked corn. Pine grosbeaks will come for sunflower seeds. Northern cardinals will come for sunflower seeds and peanut butter. Common redpolls will come for thistle seeds and wheat. American tree sparrows will come for millet and cracked corn. Purple finches will come for thistle seed, millet, and sunflower seeds. Brown creepers will come for suet. And quail might come, and grouse and pheasants and rabbits and squirrels. They'll all come—if you invite them. It'd be a shame to deny yourself the pleasure of their company and them yours.

Notes

18 He fishes not the trout waters of fame and fable, this fisherman, but rather tiny, often unknown, streams of mystery. He is a masterful reader of waters, he approaches trout-holding holes without disturbing the order of things, and he presents his offering to fish in a most natural manner.

He uses a fly rod—its length enables him to accurately place his bait around, over, and under obstacles and into currents. It allows him to keep more line out of the water, reducing drag. He uses monofilament line—it handles easily in cramped circumstances, it runs smoothly through rod guides, and it floats so freely. At the end of the line he ties a #6 or #8 short-shanked hook; eight inches above it he adds split shot to keep the bait on the stream bottom as currents carry it away.

He hooks, simply, a crawler or a worm once through its collar so it appears to a streamwise trout to be a freely-moving meal just washed into the water.

It's not quite the classic pose, I suppose, of a trout fisherman, but it is as clean and pure an experience as has been created.

Marsh marigolds spill gobs of deep yellow petals in swamps and brooksides. Earthworms take walks on sidewalks and driveways. Sora rails feed at the edge of openings in marshes and waterways. Clap your hands or slam a car door, and they might answer. Rototillers migrate from garage corner hibernation to feed on garden soil. Cautious folks just might finally be getting into the swing of spring things. No winter lasts forever, and April proves it.

Notes

April

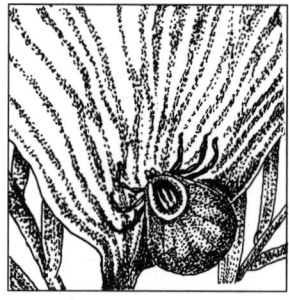

Early wood ticks are on the prowl, waylaying woodcutters and rosebush pruners. Hen mallards nest. Wood ducks are about to hatch. Raccoons hunt the cold muck at waters' edges for anything that moves, leaving their paw prints in the mud. Ever-starving shrews scavenge the same hunting grounds for insects, snails, mice, and each other.

19 While the angler in us gears up for some fine action, days and nights of grand and glorious action, the shotgunner in us sits idle, gathering dust, molding, rusting—not to be got into gear until sometime in the far-away fall future—when, as we have too little time for fishing now, we'll just as surely have too little hunting time.

And when that scarce and valuable hunting time comes we'll have to use too much of it reacquainting ourselves with shotguns and shotgunning, dusting off the dust of inexperience, Bondoing the rust spots of self-confidence, wiping clean the mildew of misuse.

Unless, of course, we right now put ourselves into spring training to become dynamic, reflexive gunners; coordinated, precision instruments of effective wingshooters; by practice, constant practice, by joining trap and skeet clubs, by shooting sporting clays, and later, turning spring practice into summer practice.

Then next fall, folks at one end of a cornfield will watch a pheasant fall, or across a bay see a mallard drop, shake their heads in amazement, and say, "Look at that shooter shoot," and they'll be pointing at us.

Notes

20 Who provides? From whose wallets come the funds for the development of strategies to maintain trout streams and deer herds? Who pays for the restoration of habitat and the prevention of further loss? Who speaks for the bears, the walleyes, and the wolves, the pine trees and porcupines? Who rises to defend the existence of eagles?

Anglers do. And so do hunters. They pay with the many millions of their license dollars. They pay with the many millions of dollars donated to Ducks Unlimited, Trout Unlimited, Pheasants Forever, Whitetail Unlimited, and the Ruffed Grouse Societies. They pay with the specially taxed dollars on each piece of hunting and fishing equipment they buy—dollars totaling well over 5 billion, and growing at over 450 million each year, dollars benefiting all wildlife and all those who enjoy it. They pay with the millions of dollars of their trout stamps and duck stamps. They pay.

It is our anglers and our hunters who care so much about our wildlife that they put their hard-earned dollars where their hearts are.

Tamaracks cover their naked branches with spring coats of needles. The more patient leopard frogs and grass frogs join their cousins the wood frogs and peepers out of hibernation and into snake bait. Otters give birth to two or three blind and helpless kits in riverbank dens. Walleyes spawn, and smelt are due to run any time now. The basic silence that began back when November took a big icy bite out of everything is definitely over. Listen . . .

Notes

April

Four feet tall and seven feet wide, great blue herons fly, with slow, labored wing beats, to colonies of nests used year after year. The lobe-footed, "kuk-kuk-kuk-kukking" American coots are back to bob their heads upon the waters. The sparks of April are set aglow on red maples where red buds have opened on red twigs. It's as if someone turned a little kid loose with a box of dull crayons—all in shades of the same color.

21 Basically, bass are homebodies. In winter they congregate in deep water, and in summer they spend much of their time there, too, with occasional to frequent grocery shopping forays into shallows.

But in spring, bass fancy turns, and like birds and bees and college freshmen, they go on the prowl, leaving deep water that warmed and rested them, to cruise coves and shallows or migrate up streams and rivers searching for just the right spawning beds. It is then and there that anglers wait—and sometimes wait and wait and wait, for not all coves and shallows and not all spring-flooded rivers and streams are created equal, and catching on to a prespawning bass can be a long and lonely business.

So we must hunt, must experiment, must change baits as often as it takes—small plugs and spinners and spoons might work. Streamers and poppers could do the trick. Small underwater slugs might be the answer, or maybe it's plastic worms or crankbaits, or maybe the darn fish don't want nothin', nohow. Or all of it at once.

It's all okay to us, though. We're out doing what we were born to do. And none too soon.

Notes

22 Basically the robin gets credit as the harbinger of spring, and there's no doubt about it, it's good to see and hear that first one.

But when the pussy willows appear, we get the first assurance that winter is once again about to give up its icy hold on us.

Pussy willows are nature's early bloomers, often showing their buds before the snows sign out for the season. Pussy willows grow nearly anywhere in the northern hemisphere where the ground is moist—along lakes, streams, swamps, or roadside ditches. While they put out many seeds, even twigs or branches poked in water can take root.

We are not the only ones eager for them to show themselves, for pussy willows serve as dining tables of sorts. Sharptail grouse eat the buds, some butterflies rely on the flowers for food, and for bees they provide an early source of pollen. Rabbits, elk, moose, deer, beaver, and squirrels browse on the twigs, bark, and foliage.

And little girls, around our house anyway, simply thrive on them.

In the woods, bloodroots, which do bleed a kind of orange stuff from broken stems, show their showy poppylike flowers. Great Lakes steelhead should be running; crappies are moving into the shallows; and mosquitoes are up and at us. The Big Dipper rides high. Whitetail bucks show signs of antler nubbins. Mars, a god of fields and growing things, is a morning star. The sharp teeth of cold nights are now dull and worn.

Notes

April

If the popple buds are as big as a thumbnail, as big as a nickel, the smelt are running. The suckers too. Aphids, caterpillars, and beetles pop out just in time for meat-eating migrating birds. No accident, really. Elms bloom, grackles build nests, and leopard frogs call. In a nice piece of timing, the first batch of bumblebee eggs have been laid and will hatch out just in time to enjoy and pollinate the first batch of apple blossoms.

23 I don't suppose you've ever gone camping without some rain either. I don't suppose we ever will. Rain, it seems, forever lurks dryly, just under the horizon, waiting for campers to come along, and when we're caught between a rock and a campsite, it slips up and douses us good. Which is okay. Most everything can be hung out to dry, eventually, and all will continue to be hunky dory.

All except the boots. They take forever to dry, and the world holds not one worse thing (besides crawling into a wet sleeping bag) than putting on wet boots. It's also hard on the feet—and the boots. To speed up the boot-drying process, here's what we do. We clean them as best we can, in the field, and wipe them as dry as possible, inside and out. We then put them, unlaced, upside down on sticks near but certainly not too near the fire. We gather a panful of clean, small, smooth pebbles, which we heat in a pot on the fire. When these pebbles are warm, but not too hot, we pour them into the boots—repeating as often as necessary, and not forgetting to pour the pebbles out before we put our feet back in.

Notes

_____

_____

_____

_____

_____

_____

24 We owe it to ourselves to fish for early-run suckers. For one thing, the season isn't open yet for many of the real fish, and for another, it helps keep the sucker population down some, so they don't get so all-fired pushy when we do start fishing for real fish.

Trouble is—what're we going to do with them once we've got 'em? Around our house smoked sucker is a gourmet's delight, and pickled sucker is nearly as heavenly. For this we take about three quarts of filleted sucker cut up in one-by-two-inch pieces and put them in a crock or plastic ice cream bucket filled with one-half cup of noniodized salt and enough water to cover the fish. We refrigerate that for twenty-four hours, then drain the liquid off. Next, we dissolve three cups of sugar in one cup white vinegar, heat and cool it, and add one cup white port wine, two hefty sliced onions, and one-half cup pickling spices. This, too, we bring to a boil and let cool. Finally, we put the fish and the onions in alternate layers in jars and pour the solution over it all and refrigerate. Pickled sucker tastes so good it's almost sinful.

Toads call with toad-sounding calls. Flycatchers arrive to catch the first insects to really take flight. Cassiopea, "the lady in a chair," is rather easily seen on the side of the North Star opposite the Big Dipper and about the same distance away, her fine brightest stars forming a kind of sprawling, lazy W.

Notes

April

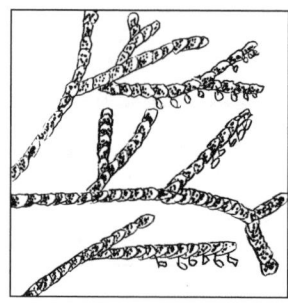

Red cedar trees shed pollen. Hummingbirds head this way, just keeping up with the first bloomings of spring-pregnant nectar-filled flowers. Leo stands high in April's night sky. Otters with their two or three kits, muskrats with their half dozen, and raccoons with their five hunt streambeds for clams and crabs.

25 Although it seems to me I stock my tacklebox to overflowing with sinkers before the season begins, within an hour or two into opening day, I'm searching for the little buggers in the dark corners of my tacklebox like a candy-hungry kid hunts for nickels under couch cushions.

Lucky for us who have more time than money, we need only a little equipment to make our own sinkers, only a bit of free time and not one iota of creativity. We need some lead, a stove to melt it on, a pot to melt it in, a ladle to spoon it, a mold to spoon it into, and a cold, wet April afternoon. A couple of fishing buddies are appropriate paraphernalia. Deluxe, thermostatically controlled melting pots, multiple-cavity molds, and other accessories are available for upscale sinker-makers.

You must take care when handling the hot stuff. And you also have the danger that once they begin, sinker makers get carried away with talking and such heavy sinker making that they don't know when to quit. The other afternoon we made, I think, a million of them. Enough to last us through a whole weekend. If we're careful.

Notes

26 Each of us enters into the great out-of-doors for reasons quite our own. But what many of us go for, much of the time, is the grand aloneness of it, the chance to breathe untouched air, to stretch our hearts, to slough off the calluses of responsibility, the scabs of routine. It is a good way to go. But, at the same time, we should not be too selfish in our goings, at least not always. Sometimes we ought to share the out-of-doors with someone in no position to get out alone. Many among us who cannot see appreciate, no less than the sighted, lake breezes and smells of just-caught fish sizzling on a camp-fire. Our elders, so often left out and left behind, can be fascinating companions on slow boat rides down lazy rivers. It is within our power to expand the range of some child who uses a wheelchair, with a drive to where deer browse beneath piney pines; and sassy squirrels and wildflowers can send the heart of a person with developmental disabilities soaring with eagles. We can do that. You and me.

Almost the same size as eagles, turkey vultures soar, as if off balance, hunting carrion or roosting on utility poles, in dead trees, or beside roadside kills. Their naked buzzardly red heads are just right for poking into dead things. On the brighter side, sandpipers are busily arriving and blue-winged teal are too. And fiddlehead ferns unfurl.

Notes

April

Brown thrashers, secretive, and shy, haunt woodlots, hedgerows, and gardens. Roots of cattails silently feel their way along the bottoms of bogs newly freed of ice, to find new toeholds for new cattails. Flickers are paired or pairing off like good passengers on the ferryboat of spring, just like the ruby-crowned kinglets moving through. Dandelions brightly bloom in a basically colorless world; they'll be ugly weeds in a week or two.

27 What do we tell a kid who wants to use the fishing boat and motor for the first time—all alone? Do we say, "Sure kid, have a good time." And then go back to our nap or the Sunday papers. Or do we say, "Be careful, kid. Many boaters are killed each year—mostly because for just one second they were careless; you can be zooming along as nice as you please and hit an underwater stump and be thrown out. And untended running motorboats tend to circle back to kill a swimming boater.

Do we tell her to stick with the boat if it swamps or springs a leak, because shore always seems closer than it is?

Do we tell her to watch out for the other guy; to watch the weather and to head for safety at the very first indication of a storm; to not become a danger to others with her own carelessness; to never overload a boat, and to never board one without a life jacket?

Do we tell her to be so, so careful, because good fishing partners are hard to come by, and we couldn't stand to see something happen to her? And do we, then, show the kid with our own good example?

Notes

28 When you come right down to it, opening-day walleye fishing is about as good as it gets, because later, when the water's warm and the fish slink to deep holes and hidden bars, it'll take more skill and more luck to do as well.

And of all the secrets to catching walleyes on these opening days, the one about anglers being willing to move around is the best. This isn't summer fishing, yet too many of us head right to some reef-and-drop-off combination spot where we caught fish last summer (and most likely will do so again this summer) and we hang in there forever, whether we catch anything or not. But now walleyes are moving, and if they've spawned, it's all the better for anglers working shorelines in waters with gravel bottoms that drop off into, say, three to six feet of water, where hungry fish roam filling empty bellies.

Early-season walleyes usually stick together, working in schools that take some hunting for. Many folks find them by drifting with the wind and trailing bait and/or casting toward shore. However we do it, we should take a kid along. Early-season walleye fishing, when it's good, and it always is, is just too much fun to go it alone.

Some wild asparagus is just high enough to cut. And as usual, we can't remember where most of it grew last summer. We'll map it out this year. Dutchman's breeches, those drooping delicate sprays of waxy, yellow-tipped flowers, are at their blooming best. Blue jays build nests. It is hard to believe there are atheists in April. Creation is taking place all around us.

Notes

April

Black bear cubs are about the size of house cats. Ring-necked pheasants lay eggs. Yellow-rumped warblers pass through, on their way to Canada, I suppose. Ravens build nests. Flickers feed on ants. Grouse drum. And painted turtles hurry from shadows to April's warming sun. Anglers, as far as the eye can see, having put new line on ready reels, practice casting as far as the eye can see.

29

It's not new news, and the signs are heavy all around us. If we do not see them, then ostrichlike with heads in the sand, or childlike with pillows pulled tightly against bad dreams, we do not want to. But our Mother Earth is hurting, hurting to the point that she can take it no longer.

We are not speaking, here, of prairie potholes, low duck hatches, or winter deer kills, and not even of beer cans along the road, but of the whole thing: water, air, falling acid rain, holes punched in our one and only ozone layer. We can do something about this. More than we are now. We have to. We, those of us who love the out-of-doors, number in the millions. Joining together, speaking with one voice—loud, clear, unyielding, wise—we can commit ourselves, take united stands against live-for-today, to-hell-with-tomorrow mentality. We have to care, to make ourselves aware, to fight a very good fight.

It is good to celebrate a designated Earth Day, but it doesn't mean a thing unless we make every day an Earth Day, and we do it now.

Notes

30 Little sisters just take naturally to bossing little brothers around. Listen to a second-grader teach a pre-school sibling the fine art of pan-fishing on the dock at their grandparent's place.

"Your bobber should be about the size of a nickel," she says with the hard-won experience of her years. "And you should have just enough split shots on your line to almost sink it. And keep those weights up under the bobber and nowhere near the hook."

And, "Oh gross," she groans, "that hook is too, too big. For panfish it's absolutely imperative (Did I say she is a bright second-grader?) that you use thin wire hooks, and only #8s or 10s. Get rid of that leader, too, and that swivel," she adds, throwing her knowledge around. "They don't work with panfish. Tie the hook right to your line—as soon as you learn to tie.

"And get rid of that horrid line; use only four-pound test. And don't cram that worm on your hook," she frets. "Hook it once, real light, right through the middle, so it'll wiggle on both ends."

Smart kid, that second-grader. Takes after her dad.

Well, April wasn't all so easy, but she wasn't so bad either. She chilled us, wetted us, and teased us. But she warmed us, dried us, gave us hope, and made us smile. She brought back woodcocks, the geese, and quite a few ducks. And melted some ice. She returned some flowers. And she got us from March to May. April sets the stage, May opens the curtains. April plants the seeds, May takes credit for the harvest. That sounds dramatic, but April does that to folks.

Notes

May

May

May hides a beehive of activity under a mostly affectionate nature. Who among us can resist the urge to stir out into May quite a little bit, even if it means, sometimes, hunching down into warm jackets to shut out stubborn reminders of the season just past? Under the Flower Moon May sets up a new season with warm days, warm rains, long hours of sunshine, and thundering stampedes of blossoming wildflowers.

1 It's May already! And you know what that means. It's time to get serious about this fishing business. Time to get on the water and smell the sweetness of the great outdoors.

Time for egg hatching—bluebirds and mallards. Time to swat mosquitoes and pick off wood ticks. Time to dig some worms. Time to take down the storm windows and let the fresh air in.

Time to take the Christmas wreath down from the front door. Time to go barefoot. Outside. Time to feel muscles pulling on paddles and listen to the slight swoosh of river water against the gunwales.

Time to change the spark plugs in the lawn mower and the chain saw and the outboard. Time for a fish fry and time to taste the first new strawberries of the season.

Time to attack dandelions and crabgrass and hunt down coffee cans full of grasshoppers for trout bait. Time to smoke some suckers. Time to wrestle a catfish to shore and time to take the kids on an overnighter. Time to put away snowshoes and skis and time to smell the flowers.

Notes

2 In the predawn dimness, Joe crouches, taking inventory of his preparations. He's put himself in turkey country, he's sure of that. He's been talking turkey all winter, and he's confident he can call a turkey off a Thanksgiving Day table.

He is totally camouflaged. The mask he wears does not obscure his vision; when the bearded bird of his plans comes into view, he will see it.

He has made a wise choice of shotgun, a tightly choked twelve-gauge pump with a short barrel: not so heavy that he cannot hold it steady for the several minutes it takes a turkey to move into position, and patterned to put enough pellets into the head and neck area at the thirty-five yards he plans to shoot.

Sitting is what a turkey hunter does more of than anything else, so he's comfortably parked on a soft cushion. He will not suffer an aching need to shift around. And he's covered himself so he'll not have to heed an untimely call from nature.

Then from a roost across a ridge, a gobbler gobbles on time and in place, and Joe, his face well hidden, smiles a smile a mile wide.

Male and female mayflies cling briefly to one another before dropping weakly back into the water to eager trout. May lures hikers out and then sends mosquitoes to plague them and sets up wood tick ambushes. Chimney swifts are back, and basswood trees leaf out. Sugar maples do, too. Brown thrashers build nests. Large, soaring red-tailed hawks drop to ground level, sinking their talons into mice, chipmunks, and snakes, and rabbits, of course.

Notes

May

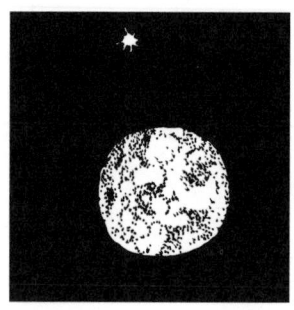

The bright star above the moon is Spica in the constellation Virgo. Skunks give birth to little stinkers; bluebirds are egg-sitting, or is that setting? Gray squirrels nurse their young. Dandelions mass for lawn assaults. Ants get into this spring thing and into the kitchen cupboards as well. Puffy cumulus clouds provide perfect concert sites for harp-playing angels, who in May would no doubt trade places with us.

3 Those of us who fish for bluegills under the ice and have stowed away our ice-fishing gear for the season ought to drag some of it out again, for those size 10 and 12 "teardrops," small ice spoons, and tiny bobbers we used last year will serve us well now.

To clear two-pound test line, we can tie a teardrop, or a same-sized plain hook if we like, and attach a very lively red worm, or in lieu of that, a waxworm or maggot. Then we can set the tiny bobber so that the bait will hang just off the bottom. Unweighted, the light line, hook, and bait will slowly drift down.

Using small, light tackle for big bluegills makes sense; the dumb, aggressive ones got eaten a long time ago, and the big ones got big by being oh-so-cautious.

Weedbeds, especially near drop-offs, can be prime locations for bluegills, though during the morning and evening hours they tend to move to shallow, brushy shorelines, sinking into deeper waters during the day.

Big bluegills will swallow those little hooks, so we're bringing along a needle-nosed pliers. We'll need them.

Notes

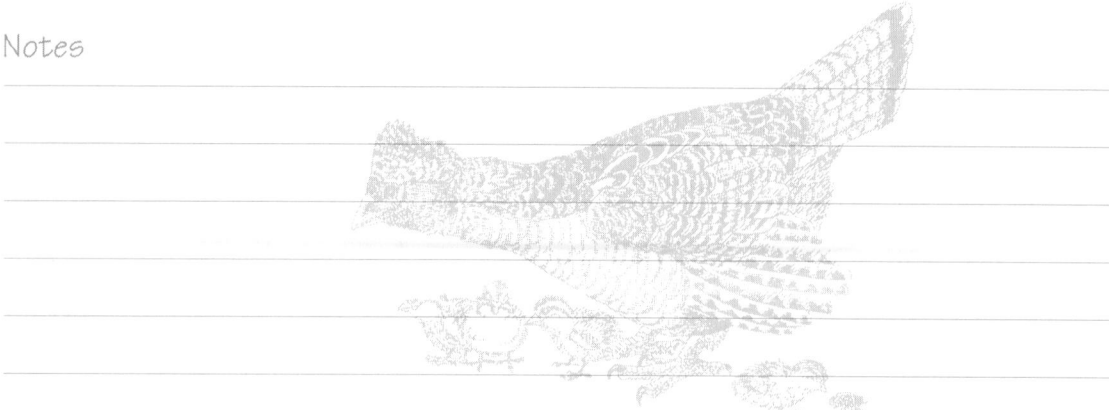

4 As the snows of spring-winter melt away, members of our hunting gang drift out to the shack on sunny springtime Sundays to check things out and talk things over. Out near the outhouse a couple of the new boys noticed scars on some leafing-out saplings—"rubs," announced the Professor. (Most camps have a guy like him—someone who knows a lot and isn't afraid to let the rest of us in on it.)

Anyway, the Professor said it wasn't much to get excited about since every buck can make dozens of them in a season.

He went on to tell us that this rubbing on trees with antlers in the fall has nothing to do with polishing them or working off sexual energy, but shows other bucks what a big, or little, shot he is—his rank in the local pecking order: young bucks make rubs on one-inch trees, middle-sized ones on bigger, and heart-stoppers on those up to four inches or more.

According to the Professor, once a buck makes a rub, he doesn't come back to it on purpose, so hunting over one doesn't do much good.

Juneberries, also called shadberries and serviceberries, bloom their drooping flower clusters of blooms, making May's world a better place. Some lilacs look serious about blooming too. Though they're not technically wildflowers, they make us feel a little wild in springtime. So they qualify. It's hard to look at lilacs without thinking of all those abandoned farmsteads, each with its loyal lilac bush still standing.

Notes

May

In spring, male wood turtles spot female wood turtles; they turtle-race toward one another with necks extended and heads held high. Before they meet they stop, swing their heads at each other for an hour or two, and decide they're in love, and then they retire to the privacy of a stream to mate. Another rash of spring fever breaks out. For some of us it is a lingering malady.

5 By now, all but the most reclusive indoorsmen have scratched at a first mosquito bite of the season. It didn't just happen; that mosquito traveled quite a road, from egg to itch.

She began life as a nearly invisible egg laid in water. Within a short time she grew into a wriggling larva, feeding on algae and microorganisms, breathing surface air through a tube. In her pupal stage she traded the tube for a pair of respiratory "trumpets." She was active, capable of tumbling out of the way when disturbed. At just the right moment, she floated to the top, her pupa skin split open, and out she crawled, a full-grown mosquito, who immediately began to hunt us down.

All this happened in the course of a week, though as an egg she could have overwintered, frozen solid, or lain dormant for a half dozen years in a dry spot, waiting for rain. And for us to come along. Now with our blood, needed to produce eggs of her own, she'll go find a wet spot to begin the process anew—another generation of mosquitoes to create itches of their own.

Notes

6 It's been awhile since I've been out fishing with my Uncle Jake, so he's in a good mood. Until I hook a big one and it gets away. Old Jake is pretty good about it too, as it takes a whole five seconds for the veins on his nose to turn blue, and he starts his sermon on how to land big fish.

He puts his pole down so he can use his hands for punctuating. "Your hook was too dull," he says, and "You shouldn't use whippy rods like that when yer fishin' big fish—ya can't set the hook with 'em. And speakin' of setten' the hook, when ya set it ya gotta set it good. And ya gotta set the drag before ya hook a fish, not while yer pullin' it in. And when's the last time ya changed that line? And ya never try to horse a big fish in, it puts too much stress on the rig. And ya never give it any slack a'tall. Ya didn't give it slack, did ya? Ya gotta stay in charge; ya can't be daydreamin'."

Now all of this is sound advice indeed, and I take it to heart, and for the last couple of minutes Jake's line has been heading hot and heavy out into deep water.

And me? I don't say nuthin!

Mostly from Mexico and down to northern South America come orioles to nest and to sing in flutelike whistles. A female dragonfly drops to touch the surface of warming waters in a series of dotting dribbles. At each dot she drips a tiny egg that sinks to the bottom. And robin babies are being born. Bloodroot blooms snowy blooms. Anemones (a much better name for them is windflower) nod brightly in the breeze. May is worth the wait.

Notes

May

With their three broad leaves and three boasting-white petals that'll turn pink with age, white trilliums strut in the woods. Trilliums look nice, but they stink. Lawnmowers move out from hibernation. The whine of their mating calls sounds across the land, bringing others of their breed out to fatten on greening, growing grass. Every day in November isn't Thanksgiving Day, yet every day in May is a May Day.

7 Old fly-fishing hands may want to go for coffee now. This is for the rest of us. Most of us come to fly-fishing after years of throwing heavy lures out on the water, about as far as we can throw a softball, with a spinning or casting outfit.

If we fail at first with a fly rod, it'll be because we are trying too hard. We've got some unlearning to do.

With fly-fishing it's the weight of the line that takes the lure out, not the other way around. Here the reel only stores the line. We don't cast the line off, we strip it off. For a regular cast we'll take about twenty feet off the reel. Then we make a series of fake casts—to work it out a little bit at a time. When all the line is out there (somewhere), we cast for real. Beginning with the rod tip at eye level, we lift the rod quickly pulling line off the water. When the rod is vertical we pause while the line straightens, and as it begins to pull on the rod, we bring the rod downward smartly—dropping softly a near-weightless fly right over a nifty little trout.

A bit clumsy at first? Sure is. So was your first kiss.

Notes

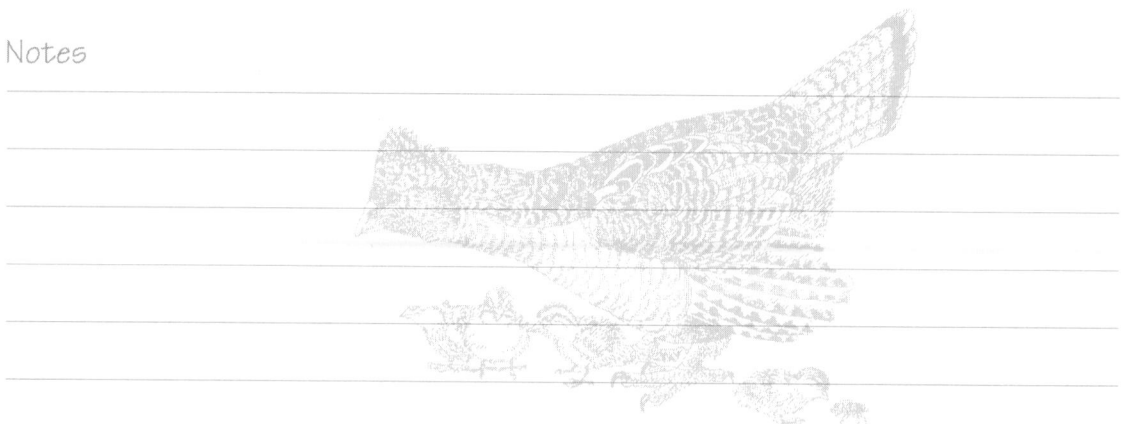

8 A number of us who write and speak on the subjects of hunting, fishing, camping, and general enjoyment of the great out-of-doors help to perpetuate the myth that the majority of those who take part in such activities actually give a damn about this outdoors we so freely use. We ought to apologize for it, because, to a great extent, it's just not so.

Take a look:

Check out the nearest boat landing. Count the empty bait containers, beer cans, masses of tangled monofilament line lying about. Anglers did that.

Check out the picnic areas close to you and count the paper plates, cigarette butts, soda bottles, and plastic spoons that never made it to the garbage can close by. Campers did that.

Check out the candy wrappers on the hiking trails, the shotgun shell casings on the back roads, the McDonald's or Hardee's containers that clutter every mile of highway and byway.

Check it out . . . and weep at the disgrace.

The first mallard ducklings are born. Cabbage butterflies are at it again. Tree swallows skim swamps, swallowing thousands of newly hatched mosquitoes. Spring warblers migrate. Pin cherries bloom, along with lady's slippers, pitcher plants, columbine, and, best of all, blueberries.

Notes

May

Up from Mexico and Puerto Rico come hummingbirds. Farm kids, and those who wish they were, play hooky to explore creeks for brook trout. Ruffed grouse still drum. Muskies spawn, and blue-winged teal are still coming in. For folks without pine trees, it is now possible to sit in the shade of other trees, if we pick the right trees and aren't too fussy, and accept a not-too-literal definition of the word "shade."

9 If, say, some kids, new at it, asked me how to catch walleyes, here's about what I'd tell them. I'd say that walleyes are migratory by nature, so go hunting them. If you get no action here, try over there. And that one was caught over there last week doesn't mean a thing now. Though it can.

I'd ask them to study a map of the lake to help in the search and to not forget that the fish is associated with rock and gravel structures, but also uses weed covers. I'd ask them to fish at night, if their curfew allowed it, or at least the first few hours after dark or the hours before dawn.

I'd ask them to be versatile and flexible, experimenting with baits and lures until they find the right combinations for the moment. I'd ask them to be quiet in their approaches, their casts, and the dropping of anchors. For my sake, I'd ask them to keep their radios down. I'd ask them to fish as often as they can to get a feel for the sport, to learn respect for the fish. I'd ask them to keep in mind that walleyes do not read tips on fishing and often do not follow the rules.

Then I'd try to follow my own advice.

Notes

10 In medieval myths the northern pike was a monster capable of swallowing swans and mules and, on a particularly bad day, their riders as well.

It was called "Luce," the water wolf. Anglo-Saxons compared it to the ancient weapon the pike, and it became, scientifically *Esox Lucius*, loosely translated: "Pitiless Pike."

Ancients believed it was bred from weeds and hatched by the heat of the sun. They believed that its heart and gall could cure fevers, its powdered jaw bones could cure pleurisy. Ashes from burned pike were used to dress wounds. Their bones were worn as amulets to ward off evil witches.

The sight of a pike feeding before noon was a very bad omen, indeed. And even to this very day, the sight of an angry twenty-pound northern at the end of a piece of stretched monofilament line makes the heart pump, the blood boil, and the eyes bulge.

Usually noisy and conspicuous with their "kill-dee" or "dee-dee-dee," from their nests of gravel, killdeer stay very, very quiet now. Their babies are hatching. Killdeer are fun to watch, with their broken-wing trick to lure intruders away from their nests. Meadow violets bloom in the pastures, and other violets bloom everywhere else. The dandelions are not as pretty as they were a couple of weeks ago.

Notes

May

June bugs are on the wing, which seems something of an exaggeration. Orioles waste no time to get to the business at hand. Already they're so carefully, so skillfully, weaving what will be a soft pouch of a nest. They'd like half an orange, if you've got one to spare, or a small cup of water and grape jelly.

11 When we speak of wetlands, we might be speaking of sedge meadows, which are more generally damp than wet. They are springy peatlands covered mostly by grasslike sedges, the surface of which is at or only slightly above the water table. Clumps of low shrubs dot the mainly treeless meadows. These oh-so-fragile wetlands, viewed as useless, empty wastelands by some, are beautifully alive and provide homes and visiting areas for wrens, Le Conte's sparrows, shrews, meadow voles, leopard frogs, mallards, teals, sandhill cranes, northern harriers, common snipes, short-eared owls, lizards, snakes, and bitterns—for starters.

Many sedge meadow dwellers spend their time hidden within the thick grasses, rushes, and vegetation that characterize this habitat. Here they fly or creep or crawl or swim, nesting, mating, raising their young, eating, sleeping, and dying. So. When we speak of filling in wetlands for worthy roads or drainage projects or shopping malls, we might be speaking of filling in sedge meadows and all they are. Forever.

Notes

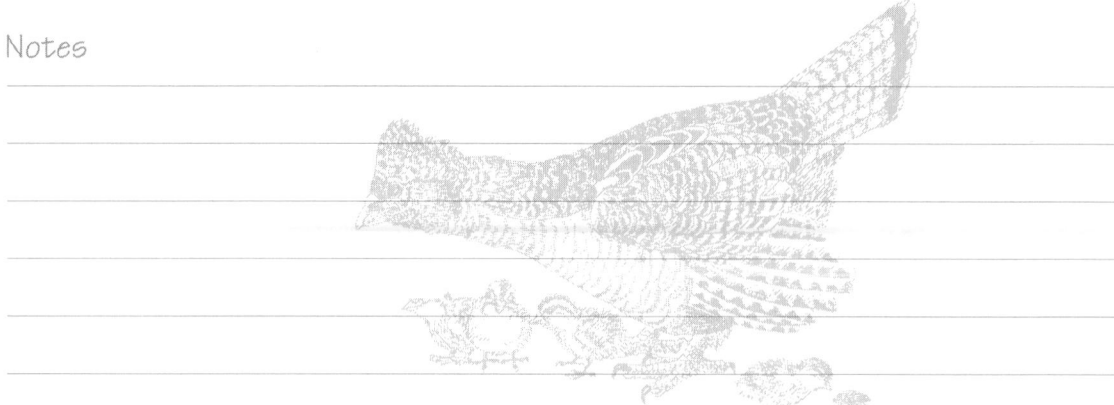

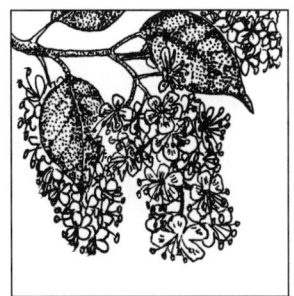

12 My Uncle Jake, like many folks who are hooked on fishing, is hooked on fishing for smallmouth bass. For most everybody, these tenacious fish, with the fiery eyes and heart to match, hold a special appeal. Jake says they are worth whatever it takes to find them.

This fascination with smallmouth bass never leaves Jake, but it heats up each spring and advances in stages through the season. Each stage requires different techniques and tactics.

In the early spring, here on Lost Lake, bass are most active where the surface of the water tops sixty degrees Fahrenheit. Spring rains and runoffs muddy much of Lost Lake in this early season and spoil the fishing, so Jake not only looks for warm water, he looks for clear water, too. He also looks for underwater humps and bars where the bottom quickly drops deep. He likes rocky bottoms.

If that's not enough, Jake says smallmouth avoid direct sunlight in early spring, so he fishes them on overcast days when cover requirements aren't so critical.

This all seems a lot of monkey business, but Jake doesn't mind.

Wine-making, jelly-making chokecherries bloom. Honeybees complete their spring housecleaning—dragging those bees who didn't make it through the winter to the hive front door and dumping them out. Indigo buntings, so blue it hurts your eyes to look at them, arrive. This is a good time to go valley watching, which means to climb the biggest hills around—we don't have mountains here—and look at all the greening up down below.

Notes

May

Crane flies, those comparatively enormous mosquito-looking creatures, walk on spindly legs over muck and mud, touching the tips of their bellies to the stuff every few seconds, depositing an egg at each touch. This is the peak of the sometimes hard to see but always easy to hear vireo migration. Some of the first Canada goose goslings hatch. The special flight of barn swallows is worth a second glance and a third.

13 On a rainy afternoon, Sigurd Olson's words float and bob from the page. "The way of the canoe," he writes, "is the way of the wilderness and of a freedom almost forgotten. It is an antidote to insecurity, the open door to waterways of ages past and a way of life with profound and abiding satisfactions." Yes. It is. It does.

And in later pages, more pressingly perhaps, Rudyard Kipling urges, "Something lost behind the ranges, something hidden, go and find it. Go and look behind the ranges, something lost behind the ranges, lost and waiting for you. Go." Yes. Yes!

And yet later, Robert Service pleads, "But can't you hear the wild? It is calling you. Let us probe the silent places, let us seek the luck betide us; let us journey to a lonely land I know. There's a whisper on the night wind, there's a star agleam to guide us, and the wind is calling . . . Let us go." Yes! Yes!

Enough of this reading! And enough of this writing! Go. Indeed let us go. You to where your heart leads you, and me—since my luck runs north, I'll go that way, and we'll catch you later.

Notes

14 Back when the earth was a kid—still in sneakers and blue jeans—there roamed the unique, beautiful pronghorn—then and now no antelope at all, but the only one of its kind in all the world.

The fastest running animal in North America, pronghorns can reach speeds nearing sixty miles per hour, and can run at half that for miles. With a little head start, fawns two weeks old can outgo a hungry coyote.

Pronghorns grow horns, not antlers, and are the only horn growers to shed their horns each year and to grow forked horns. The does grow them, too.

Though they'd probably rather not, pronghorns can go days without a drink. Pronghorns roam the flatness, the wide open spaces where the sage and prairie grasses rule, where it uses its phenomenal eyesight as its primary defense. Large, protruding eyeballs set on the sides of its head allow it to see, and sharply so, to the side, straight ahead, and behind, making sneaking up on one a chancy piece of work.

Hundreds of tiny tent caterpillars hatch from egg masses laid last fall on apple and cherry branches. Right away they're building communal tents to which they retreat after a hard day of leaf eating. A male sulfur butterfly that happens on a female chases her straight up in the air. They look like a couple of dry leaves caught in a whirlwind. A pair of little salamanders, reddish orange, about the size of a ring finger, stroll along the garden's edge.

Notes

May

Belted kingfishers bring fish to their young at the rate of one every fifteen or twenty minutes all day and half the night long. Later, they'll withhold food to lure the young out of nests dug out of the banks of rivers. Nesting catbirds, cousins of mockingbirds, mimic their neighbors, pretending to be intruders, getting everybody all upset. Out in the meadows and more open spaces, sun-coated buttercups are about to break out.

15 We all have our own ideas of what heaven's all about. Now I'm not knocking the sitting-on-a-cloud, harp-playing-for-eternity version, but I personally prefer this one.

Let's say it's about noon. We've been fishing all morning, with some success, and it's time to take a break and treat ourselves to a quick and easy shore lunch. We've come prepared, of course. First, we'll start a small fire. Then we'll fillet or steak our fish, sprinkle it with salt, pepper, and lemon juice, wrap it tightly in heavy foil that has been coated with butter, and place it over coals.

We'll turn each package often with tongs and cook them fifteen to twenty minutes. If we feel particularly fancy, we might open a can of beans and set that in the coals, too, and enjoy the whole thing with fresh bread slathered with butter (when you're talking butter, there's not a better word than "slathered").

Then we'll clean up our mess and take a nap before we get back to the serious business of fishing.

If this isn't heaven, it's as close to it as some of us are likely to get.

Notes

16 A duck is not a duck when it's a fool hen, a mud chicken, a white bill, a water guinea, a moor hen, a marsh hen, a mud duck, a mud hen, or a coot (it's all the same bird)—and though it looks like a duck (more or less), and feeds like a duck (tipping like a puddler and diving like a diver), and flies like a duck (when it finally gets itself off the water), and lives like a duck (in lakes and marshes), and migrates like a duck (great distances), it's not a duck at all.

On the one hand, the coot's so like a duck but is not a duck, and on the other, it is also very like a chicken but, of course, it's not a chicken—though it has a beak like a chicken's and short wings like a chicken's and when it swims, it has the annoying habit of bobbing its head back and forth like a chicken does when it struts across a barnyard.

No. A coot's a coot "for a' that" as the poet said—its own bird, of its own feather, of the rail family.

Certainly as skinny as a rail and as crazy as a . . . well, you say it.

Baby gray squirrels are out of their nests to give the world a once-over. Scarlet tanagers, called fire birds or black-winged redbirds, eat gypsy moths and tent caterpillars by the dozens. They're worth their weight ten times over in chemical pesticides. And they don't cost a dime. Chokecherries hang out their fat, fluffy, bee-covered blossoms. Beetles beat their buzzing heads at porch lights.

Notes

May

Tiger swallowtail butterflies cruise garden and lawn. Monarch butterflies lay eggs on milkweed buds. A male damselfly carefully lowers his mate into the water to lay eggs. At a signal from her, he'll lift her out again. Cabbage butterflies lay eggs on, what else, cabbages. Common tree frogs call. Morel hunters haunt traditional morel Maying grounds. Bitterns prowl wetlands in search of fish, frogs, and crayfish.

17 As the earth stops growing with labors of spring and heats up into summer, there happens a most remarkable thing—the mayfly hatch. Mayflies begin life, dully enough, as nymphs, as wigglers, lying on lake and river bottoms in tiny U-shaped burrows.

There they grow, changing skins to accommodate the growth; and then on a magical warm evening, before the rise of a soul-dissolving moon, they break from their dens and swim to the surface, to struggle free of the water and their confining skins, to become duns with wings, large, beautiful, fragile. Briefly, duns ride atop the water to dry, and then they hie to treetops to hide.

In a couple of days, in a blessing that is also their downfall, duns become spinners and abandon their hiding places to gather over the waters in magnificent mating flights, moving upstream in swarming clouds. Silently, then, females drop to the surface to lay eggs that sink to the bottom for another go at it, while exhausted males and females fall to the water, wings outstretched in surrender, to die, at which point the entire trout population rises to the occasion.

Notes

18 The moose, it is argued, was put together by a committee—one, some have said, with little eye for beauty.

If so, the committee in charge of wading in deep water, crossing bogs, running through deep snow, and stepping lightly and quickly over fallen trees gave the animal long, long legs. The committee in charge of not sinking out of sight in oozy lake and river bottoms and swamps gave it large, splayed, bigger-than-pie-plate hooves and well-developed dewclaws. The committee in charge of stripping bark and pushing down trees for supper gave it a big bony nose, and the one in charge of hearing everything within five miles gave it equally large ears. The committee in charge of draining water from its neck when it raises its head out of the water wrapped a hair-and-hide ropelike bell around its neck. And the one in charge of "get out of my way buddy" made it up to seven feet tall at the withers and eighteen hundred pounds in weight, with a set of antlers the size of the federal government, and a lousy disposition.

But that face. If it's a face only a mother could love, you tell it.

Thirteen-lined ground squirrels, which seem never to get enough to eat, hunt insects. They go bonkers over grasshoppers. In woods and swamps, jack-in-the-pulpits, sometimes called Indian turnips, and related to skunk cabbages, show off tiny flowers that'll give way to clusters of scarlet berries. They're pollinated by gnats and blackflies—the only time these twin monsters from hell do right. Wild strawberries bloom promises of great value.

Notes

May

By either the pair or the flock, sandhill cranes dance a breathtaking dance of courtship: circling slowly, bowing to one another, and then suddenly springing up to fifteen feet in the air with their wings thrown back, often whirling about completely and then gently bowing again on the rebound. This can go on for hours.

19 Mostly, we handle the tornadoes of life. The earthquakes. It's the little things that push us over the edge. That drive us to drink. The little things. Like trying to pull apart stuff that doesn't want to be pulled apart—like sections of a fishing rod. Twisting and turning with a pipe wrench won't do. Beating it with a hammer is slightly worse, though it makes us feel better.

It's better to do it this way. Stand with your feet slightly apart and knees slightly bent, place the stubborn rod behind your knees, take hold of each section—a hand outside each knee—and pull, using your legs and thighs for leverage. Suddenly the sun is shining, and all's right with the world.

Another evil situation occurs when two or more plastic buckets stacked within one another become quite, quite attached. To separate them with a minimum of aggravation, sit down, take ahold of the top bucket with your hands, put a foot on each of the outside edges of the bottom bucket, and gently push straight out with the feet.

And that's all there is to that.

Notes

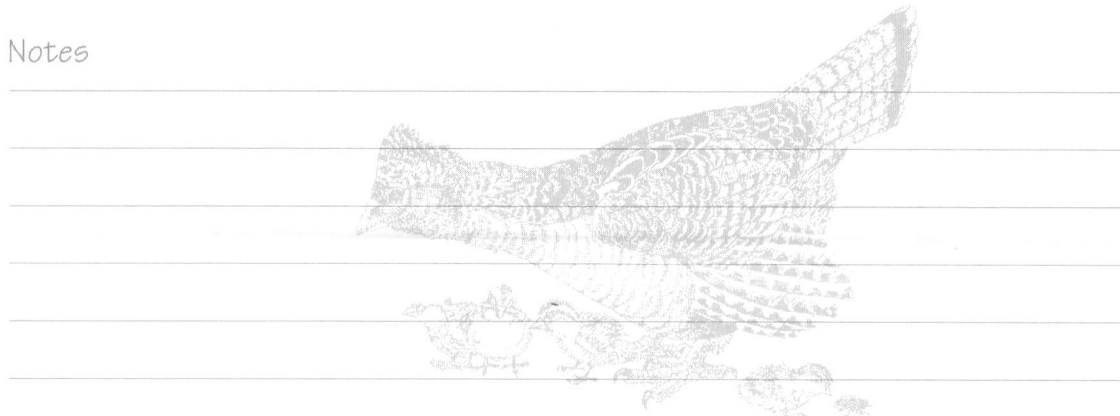

20 It's hard to believe that target shooting once ranked among the greatest of American spectator sports and that champion shooters were treated as royally as today's quarterbacks. Shooting then was a wholesome, red-blooded, all-American thing. Even today, probably more nations compete in Olympic shooting events than any other.

Target shooting can be a family sport as well, and it should be—none are safer. Special events and classifications include every member of the family, with handicaps given in much the way the local bowling league does—to keep things even.

There are several types of target shooting. "Small-bore prone," for example, is most popular among senior citizens, who blow holes in the I'm-too-old-to-try-it theory. The NRA, Boy and Girl Scouts, YMCA, 4-H, Boys and Girls Clubs, as well as patriotic organizations, churches, and civic organizations sponsor shooting leagues.

You've got to admit it beats the heck out of sitting in front of the TV growing extra layers of fat. Maybe you and your family should give shooting a shot.

Those born now are born under the second sign of the zodiac, Taurus, the bull, with the V-shaped cluster of Hyades its face, Aldebaron its right eye, and Pleiades forming the shoulder. The constellation also includes the Crab Nebula, a cloud of gas. Looking like miniature bamboos and related to tree ferns that hundreds of millions of years ago towered over dinosaurs, horsetails grow on damp edges of streams and ponds.

Notes

May

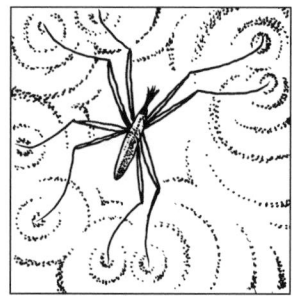

Water striders are those long-legged insects that skate across the water, their four back feet providing flotation. They slide over to another insect caught in the water, poke a hole in it, and suck it dry. Males find a neat plant or piece of wood and invite females to lay eggs there. Nymphs of mayflies creep over stones and weeds at the stream's bottom to feed on algae.

21 Now, I like folks as much as anybody and better than some, but trying to fish on a lake with ten thousand other people is a source of irritation to me and a fly in my ointment (that'd be a dry fly). But it's a fact of life that if we can't fly to some remote fishing paradise, at times we are going to fish in very crowded waters. So, let's accept it, quit worrying, and beat those other folks at their own game.

We'll get there first, be ready, have everything set, go to bed early, and get up a few hours later, so by the time the sleepyheads get down to the water, we'll have a couple of fish on the stringer and a hot spot anchored down.

And we'll head in early, too, so when those other anglers hang it up after a long day on a busy lake, and the skiers quit, and the swimmers go home, we'll come back and do it all over again, mostly by ourselves.

We'll have done our homework to the point of knowing what's a hot bait and what's not, and though we'll be flexible, we'll know what's what.

Notes

22 Fortunately, few of us are the kind of camper who still chops down trees at each campsite, digs ditches around the tent each night, pounds nails in trees, or leaves garbage to pile up or blow about in the wind.

We care enough, most of us, about our great outdoors that we cut only a few boughs or take only a few handfuls of moss to cushion our night's sleep.

We dump only a little soapy water into the lake, we pick only a small bouquet of wild-flowers, build only an occasional roaring campfire, and pick up most of our waste.

Of course, if a thousand of us do the same, it means a thousand armfuls of boughs or handfuls of moss are picked. It means a thousand dish washings in the lake and a thousand bouquets picked and a thousand too-big campfires burning needlessly a thousand trees and a thousand little bits of garbage.

We care so much, many of us, about our great outdoors, that we're loving it to death.

Down an open, dusty trail, the gray foxes leave well-worn trails from dens to hunting grounds. Grays can move along at nearly thirty miles an hour when they have to, exchanging, as it were, a fox-trot for a fox-gallop. Wild mustard shows off its four-petaled yellowness. It looks nice in the ditches, but as the son of a farmer, I'll take mine plain.

Notes

May

Morel mushrooms spring from warm, moist grounds of woods and orchards. Find them in the summer and fall and they'll kill you because they're probably false morels (which can also be found in the spring). Those mayfly nymphs of yesterday? They can wait months or years to reach adulthood, an adulthood all of twenty-four hours long. Snapping turtles lie in watery ambushes, awaiting fish or insects or ducklings whose luck has run out.

23

It's a quiet trip, generally—this float fishing. Easy. Gentle. Different. And quite wonderful.

With an early morning start, a couple of anglers push off in a sturdy canoe, packed with a day full of hope, into a river full of adventure. Drifting lazily, silently over deep pools, around sheltered bends, through towering pines, and over shallow riffles, one of the two casts as the other paddles only enough to control the course.

At lunch time we ease our craft onto a bank, build a small fire to fry fish, heat beans, and boil coffee. Maybe we take a nap.

When we're good and ready, we set out again to drift through the afternoon, catching fish, jumping ducks, surprising deer, startling beaver, listening to song birds, and catching more fish.

When we get as far as we're going, we camp for the night, or we beach at a take-out point, load our gear into a vehicle one of us left before the sun rose, and ride the starlit night home.

Sound good? There's a river just like that near you, too. And it sure beats hoeing tomatoes.

Notes

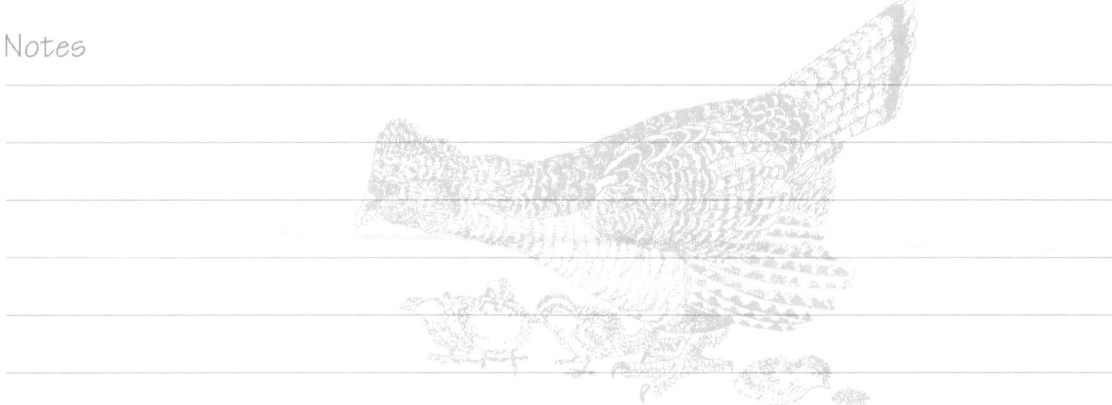

24 The Ojibwa started it, using *mas* for "ugly" and *kinonge* for "fish." Now it's known as maskinonge; muskellunge; 'lung; pike muskie; blue muskie; spotted, jack, tiger, or great muskellunge. Or just plain muskie. Though often, when hooked, it's referred to as "ohmygodigotone."

It's a solitary, ornery ambusher, living in weedy waters. When it spots a meal, it coils into an S shape and strikes like a snake from behind, grabbing its prey broadside. With shakes of its head it brings it closer to its mouth to be swallowed head first.

It'll take the toughest plug we have, chew on it, and spit it right back at us.

Largest of the pike family, it grows to sixty, seventy, and some say one hundred, pounds. Its body is six times longer than it is deep. The front of its head is scaled and shaped like a duck's bill.

It spreads a horrible disease called muskie fever, for which there is no cure.

If you catch one—let it go to grow to catch another day. If you dare.

Blackflies poke holes in the bodies of innocent hikers, campers, and anglers. Convocations of carp spawn in the backwaters of lakes and ponds. Snails fasten little jellied capsules of eggs on underwater rocks and sticks. Whippoorwills, feeding on insects they catch on the wing, are "whip-poor-willing" tonight. Half of a whirligig beetle floats atop the scum on ponds, and half under it, one set of eyes looking up and out, another set looking down and deep.

Notes

May

The courtship rituals of birds are usually unique and always fascinating. Watch an evening grosbeak, for example. A female pretends to be a helpless little bird while a male must feed her and dance with his bill and tail up and his wings spread wide and vibrating—you know, like they do at the prom. In ponds, zooplankton, water fleas to unscientific us, live out their busy little lives grazing on suspended algae.

25 You say you've got yourself in a pickle? That you're full of bug bites and you're itching like crazy? That the kids used all the goop to ease the itching on the cat and you don't know what to do? Well, buck up, friend, and dab a pinch of toothpaste on each bite; and in the time it takes to work a fishing hook out of the carpet, your itches will be a temporary thing of the past.

And you say you dropped your tackle box off a cliff and cracked it good, and you can't get a new one till your birthday, which is a long ways off? Well, buck up, friend, and fill the crack with plastic pipe-joint cement.

And you say you've got blood stains on your new hunting jacket that you're just never going to get out? Well, buck up, friend, and sprinkle some meat tenderizer on the culprit spots before you wash the coat, and it's new again.

And you say you forgot the bottle opener and you're thirsty? Well, just catch the bottom tine of a fork under the edge of the cap, stick the blade of a knife between the two tines above it, and pry down with the knife.

That's all.

Notes

26 How do you catch a northern when you really need one? Well, a good many good folks fish in slow-moving streams or in shallow, weedy waters in lakes, in beds of lily pads, over underwater patches of sand grass, along stumps and under tangles of driftwood, and near shore in small weedy bays.

They use irregular retrieves, vary trolling speeds, and fish with sucker minnows, spoons, jigs, plugs, and plastic worms—or frogs, and combinations thereof, in big sizes, small ones, and those in between. They use leaders, or live dangerously and go without, but they for sure use snap swivels to make bait changing fast and hassle-free.

If one method doesn't work, they try another; if one spot isn't producing, they go to another; if the lake's no good, they head for another. And when a northern hits, they sock it to him good into a tough bony mouth. Or with live bait, they wait a bit to give the fish a chance to turn and chew it. And they know the northern's a sleeper, often coming easy to the boat—until it sees the boat, when all hell breaks loose, and too often the fish, too.

You try a little of this, a little of that, and you need to get lucky.

In the marshes and bogs and swamps, cattails shoot new shoots and stalks into new cattails. Cold-blooded salamanders explore forest floors in search of insect-food. Oh-so-fragile mayflies hatch just like they did in the days of the dinosaurs. It's true, they've been around that long. Fox snakes, the fakers, beat their tails on the ground, hoping to sound like rattlesnakes and scare intruders away. It works on me.

Notes

May

Fireflies dance on the garden's edge tonight down by the mailbox. Slowpoke turtles desert the safety of ponds and streams to dig shallow pits in warm sand with their hind feet, laying their eggs in them and then filling them up and tamping them down again. Eggs that'll take the sun all summer to hatch. Hognose snakes stand straight up and look mean to scare us away. If that doesn't work they roll over and play dead.

27 Being a lover of, and a doer in, the great out-of-doors can be a dirty business. We are forever cleaning, scaling, plucking, gutting, shucking, filleting, gathering, setting up, taking down, oiling. We wade, tramp, crawl, creep, climb, and float. We dig for worms.

And where is the soap when we need it the most? Nowhere.

Here's how to take care of that. Go into your sock drawer and pick out one of the many without a mate. Choose a long one. Drop a bar of soap (the floating kind is easiest retrieved if dropped into water) down to the toe. Tie a knot in the sock above the soap. This thing can be hung in a handy spot—from a tree in camp, the tailgate of a pickup—wherever our dirty business takes us.

To wash our hands, we simply drop the sock in water and scrub. The suds come right through the toe.

Of course we'll still have to dry our hands on our shirttails, but we can't have everything.

Notes

28 Basically four types of huntable turkeys live in the United States of America, each more or less allotted its own territory, and each slightly different from the other, yet each equally magnificent on the ground, in the air, or in a bed of wild rice on the supper table.

The best known is the Eastern. It inhabits the entire eastern seaboard and west to Texas and on over to Kansas and Iowa and into Wisconsin. It's a large, bronze bird. And there's its somewhat smaller lookalike, the Florida turkey. You've correctly guessed its home range. The Merriam is a dark bird, but it has white tips on its tail feathers and on its lower back, giving it the black-and-white look so fashionable in some circles. It's at home in the southern Rockies and as far north as Montana. Finally, the Rio Grande is native to Oklahoma, South Texas, and up to Nebraska. Turkeys—from upland woodland to swamp, from mountain to prairie, from sea to shining sea.

And in the spring, their top priority is mating, so the hunter who most sounds like a sexy hen has the best chance of meeting a tom, for the turkey language of love is universal, too.

Monarch butterflies, now that milkweeds are starting to look like milkweeds, continue to come from way down in Mexico. Actually they didn't start out there, but were born along the way. Ladybugs attack aphids, mealybugs, and scale insects intent on eating up the good stuff growing in the garden. Inch-long damselflies, propelling themselves with bursts of water from their bellies, fiercely snag mosquito larvae with hinged jaws.

Notes

May

Woodchuck youngsters follow their fussy mother from den to den to den until she's satisfied she's got it right and that she's left a new batch of fleas behind. They feed along the way on dandelions, and the clover and alfalfa of frustrated farmers, and new-begun garden stuff. Whitetail bucks show signs of wall-hanging material, gift-wrapped in soft velvety moss.

29 With time limitations and families and job responsibilities being what they are, many of us who fish and hunt often find ourselves in quick-fish, quick-hunt situations that, despite the best preparations and the best of intentions, become no-fish, no-game situations.

Say if I, for instance, was put down in the middle of New York City to find Joe Schmo. I wouldn't know where to begin. That's much the same situation hunters hunting in new country and anglers on unfamiliar waters face. Despite maps and charts, it's big country out there and big waters, and time-limited folks can't cover it all with adequate bring-home-the-bacon accuracy.

The answer, of course, is to hire a guide. It'll be money well spent and a job that ought to be done well ahead of time. Chambers of commerce and fishing and hunting lodges make good sources. Talk or write to the guide personally. Ask for references, understand exactly what's expected of each of you under all circumstances. After all, we wouldn't want to go to New York looking for Joe, only to find out that he's moved to Duluth.

Notes

30 A heap of fish that bite never get hooked, or get hooked but never reach the net, or get netted but drop right through, and it has more to do with the fisherman than with the fish, though the fish gets the better end of the deal.

Good anglers with good tackle lose fish, but too often a gone fish is lost to gear that's out of shape or out of fashion. Most of us change lines once in a while; the good guys and gals do it after every twenty to thirty hours of use. They stay away from Brand X, use the correct pound-test for the reel, and, to prevent twist before the first cast, spool it on right.

They know their knots. They tie them right or they tie them again. They cut a half dozen feet off the terminal end every hour or so. They set their drags perfectly. Their rod guides are free of nicks, their reels are clean, well-oiled and greased, and firmly in place.

Their hooks are dangerously sharp. The snaps and swivels on their leaders and lures are sound. Their nets are as good as new.

So that when that once-in-a-lifetime fish decides to strike, their iron's red-hot and ready.

The lady's slippers still bloom. More not-so-baby robins are out of their nests. So are grackles, which is not necessarily a cause worth celebrating. American elms drop their seeds. Deer fawns stay very close to mothers. Wild grape vines show their first flowers. Wild asparagus hunters have field days. Trout anglers boast of good streamside times, and folks after walleyes burst with pride.

Notes

May

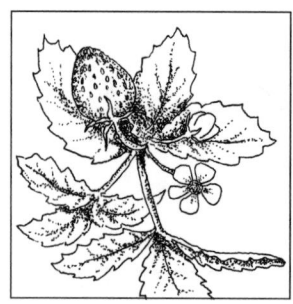

The first wood duck ducklings drop from high nests and bounce a couple of times, and make their way to water. Wild strawberry plants continue to promise explosions of goodness with little white blossoms. Barn swallows nest. Our world's almost green again, which sets off the blue of the skies and lakes nicely. And I heard a loon last night. So was May a month of May baskets? Or May days? It sure was.

31 Let's say it's a Sunday in the spring, maybe after church or maybe after Sunday dinner dishes have been put away, and all the couches and easy chairs are filled with half-napping baseball game watchers or Sunday paper readers.

It could be Junior or Sis, but most likely it's Mom with one of her don't-give-me-any-sass looks who suggests a Sunday drive in the country. If it's Mom, we go.

As we cruise down the highway, Sis points out a meadowlark, with brilliant yellow breast feathers and black collar, sitting on a fence post. As we pass through a lowland woods, Grandmother points out hundreds of white flowers with a distinctive three-petal shape. "Trilliums," she says.

Along a marshland area we hear a high-pitched peeping from a chorus of a thousand voices. "Them's spring peepers," says Junior, whose knowledge of wildlife is better than his grammar. As we leave a wooded area near nightfall, a large broad-winged bird flies across the road like a silent shadow. "A great horned owl," yawns Dad, getting in his two-cents worth as we enter the lighted city. And June.

Notes

June

June

When June comes to the great out-of-doors, the party for the most part is over. All that riotous living of April and May—all that courting rigamarole, all that showing off, boasting, fighting for lady fair, mating, nest building, egg laying, and baby having—is over. The moon in June is the Strawberry Moon. Strawberries. "Doubtless God," wrote William Butler, "could have made a better berry, but doubtless God never did."

1 It's June already, summertime. Some of the time. Time for long days, and much too soon, time for shorter ones again. Time for picnics and walks along the beach and cool nights on the porch swing. Time for slow boat rides at dawn, hard hunting down-deep walleyes.

Time for weinie roasts and ghost stories around campfires. Vacation time, some of the time. Time for loon calls and strawberry shortcake.

Time for weeding and mowing. Weeding and mowing. Time to shore up the sagging dock. Time for canoeing and hiking and skipping stones on quiet bays. Time for mosquito swatting and bass fishing. Time to tease crappies from deep holes and dare northerns from weed beds.

And time for muskie hoping.

It's time for lemonade and iced tea and sunshine. Time to fill the hummingbird feeder, I'll bet. Time to make time for school-free kids and time to get the old folks out where the sun can warm their bones. It's time to pick a flower for a lover. And it's time to pick an old dandelion and blow its seeds to the four winds, expecting all our troubles to go with them.

Notes

2 To some Native Americans, counting coup, touching an enemy without killing him, was the greatest honor. So it is with many of us who fish for muskie, who believe that a muskie must be judged only on its value as a challenge, that it is too honorable a fish to be caught only once. For us, the thrill lies in the chase, the catch, not the kill.

To that end, we use artificial lures to avoid deep-hooking the fish. A muskie can swallow a sucker minnow, hook and all, a long way into its belly, making it nearly impossible to remove without great risk to the fish. Despite the pleasure we feel at hooking such a trophy, we also stifle the urge to prolong the excitement by overplaying the fish, potentially harming it. And we suppress an eagerness to bring it in too quickly, also potentially harmful.

Most fishers of muskies don't expect a lot of action. We count our successes in other ways—reaching for the high challenge and the fascination of pursuit. To us, there is more honor in fishing for muskie and catching nothing than in fishing anything else and catching nothing.

June is family month in the great outdoors—a time of protecting, feeding, caring, rearing. Baby chickadees begin to leave nests. Spotted, nearly odorless fawns lie motionless on forest floors. Hen grouse dust bathe their babes on lonely backwoods roads. Mother mallards herd ducklings through growing cattails, while papas haven't a care in the world. And bluebirds, noses to the grindstone, fetch grasshoppers, crickets, and beetles to their babies.

Notes

June

Baby loons hatch to hitch rides upon the backs of their doting parents, who catch for them fish and floating insects. Fireflies light their lanterns over bogs of flowering laurels and rosemary. Blackberries and raspberries blossom. So do the grandest of all flowers—wild roses. Pheasants and Hungarian partridges continue to incubate eggs on the ground, in shallow depressions. Some mallards are hatched; some are hatching.

3 Keeping live bait lively alive can be as challenging as backing the boat trailer into the water on the first try. But basically all it takes is a proper temperature and a favorable environmental substitute.

A clever fisherman, like my Uncle Jake, doesn't overload his bucket with too many minnows; he changes the water often, trying to keep it around fifty degrees by adding ice, and uses aerators when the lake's a long, long way off.

Fifty degrees is the key to keeping worms and crawlers fit, too. Most of us keep them too warm and/or too wet, and dirt's not as good for them as damp moss or the boughten stuff—to which ice is added as needed. Leeches also need water close to fifty degrees—water that should be changed often, unless it is the city chlorinated stuff, in which case they'll be dead before the need arises. Crayfish can be kept at fifty degrees in damp moss. So can frogs.

Of course, we don't want to keep live bait around too long, or the kids'll start to name them, which makes the sticking of hooks into their hides something of a ticklish situation.

Notes

4 When Hamlet cried aloud in anguish, "To sleep; no more; and by a sleep to say we end the heartaches and the thousand natural shocks flesh is heir to. 'Tis a consummation devoutly to be wished, " he was, according to some experts, out of sorts after a lousy night out on the floor of a tent. Really, folks, it's not necessary.

To ensure pleasant dreams beneath the wandering stars, we need but to choose the mattress—a one-and-one-half-inch-thick pad that contains one and one-quarter inch of open cell foam and one-quarter inch of ensolite.

And we need but the right sleeping bag to put upon it. We need a sleeping bag suited to the conditions in which we find ourselves. We need to shake it out and air it out between sleepouts. We must not wear our day clothes in it either.

And we must ever regulate the flow of air within the tent by keeping zippers open on upper windows to allow dampness to escape.

That's all.

G'night.

Larkspurs continue to show pretty little blue and white clusters of flowers, though they won't for too much longer. Chokecherries, shrubby members of the rose family, bloom. Mourning doves are egg-sitting on loose platforms of twigs on the ground or in trees. They'll raise two or three broods this season, and take until nearly September to do it.

Notes

June

5 Though summertime walleyes can be caught at any time, the peak feeding times of an hour before to an hour after sunrise and sunset bring the best results to most of us. But even those times offer some curious challenges of their own.

In the spring and fall, there's not as much natural forage in the water—not so much food available for predator fish like the walleye, which must spend more time hunting down its meals and must travel greater distances to fill its belly. Technically, fishing is easier then.

But in the summer, when prey density reaches its highest, walleyes quickly and easily find plenty to eat, and may not be particularly hungry when our lures pass by, requiring us to more carefully mind our Ps and Qs. And to make it more interesting yet, summertime walleyes do not spend as much time over their familiar haunts of rock and gravel bars where we're used to fishing them, but move instead into the weeds where their groceries are. Which is where we must be, with free samples of jigs tipped with leeches or crawlers.

Notes

6 What we do is make a target frame by laying a couple of six-foot furring strips side by side four feet apart and fastening two crosspieces to them—one near the top and another four feet below it. On some four foot by four foot squares of paper we draw a thirty-inch circle and mark an X in the center of it. We note on each target the gun we are using, the range, the choke, and the shell. We tack one target to the frame and stick it in the ground, and we shoot from forty yards and count the BB holes within the circle. Using a new target each time, we do the same at thirty yards and at twenty. We do it with the No. 2 we use on the geese, the No. 4 on the ducks and pheasants, the No. 6 and No. 8. The results are often eye opening. If we know how many BBs are in each shell and count how many hit within the circle, we know how big a hole we put into the autumn sky when we pull the trigger, what to expect from the gun, at what range, with which shells with each choke. It's called patterning and it can get more complex, can get boring and use up some shells. But if we all get together at the shack and do the job as a team and top the day off with brats over the coals, it'll be a picnic.

Bumblebees celebrate clover blossoms. They know what they're doing; it is a cause worth celebrating. Tadpoles explore shallow shorelines where yellow water lilies rest afloat; and blackflies, the true curse of Adam's sin, continue their miserable existence. Pairs of barn swallows carry insects to newly hatched chicks. Sharptails erupt in frenzied, prancing courtship rites on traditional dancing grounds. You'd think they'd be done with this by now.

Notes

June

Baby wood ducks hatch, hesitate, hop from nest holes, fall in behind mother, and run helter-skelter for the water in a frenzy of alliteration. Cedar waxwings court each other now by passing berries back and forth to each other in a "you take it; no, you take it; no, you take it" sort of a game where they both end up winners. This morning, the Professor said that a few million years ago there were froglike things with heads as big as donkeys.

7 As we travel traplines into the bush, paddle rivers to nowhere in particular, sleep under gorgeous half moons, or jig days away in ice shacks, our souls are filled with peace and contentment, but our bellies growl with complaining emptiness. To shush the growling, make some hot and hearty stove-top frypan corn bread.

At home mix together one cup each of cornmeal, whole wheat flour, and powdered milk, two tablespoons of sugar (if you've got it and want it), one tablespoon of baking powder, and two tablespoons of powdered egg.

On the trail, when the growling starts, mix in one-third cup cooking oil and enough water to make it the consistency of pancake batter. Then pour it into an oiled, preheated cast-iron pan. Cover it and cook it on the very lowest heat you can get—raising the pan off the campstove or coals if you have to. It'll take some time cooking—anywhere between an hour and two—but served hot, coated with butter or syrup, all by itself or with a plate of beans (or whatever you've got in the bottom of the pack), it'll make the filling of a belly about as good as the filling of a soul.

Notes

8 Debunking the myth that anglers are all wet, many of us—so we can get ourselves into the best possible positions to cast flies and lures, or cast to fish we cannot reach from shore—opt for waders.

And we opt for good waders, for waders not as comfortable as possible make fishing more of a pain than the pleasure God intended it to be. Waders should fit—should not be too light, nor too heavy, nor too hot for conditions. They must offer the wearer freedom to step over logs, straddle boulders, and climb steep banks.

As an aid to keeping ourselves upright during the wading process, some of us further opt for the security of a wading staff—either one we cut ourselves or a commercial one. And if the inevitable does occur and one of us takes a dunking and becomes all wet, we don't panic or fight the rapids, but allow ourselves to go with the flow, letting go, if necessary (gasp), of our fishing rods, content that eventually the current will take us to shallow waters and that even all-wet anglers eventually dry off.

Luna moths are on the wing, or were last night, as a half dozen of them are on the lawn this morning. Tiny brook trout, spawned last fall or earlier this spring, try their best to grow into bigger brook trout. Trumpeter swans and ringneck pheasants hatch. Smallmouth bass spawn. Daisies start to make a stand.

Notes

June

Ant lion larvae—we call them doodlebugs—looking like fat little half-inch-long lice with enormous jaws, build funnel-shaped ant traps in dusty soil. Wild iris, quite correctly named in ancient Greece after the rainbow, blooms. Monarch butterflies feed on clover blossoms, and painted turtles lay eggs. In a frantic show of righteous indignation, robins try to drive crows, intent on making short work of robins' eggs or little ones, from their evil mission.

9 It depends on who you talk to, but folks around here claim the best time to go fishing is when the barometer is rising, or just before a storm, or just after one, or during the dark of a moon, or when the sky is overcast.

Or when cattle are up and feeding, or deer are moving, or when oak leaves reach the size of squirrels' ears, or at the first light of day, or during the hour or two before dark, or right after a rain, or just before one, or during a steady drizzle.

Or just before fish spawn, or just after they finish, or when the water rises or as it begins to drop, or when a breeze ripples the water.

Or in the midst of a hatch—any kind of hatch—or when spiderwebs hang tight, or when ants build high mounds, or when my Uncle Jake gets a crick in his back or his right leg gets stiff, or when the boss sends you out of town.

Most of us do agree, though, that the best time to fish is today, because if we wait till tomorrow we'll find they were biting yesterday, which is—well, you get the idea.

Notes

10 Many consider them to be other than great sporting fish, but perch can provide fast action any time of the year, bite on nearly anything, exist about anywhere a fish around here can, and taste about as good as any fish does. They're yellow perch, but folks call them coon, ringneck, jack, and striped perch.

Generally considered panfish, perch resemble, in both appearance and taste, their close cousins, the walleyes. And like walleyes, they're wandering nomads and travel in schools. Other fish get big by eating perch, lots and lots of perch—perch eggs, perch minnows, little perch and big perch. Perch eat other perch. Which seems okay all around, since they reproduce so well.

Perch eat nymphs, crayfish, hellgramites, minnows, crickets, grasshoppers, and leeches. They'll bite on all of it and jigs, spinners, spoons, flies, and good old garden-variety earthworms.

They're usually a foot or two off the bottom and, on a light outfit, provide enough action. More than once, perch have saved the day for otherwise skunked anglers. They're a favorite during ice-fishing season, too, but let's not think of that now.

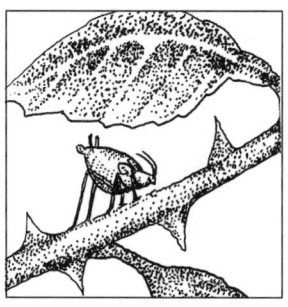

From eggs laid last fall come little aphids, which poke their beaks into plants and suck the juice out. They, in turn, expel "honeydew" that is shlurped up by ants, which protect the defenseless aphids from whatever of their enemies ants can beat up. Cattails bloom. White water lilies follow suit. Bobolinks egg-sit in saucerlike nests. Female bats don't scoop up mosquitoes with quite the same agility they did last month, since they're loaded down with babies.

Notes

June

Deerflies have replaced blackflies as scourges upon humankind, especially the outdoor kind. They rob us of peace of mind and chunks of skin. Red-tailed hawks patrol the skies, searching for chipmunks, mice, and snakes for their hungry pairs of youngsters back at home in their scraggly nest. A June bug that somehow made it into the house lies upside down in a futile attempt to do the backstroke across the kitchen floor.

11 Float-fishing down a river is not the most efficient way to float down a river—what with always stopping to fish. And it's not the slickest way to fish either—what with a hurry-up current carrying us past the finest of fishing spots. But, gadzooks! Is it a nice way to combine these two fine enterprises.

While many lakes are heavily fished, most of our rivers (not counting trout rivers) are underfished—especially for such praiseworthy prey as smallmouth bass and walleyes. For that reason alone, rivers are worth a second glance, or three.

And rivers, such rivers, each with its own disposition, its own mystery, its own tentative hold on its own water—water chuckling, giggling, spitting, jiving; water frowning, and glass-like, fooling; water seeking the sea.

Rivers, each with its own scenery—scenery that is never the same for more than a minute—motion-picture scenery of cliffs that hold watching water gods, of trees that have seen so much and tell us none of it, of birds and beasts.

There are fish-full rivers near all of us, and all are calling. Calling.

Notes

12 A bowhunter comes to grips with himself (though this himself could as easily be a herself, so adjust your pronouns accordingly). After some pondering, this bowhunter has come to the conclusion that he is not as tough as once he was (or thought he was).

So he's traded in the bull of a bow he's been hunting with, the one that bruised his fingers and turned his arm and shoulder muscles into Jell-O.

Now that he has matured, he understands that if pulling back on a bowstring makes him shake and quiver, he will not hit a darn thing with it, let alone a deer that comes up to him when his heart is bang-banging in his ribcage. And he's proved it.

He's aware, now that he's older, that like a hunter who shoots too big a gun, a gun that knocks him for a loop at the firing, he'll flinch, too, when he lets an arrow go from too big a bow.

So, with his new-found wisdom, he's got himself a bow he can handle. And if the draw-weight of his bow matters to anyone, he figures he can fudge the difference.

Canada geese are particularly vulnerable now as they molt, losing their flight feathers. Grounded. In thick-headed maneuvers, grape-big June bugs continue to launch attacks on porch hanging lightbulbs. Hungry crows make short work of the eggs and young of other birds. Some small ponds and streams lose water, running dry—causing, I imagine, some concern to tadpoles and trapped trout, the latter causing concern to me, too.

Notes

June

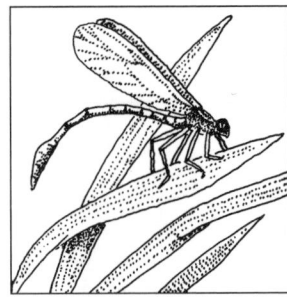

Male damselflies sport bright green metallic bodies and black wings. Females, mostly brown with a white spot at the tip of each wing, perch on leaves to ambush passing mosquitoes, scooping them up in baskets formed by their hairy legs. Three-month-old baby foxes play around like kids at recess. June is a generous month, a family month, a month of protecting, feeding, caring, rearing—and certainly a time of growing.

13 There's more to catfishing than merely flinging bait out in the current, into a pool, and laying back until a hungry fish comes by. Catching cats, plenty of cats, requires a knowledge of rivers and their structures and an understanding of the fish. Anything in the river that disrupts the natural flow of water—submerged trees, midcurrent rocks, logs, shallow riffles, or sharp turns might hold a catfish or three. There the fish rest easiest against the current, in places that draw into their eddies easy mealtime pickings.

Catfish feed mostly on or near the bottom, so catfishing folk put egg-shaped sinkers on and tie barrel swivels below them. They add a foot-long leader, to which they fasten a #1 hook. And to that the bait of their choice.

When catfish feed on insects, nearer the top, the logical move is to fish shallower, using a bobber to lift the hook off the bottom, pitching the rig above the eddy and maneuvering it to where the fish lie.

Good catfishers take plenty of gear, for if they're not hanging up or snagging, they're not trying hard enough.

Notes

14 It began with the first caveman, when his significant other forgot to pack a sharp rock or pointed stick as they set out for a weekend of getting away from the rigors of cave life. It has continued to this day.

Not once in the whole history of getting away from it all has a camper gone camping without having left a piece of equipment back at the cave. Not once. Not ever.

It'll be a tent peg, toilet paper, stove fuel, salt, spatula, flashlight, or rope. It'll be duct tape, saw, or biscuit mix, but something gets left behind.

Too many campers rely upon their memories alone to get them safely and comfortably in, out, and through campouts. They don't make lists. Campers must make lists and carefully check off each item as it is packed. They must check it twice.

And there's not an outdoor writer worth a hoot who doesn't supply readers with such a list of essentials, which must be taken on outdoor excursions. Many put squares next to each item for checking-off convenience. I want to do that for you. I want to be worth a hoot.

But I've forgotten my list.

Pealike yellow and purple flowers of rootless bladderworts show prettily above the water in shallow lakes and ponds, while below the surface they trap insects in tiny bladders and eat them slowly. Black bears mate now so they won't have to bother with it in the fall when they'll be busy eating, putting on fat. June-dewy mornings come early, but slowly, allowing us all, bug and bud, tomato blossom and you and me, time to stretch and rub the sleep from our eyes.

Notes

June

Lady's slippers open their moccasinlike flowers. Hummingbirds finally get around to nesting, the males flying loop-de-courtship-loops, defending feeders, driving away intruders, while the females line Ping-Pong-ball-sized nests with spiderwebs and lay tiny garden-pea-sized eggs. Moose wade belly deep into water, feeding on sodium-rich water lilies. Baby partridges play follow-the-leader behind fussbudget mothers.

15 The "hope that springs eternal" springs not only within the breasts of those who swing at baseballs; it also springs beneath the vests of walleye anglers. With each and every cast. We forever figure that if only we had this lure or that gadget, we'd put up even money we'd get a hit every time we're up. And sometimes we do, but most times we, well . . . strike out.

If there is a secret to catching walleyes, it lies mostly with the weather and it's the anglers who know the weather patterns and conditions that set walleyes off on feeding binges that'll score most often.

Ideal weather conditions for walleye catching may come along only a few times in a season, and we'll know when that is by paying attention to the forecasts.

What we'll look for is a consecutive string of warm, sunny days—the longer the string, the better. Then we'll look for a good teeth-rattling wind. Then we'll look for a storm brewing. Then we'll gather the gear and go walleye fishing, because we're going to hit home runs all day long. I hope.

Notes

16 Becoming a father is easy enough, but being one is something else again.

A father must be strong enough to carry a kid the last mile to a secret fishing spot but gentle enough to remove a hook from a small boy's trembling hand. A father must be patient enough to straighten little fishing poles' tangled lines every fifteen minutes or so and not complain—too much.

He must be brave enough to put worms on hooks, yet understand a child's hesitancy to do so. He must be clever enough to know just where the fish are biting, but humble enough not to brag about it. He must be funny enough to laugh when a big fish breaks his line, yet serious enough to let a little girl cry on his shoulder when one breaks hers.

Being a father means taking the kids along, unhooking Mister Twisters from branches, and looking the other way when a favorite $8.95 whatchamacallit gets snagged on the bottom while his rod and reel sit idly in the boat—and enjoying it.

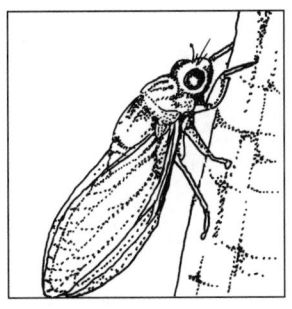

Sounding like so many matchboxes full of sand being shaken hard and fast and fairly long, fresh cicada gents call out to cicada lasses for a summer frolic. Call her brown thrush, fox thrush, maris, sandy mocker, ground thrush, French mockingbird, or, as we do, brown thrasher, this long-beaked, bright-eyed beauty feeds her youngsters as many as six thousand insects a day.

Notes

June

Red-orange salamanders lay a half dozen eggs or so under logs in damp woods. Red squirrel pups, fighting like a bunch of spoiled kids, get fed up with one another and leave the nest. Some say their parents throw them out. Lady nighthawks incubate eggs on the ground without benefit of nests. Young robins, fresh from the nest, hop behind mothers, begging for worm-snacks, too lazy to find their own.

17 This complete meal serves as a handy shore lunch when the fish aren't biting, and it is our traditional first supper of a camping trip.

Before we leave home, for each member of the party we wash and thinly slice one potato and peel and slice one small onion into quarter-inch slices. Then, depending upon the proximity to payday, we partially cook a big hamburger or a decent-sized steak and wrap it in strips of bacon when it cools.

On a large piece of really heavy-duty foil we alternate layers of the potato and onion. On top of that we put the meat. On top of that we sprinkle fresh or frozen corn and peas. On top of that we add seasonings and maybe some catsup.

We wrap it all up tight and keep it cool until we're in the field and nearly hungry. Then we let the thing cook on hot coals for an hour or so while we set up the tent or take a nap. And if it's raining, lightning, thundering, and you can't go camping, this'll work as well in the oven or over charcoal. In which case, you invite a few mosquitoes, a half dozen ants, and you've nearly got the real thing.

Notes

18 Violin winds abruptly become the roars of a thousand locomotives, puzzled thunder breaks into thundering bedlam, and smells of rain swim backward in time and bring the sun to its knees, for not even the sun can bear to watch tornadoes dropping from the sky, viciously turning and twisting.

If we're fishing or camping, pulling weeds or driving to work, and we hear of a tornado watch, it means that conditions are right for one to develop, and we should stay tuned in and alert. A warning means that a tornado has been sighted or will be soon, and we get to shelter. We don't outrun a tornado—not on foot, not in a motor vehicle—such attempts are foolhardy and fatal. We get inside if we can, to a basement, or lacking one, to an inner closet or bathroom without windows—we stay away from windows. If a tornado catches us in the open, we lie face down in an open ditch or depression, covering our head and neck with our hands. If we're caught in a vehicle, we stop it, get out, and do the same thing.

There is no courage in the face of tornadoes, no speed, there is only the serious matter of preservation.

Some robins are on their second go-round in cup-shaped nests of grass and mud filled with four eggs of robin's-egg blue. Buttercups bloom gold all over the place. Fiddlehead ferns uncurl their curls. Growing baby brown bats cling to their mothers who must work harder and harder as they go about insect hunting. Baby ducks panic at a frog's jump or floating turtle. Partridge mothers send little puffball partridges scatter-hiding at any sign of danger.

Notes

June

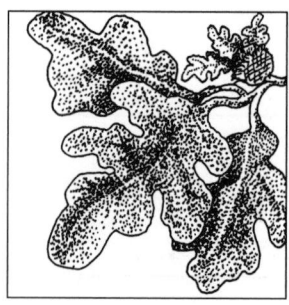

Oak leaves rustle in a great green busyness. An average oak tree gives off, so we've heard and do believe, one hundred fifty gallons of water on a hot summer's day. Porch sitting at sundown, we can't help but sigh and wish it wasn't quite so true that in a day or two— say it isn't so—the days will begin to shorten.

19 The difference between catching northerns and catching really big northerns is often a matter of luck. But sometimes it's a matter of thinking big, and a matter of having a trick or two up your sleeve.

Trophy-big northerns often leave weedbeds to lesser fish and roam the big open waters where they reign supreme. Trolling such open waters is alien to many who fish for northern, and it takes some practice to adjust the crucial trolling speed to maintain lures at the right temperature depth.

Catchers of these trophy northerns use heavy spoons that produce slow, wide wobbles if they're going deeply deep, or long thin ones that produce a faster wobble and a tight flash for less so. They use big-lake spinners and just as big deep-diving crankbaits. They use wire leaders on everything. They have the option of "flat lining," running a lure straight behind the boat, or using downriggers and planer boards to put lures exactly where they want them— out of the wake. And they hang their catches on the wall.

It's not deep-sea fishing, but it'll do, it'll do.

Notes

20 So often it's the little things that count. The small, quiet, gentle things—a smile, a single rose, a sliver of a moon, a sky, a twinkling star, a ray of light sunshining through the clouds.

The little boats get us into little out-of-the-way seldom-fished honey holes of lakes. The little motors let us slip quietly atop feeding schools of fish. Often the little baits catch the biggest fish, the little bobbers tell the greatest tales, the little streams hold the greatest thrills.

Giving a little oil to a summer-stored shotgun keeps it new. A little planning makes a camp meal great, a little care keeps a fine reel reeling and a good tent tentable. It takes a little practice for just plain old-clothes anglers to fill their creels, and fair shots to become marksmen, and arrow shooters to become archers.

It takes a little donation to save a habitat, a little urging to turn a legislator a little bit toward the right direction. And a little consideration toward fellow anglers, hunters, and campers goes a long, long way.

That's giant Jupiter, a little brighter than even the brightest star, that dominates the evening sky to the west. Young killdeer skitter-test long skinny legs. Though summer's only about to begin, some folks figure it started around the middle of May and will last until the end of August.

Notes

June

Click beetles, brownish, slender, shiny, and smooth, sometimes called snapping bugs, spring beetles, and skipjacks, often just keel over when disturbed, landing on their backs. No problem. They just pop themselves right side up again when they become undisturbed. Pretty good sport on a dull day. Their larvae are called wireworms. Young bobolinks are about ready to leave their nests. The scum on ponds and back bays oozes with life.

21

The campers in our family get a little fed up with having hot dogs and beans all the time, so the other night we tried something different. At suppertime the campers said, as usual, "What, hot dogs again?" And we said, "Sure, but we've got a dessert for anybody who cleans up everything on their plates." And then we followed it up like this.

We took half a loaf of bread and spread both sides of the slices with butter and blueberry jelly. We were generous with the jelly. Then we buttered down a heavy skillet and arranged the slices in layers. We poured a cup of milk over the bread, slowly, so the bread soaked up about all of it. Then we smeared some more butter on the top slices and tightly covered the pan and set it over low-burning coals for half an hour. This has got to cook slow.

And when the last kid licked up her last bean, we sliced the stuff, which was now like pudding, and served it up like pie alongside a cold glass of milk.

And the blessed peace that befell our campsite was like a soft whisper bobbing in the breeze.

Notes

22 Putting in to strange lakes and fishing them for the first time can be something like opening a Christmas present: at once anticipating something we've always wanted and dreading that the thing may be filled with coal. Fishing untried lakes poses a challenge, a challenge that, even without a map, an angler with a few tricks up a sleeve can meet.

One method of locating productive fishing spots in unfamiliar lakes is to troll gridlike, in parallel lines, moving first north and south over an area, and then east and west. When we get a strike, we drop a marker buoy at the spot and make a new set of grid lines closer together near the marker. Where there's one fish, there're often more.

Or we can troll in S-patterns instead of straight lines, which raises and lowers a lure in the water, keeping the marker handy. Trolling in small, then ever-widening, circles is another maneuver to become familiar with new waters. In these systematic travels, we'll find sunken islands, underwater brush piles, ledges, reefs, springs, channels, and such places as fish call heaven, as do those who hunt them.

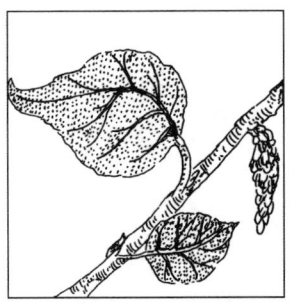

No longer winter-dormant, the once brown, knobby, bare-as-bones twig ends of cottonwoods now teem with a wondrous wealth of green aliveness. We were so busy, we forgot to watch it happen. Ever wonder how many insect eggs hatch on a June day in the neighborhood? In the county? In the state? In the country? In the world? In the universe?

Notes

June

Another robber fly, the horsefly, takes its turn at bare spots on the human body. Especially does it favor that little spot right on top of a fellow's head where there isn't quite as much hair as there used to be. Red-winged blackbirds feed their young.

23 We are attached to the waters of our lakes and rivers, tied to the sun shining on them. We sit in rowboats; we doggie paddle in the smooth waves; we fish from docks and motorboats as the sundown voices of children carry across our blue, full-of-moonlight, mortal waters. Yet we use these waters as wrecking places for broken pieces of our garbage, ice them with the acid rain of disregard. And now we mutilate even further these waters that we love, with more careless mischief. We add yet another scourge to them, one that grows so fast and with such vigor that it very quickly fills them, clogs them, chokes out native plants and animals, ruins boating and fishing. It is Eurasian watermilfoil, this scourge, and so damning is it that one single piece of one (of one part of one) left on a boat or trailer or prop will infect, infest another of our waters, leaving us nothing to do but shed a tear for what was of them and for what might have been.

Notes

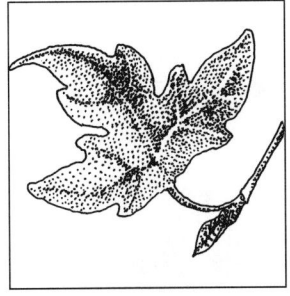

24 Surely, outside of a full canteen, a stout paddle, and a change of socks, bacon's about the most important piece of equipment on a wilderness outing. If the bacon goes bad the trip goes bad, but if the bacon stays good, well, you get the idea.

Anyway, if they do it right, hunters, anglers, campers, and those who roam just for the heck of it, far from plug-ins and extension cords, can keep their bacon fresh and mold-free for up to two weeks.

First, we get rid of the sliced, prepackaged stuff. That'll go bad fast. We need to buy our bacon in solid slabs. It's more mold-resistant, and if a little mold does creep in on it, we just scrape it off.

And to make bacon even more mold-resistant, we wipe it down with vinegar before we set out, we keep the whole chunk wrapped in vinegar-soaked cheesecloth, and we tote it in airtight plastic bags.

And then we dry the slab every couple of days by holding it briefly over the smoke of the campfire. Which doesn't hurt the taste any, either.

While the unseen miracle of maple tree roots grope down and out, the more obvious miracle of its leaves shelters birds and us on a midweek picnic. Young red-tailed hawks are about ready to test their wings. That awful purple loose-strife, filling pond after pond after pond, begins to bloom again. Porch sitting again tonight, we see stars that reach as far as the limits of our imagination.

Notes

June

Black-eyed Susans nod in what's left of June's breezes. Tenspot skimmer dragon-flies—what a nice name— mosquito-shop. The little house wren is out, too. She can feed up to five hundred spiders to her young in an afternoon—though I don't know who did the counting, nor was I there to watch.

25 This and that. Here and there. Now and then. That's a kestrel, that tiny colorful hawk perched on telephone wires or hovering helicopterlike in flight as it watches fields and roadside ditches for prey.

Freshwater fishing hooks generally come in sizes from the big #1 to the tiny #31. A pickerel pike is neither a pickerel nor a pike, but a walleye. A moose grows those great big antlers in as little as three months, making that how many pounds per day, I wonder.

A gray fox can climb trees, but a red one cannot, and a shark has no bones. Look it up. Rattlesnakes don't always buzz a warning buzz before striking. Some fish are anadromous—living in the sea but ascending to fresh water to spawn.

A longer anchor rope should be used in heavy winds; a shorter one causes the anchor to drag. Squirrels, white-tailed deer, wood ducks, and wild turkeys fatten on acorns in the fall.

And the gestation period of a possum is thirteen days.

Notes

26 Within the marvelous mystery of migration, ducks and geese fly pretty much where they want to, or where they have to—depending on the duck or the goose, from north to south and back, in four broad, sometimes indistinct, sometimes overlapping, occasionally parallel paths.

One of these, familiar to duck and goose hunters, is the Central flyway. Though it lacks the long coastlines of its sister flyways, the Atlantic and Pacific, and the intricate river systems of the Mississippi, the Central has a lot of great things going for it and flying through it. The Central follows nearly all grassland, from start to finish, yet three-fourths of the continent's redheads pass through it. Mallards are its number one bird, followed by pintails and greenwings, woodies, mergansers, widgeon, gadwalls, shovelers, scaup, and canvasbacks, all of whom call it home.

And when they go, where do the wild geese go? Line after line after line of Canadas, white-fronteds, and snows cut the evening sky, calling to after-supper porch sitters in the states and provinces that make up the Central flyway.

Those born these days are born under the sign of the crab, Cancer, lying rather dimly with no great stars in it. Cancer is called the crab because a crab moves backward and forward with equal ease, as does Cancer. School-free kids, tan-camouflaged to match the sandy beaches, carry on something awful in the water. Shall we join them?

Notes

June

Wood ticks are out and about again and still. Wrens ought to devote some time to them and let up a bit on the spiders for a while. So should the yellow-shafted flickers, who can take as many as five thousand—that's three zeros—ants in an afternoon. We always especially enjoy June, for in June no one needs an excuse to go fishing.

27 We may never score a touchdown on an autumn afternoon, hit a home run, or pass a baton in Olympic competition, but most certainly the men and women who shoulder 20-gauges through miles of falling leaves, or tote .30-06s over mountainous terrain or through foot-deep slush, or pole decoy-heavy john boats over white-capped flowages are, in their own right, class athletes.

As with any athletes, hunters, before the whistle of opening day sounds, should be in pretty good physical condition.

They should start easy—some walking or biking, some living-room calisthenics—and then move on to more vigorous, complex exercises.

If it's been too long since the hunter-athlete has seen a doctor, now is a good time to do it. With persistence and luck, all this might mean an extra partridge or two, and more important, an extra season or two.

Notes

28 Talking muskie fishing is ticklish conversation—the situation changes so fast, you sort of hate to commit yourself one way or the other. So when we speak of muskies, we must speak in broad generalities, not ignoring any of the possibilities and not expecting too much other than the anticipation that at any moment all heck might break loose.

Some folks around here start out fishing muskies in the spring in weedy, mucky flats, using suckers or chubs. Then as the water warms, the weeds come up, and the bloom comes on, they switch to fluorescent lures and move to the steeper weed lines and breaks. Still later, as the water really warms up, muskies hold deep off the weed lines and secondary breaks or hang suspended off deep breaks and midlake humps, and they move right to the weed lines early and late in the day—where waiting anglers change to hot-colored crankbaits and find the best fishing at about dawn—knowing full well that the only certainty in fishing muskies is that they'll feed the day before you get there. As in "Ya shudda bin here yesterday." Generally speaking, of course.

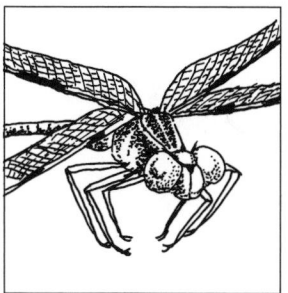

A friend of mine envies dragonflies, who, he maintains, do nothing but eat and make love. They're making love when they're flying in tandem and they're eating as they solo, scooping mosquitoes into baskets formed by cupping their hairy legs. And in March, did you figure the grass'd need so much cutting by now?

Notes

June

On the bottomlands, the basswood, or lindens, bloom their hanging, pale, fragrant flowers, to the delight of bees and neighbor beekeepers, for the nectar makes such good honey. Grackles flock. Baltimore orioles, pleased with the seasonal glut of caterpillars, take up to a hundred of them an hour to their youngsters.

29 Many of us will spend our annual two- or three-week temporary reprieve from the grindstone out fishing. It'll be time long longed for and time well spent, though if you think about it, we might want to invest a little bit of that time out on the marsh in the old duck blind.

Now, when the water and weather are warm and the place is jumping with activity, is a nice time to work on the blind, or if it's too rickety, to start over and build a new one.

Now's also a good time to study the place. Maybe the marsh has changed in the last few years. Maybe it has grown up and the ducky spots have moved a couple of hundred yards one way or the other. Maybe the water level has changed, or we'd like a better angle to the fall winds or to the rising or setting sun. Maybe we'd like more visibility. Maybe the hunting pressure has become a little heavy where our blind is, and we'd like to be a little lonelier. And maybe we'd like to do something about it.

Maybe we'd just like to get out there and watch the local duck action at work. And maybe we don't need any excuse at all.

Notes

30 When you've got yourself a campfire, you've got yourself a pal, a companion on scary nights, to lift your spirits, to hold crackling conversations with, to warm your body, dry your socks, and boil your stew.

When and where it's okay to do so—where wild fire danger does not exist, where the environment is not so fragile as to be easily scarred, where firewood sources are not endangered—there's just nothing quite like a good campfire.

And each of us has a favorite method of campfire making—personal and private. One very nice campfire doesn't require axes or saws or too much work or imagination. It involves lining up the firewood—little sticks for a quick, pretty little soup-heater or bigger ones for after-dark storytelling fires—into a starlike shape.

You keep the flame in the middle alive by pushing each stick toward the center as it burns down, so it can do its share in keeping the hope of the fire alive and warming the cockles of a heart.

On sandy roadsides and occasionally on muskrat houses, snapping turtles lay a couple dozen Ping-Pong-ball-sized eggs in nests where they've first peed to loosen the soil and then dug out with their hind feet. It's been a busy, busy month of June. Our planet has indeed swung back on its great pivot, as pointed out daily by a creeping abbreviation of daylight.

Notes

July

July

July is the month of the Middle-of-Summer Moon, the Moon of Ripening Cherries, the Buck Moon. In July bees buzz in blooming basswood trees. Papa bears hunt up prospective mama bears. Black-eyed Susans nod coyly from roadside ditches. Cottontails and robins begin second families of the season. Busy beavers harvest aspen for food and for dam fixing up. And the sun gloriously sets as only a summer sun can set—late.

Notes

1 It's July already! And you know what that means. It's summertime all the time. It's time to water the lawn again. Time to run through the sprinkler. Lemonade time. Time for watermelon desserts.

Time for a firecracker of a picnic. Time to watch the stars at night and fly them with the stripes during the day. Time to reflect. To remember. To be grateful.

It's time to remember the snowbanks of January and the shoveling thereof. It's time to do some serious planning on planning a hunting trip out west. Maybe. Time at least to dust off guns and time to go fishing in the coolness at the starts and ends of day if we can.

It's time for ball games and reunions, for great Aunt Fern once again to pinch your cheek and gush how tall you've grown, while your own kids giggle at a safe distance. It's time for a fishing weekend. Or two glorious weeks at the cabin. And time for a slow boat ride at sunset. Time to dig deeper for worms, to eat tomatoes hot off the vine.

And time to find some shade.

2 What do we do? Where do we go? When the only time we've got is in the heat of a hot summer's day, when the fish don't bite for anything?

Well, we'll go fishing, because that's what we do in the heat of a hot summer's day—when it's the only fishing time we've got. Probably perch fishing today.

We'll take a very, very paper-thin piece of pork rind—a little over an inch long and a quarter of that wide. We'll attach that to a thin wire hook tied prettily to a two- or four-pound test line. A foot or so ahead of that we'll pinch off a BB-sized split shot (half a one is better) and a foot beyond that, another one. Then we'll cast the thing out, let it settle to around perch level, and practice some patience by reeling in terribly, terribly slowly, painfully slowly. And every half a foot, we'll pause and maybe give the thing a tiny twitch.

We might catch a crappie by mistake. Or a bluegill. We might not have red-hot action in this heat, but we're fishing in this fishing time allotted to us, doing the best we can, and doing okay.

Milkweeds reach the peak of their bloom now. Grand-mothers eager to fill berry baskets enlist the aid of not-so-eager grandchildren for ritual harvests of blue-berries. Campsites are full; summer cottages are the centers of social life. Detour signs sprout up on every highway and byway in the country, and deeply rooted under-construction signs blossom where detours don't.

Notes

July

Catbirds sing after sunset. Not their own songs, though, and never quite the same one twice. Hawk eggs hatch, and baby eagles test their wings in first flights through cloudless skies. Elderberries bloom with flat-top clusters of flowers. On good days, purple martins catch a thousand mosquitoes per. Lightning bugs, living chunks of starlight, in pre-Fourth of July celebrations, sparkle over the gardens and down at the edge of Katie Lake.

3 Much to-do usually surrounds the getting of a kid's first gun. The whens and wheres and hows and whys have been coolly, if not coldly, discussed and hotly debated in households since the first cave-kid pleaded for a throw-stone and then, in an I-told-you-this-would-happen eventuality, a slingshot.

But what about the citizen who, having reached the age of reason and voting privilege, wishes to wade for the very first time into the warm waters of gun ownership? That decision too is not one to be made lightly, and it too must come only after much debate and discussion within the head and the heart of the citizen.

The would-be gun owner should examine his or her motives, read everything possible on gun ownership and the great and grave responsibilities of that ownership, and talk with friends who own guns—and, to hear both sides of the issue, I suppose, with those who do not. He or she must take courses in the handling and shooting of firearms, shooting first under the direction of experts.

If it's still a go after all that—well, we'll take that up later.

Notes

4 "Eat your peas," my mother said. "Eat your oatmeal." "Eat your spinach." "Wear your cap," she insisted. "Get a good night's sleep." "Chew your food." "Do your homework." "Change your socks." "Wear clean underwear."

Being given no choice, I listened mostly to what she said, and eventually did as she bid. Some of it even got to be a habit, and, as she predicted, I grew up fairly big, and strong enough, at least, to push a pencil.

Alas, though, Mother didn't know it all. Didn't help me where I needed it most, and left gaping gaps in my education. Retarding my growth and development then, and leaving me less of a complete angler today. Not once. Not one time did she preach to me the importance of owning a case for fishing rods. No. Not ever.

Though I have snapped rods in car doors, screen doors, and garage doors; broken them on trains, planes, boats, and bicycles; dropped them on city sidewalks, village roads, country lanes, and backwoods trails; though I have thrown good money after bad and bad after good— I still do not own a rod case. Where did you go wrong, Ma? Where did you go wrong?

Ten times as far from the sun as the earth (886 million miles) and seventy-two thousand miles in diameter (ten times that of the earth)—Saturn looks very bright, very much like a star in the morning skies these days. Of course Saturday is named after this planet, which takes around thirty years to orbit the sun.

Notes

_____

_____

_____

_____

_____

_____

July

This heat got you down? Well, these days the sun is about as far from the earth as it gets. Go figure. The southern half of the fishing folks head north to catch the big ones. The northern half head south to do the same. And the half in the middle loll beneath the shade of oak trees, not doing a thing. Sphinx moths or hawkmoths, hover over our flowers hummingbird-style. They're not trying to fool anyone and don't.

5 We took last weekend off from the rigors of fishing to gather at the deer hunting shack for annual summer maintenance duties. As we sipped some cool stuff under the shade of the old white pine out front, the Professor, who gets uncomfortable at the thought of somebody else not being busy, came along and reminded us we better get to putting up our deer stands.

It's the belief at our camp that a good tree stand is about the best deer-getting device a bow or gun hunter can use. A deer's warning system is geared to ground-level attack, at least somewhat; the tree stand puts us above its normal line of vision, and often puts our scent pattern above the deer too.

We set our stands where they give good views of approaching trails and good shot angles. Under the Professor's watchful eye, we build them safe and we build them comfortable enough to allow us several hours of fidget-free sitting. We put them a bit off the main trail. Built now, a tree stand lets the animals and the hunters get used to it early.

And folks with cameras use them all year round.

Notes

6 Smallmouth bass lead lives of double existence. By day, in clear July waters, they can be timid creatures, shying from anglers and the boats that carry them, demanding little lures, light lines, and experienced, sensitive fingers to detect tiny tap-tap strikes. But by night, under cover of darkness, these same fish can shed their shy, coat-and-tie demeanor, roll up their sleeves to expose tattoos, roam boldly, and feed vigorously, ignoring boats, caring little about lure size, and sucking up anything that smacks of midnight snacks.

Fishing in the dark can be a new, quite wonderfully alone experience. Mostly, you have the lake to yourself, and with so few distractions, the whole business seems so up-close, so yours all alone—the sound of the cast, the slice of fluorescent line against the darkness, the kerplunk of a spinner bait hitting the water, the gentle chop against the boat, the splash out there of a nice smallmouth night-dancing at the end of your line.

And the thump of your own beating heart.

On ground nests, near clumps of vegetation in meadows and marshes, young short-eared owlets get ready to leave their nests. Their low-flying, sometimes day-flying, mouse-hunting, worn out parents must feel pretty good about that. The sweet smell of clover fills the evening air. Small jungles of jewelweed—some folks call them touch-me-nots and so do we in the fall—grow in ditches and woodlots where it's damp.

Notes

July

Tadpoles become frogs. Some have to hurry or their shallow ponds will dry up on them. School-free kids get to stay up late. At night they lie on their backs in the backyard counting the stars and reaching out to them as far as the limits of their imaginations allow.

7 Cattails can grow half a foot a day. And, for the most part, it's a good thing. The green bloom spikes of the plant can be cooked as a vegetable; its sprouts can be used in salads; the yellow pollen can be added to pancake batter; its young shoots can be eaten raw, cooked, or pickled.

Ducks, geese, and muskrats feed upon the starchy root of the cattail. Muskrats use the plant to construct their lodges—which other animals and birds use as nesting and resting places. Red-winged blackbirds nest in cattails and cattails offer precious hiding places for ducklings.

Cattails grow into more cattails in two ways. New plants sprout from the spreading roots of old ones—the quick and easy way. And they grow from seeds. The brown tip (the cat's tail) can hold a quarter of a million seeds, which burst out to fly to their own nesting sites.

Cattails do so much for a wetland and its inhabitants, it's a shame they overdo it—crowding out other good plants and eventually filling it in—a definite no-no, even for cattails.

Notes

8 He's born, along with one or two brothers and sisters, in the middle of winter-heavy February to a sleeping mother who's not about to wake up just for him. At least not for very long. He's about six or seven inches from one end to the other, blind, and nearly hairless, and weighs around ten ounces.

In late March his mother wakes, moves out of the den, "woof woofs" to him—bear talk for "C'mon kids"—and he enters into the great out-of-doors.

Mother bear (papa split as soon as she got pregnant, which doesn't do much for the credibility of Goldilocks) acts as his protector, provider, and teacher through his second year, and then kicks him out.

At three he's a loner and sexually active with many girl bears taken in by his good looks and smooth line. He's boss of a dozen or more square miles of forest, swamp, and stream.

He eats nearly anything, sleeps much of each winter away, grows into a seventy-inch, four-hundred-pound hunk, lives to a ripe old age, and eventually, of course, dies, though probably of nothing serious.

Whitetail antlers are velvet-covered and beautiful. Whip-poorwills call as the sun sets, and as it rises, and on clear, moonlit nights. Sometimes they give a little "cluck" before they belt out "pur-ple RIB" a half dozen times or so. Some folks go fishing this morning just to catch a sunrise and to drink hot coffee from a thermos. Grouse, pheasants, turkeys, larks, wrens, and quail take baths in this warm July dust to clean up, remove oils, and stop the spread of parasites.

Notes

July

Little pine trees grow into Christmas trees. How many shopping days are left do you suppose? I don't give a hoot either. Half-grown rabbits eat their share of the garden lettuce. And the pastel colors of spring have given way to the red-hot colors of summer. Bull moose antlers have grown about all they're going to, which is about enough.

9 I like to see kids team playing: baseball, hockey, basketball. But all in all, I think I'd rather see them playing tennis or throwing horseshoes, or running or swimming—things that'll last them a lifetime. And fishing, of course, definitely fishing.

But kids aren't going to pick up such things by themselves. They need us to show them the way. With little kids, we won't take them hawg fishing. Big bass, big walleyes, and big northerns, even, cooperate too seldom to hold kids' interest. We'll take them little-kid fishing, catch-a-fish-a-minute fishing. And we'll let them help us in the preparations. We'll outfit them properly, with regulation life jackets and reels.

When the action slows, we'll take a break and have a snack and a cool drink. We'll talk, watch the clouds, the birds. We'll watch their own beautiful rainbow reflections in the water. We'll try to instill in them a deep respect for the wonderful world about them. And if they get tired, we'll quit for a while, for what's good for our partners is good for us, and our last casts together are a long, long ways off.

Notes

10 Often called the "bird dogs" of artificial lures, crankbaits may also be the most efficient and most versatile, and are usually pretty enough to (and should) decorate Christmas trees.

Crankbaits are made of wood, plastic, or foam, with plastic or metal lips—diving planes—at their noses. The size, shape, and angle of this plane determines the depth at which a particular crankbait will travel.

Long, broad lips set at steep angles cause plugs to dive deep, while those with small, shallow-angle lips stay near the surface.

Most crankbait users like this bait to dive deep enough to make contact with bottom structures. Which is okay. If it gets stuck on something, it can, when given slack, float backwards and up, freeing itself, for it's often the nose that's snagged, not the hooks.

The endless retrieve produced by trolling crankbaits allows us to get down deep and stay there, so important in this hot weather. Down to where the big ones lie—content to snooze the summer away.

Foolish fish.

In clover meadows, in road-side ditches, in parks and pastures, sulfur butterflies are on the wing. Honeybees work themselves to death in just six of these summer weeks; it's all they know. The queens are egg-laying machines, turning out about one every thirty seconds, over a couple thousand a day. Red foxes shed winter hair. Chorus frogs warm cold blood in hot sun spots on the forest floor.

Notes

July

Snowshoe hares kick their first batch of bunnies out of the nest and begin working on a second. Wild raspberries ripen. Poison ivy thrives. Some folks say that the juice of the jewelweed eases the itch. Acorns are noticeable in oak trees. And it seems that of the twenty-seven thousand species of beetles in this country, all of them are out and about now—clicking, scurrying, gnawing, providing food for birds, and chewing on dead things.

11 Some of you out there have decided, and it's about time, that the outdoor sporting life—you know, hunting, fishing, camping, digging worms, and so on— is for you.

Magazines and newspapers are full of advice to get you started and behind-the-sporting-goods-counter folks will fit you out. But there's no one but me to teach the most important aspect of all to the leading of a successful outdoor sporting life, which is how to pick an outdoor sporting life buddy.

This is a hard thing to do, to be done with a thousand times more care than the picking of a spouse. First, you must find someone who wants to do what you want to do and when you want to do it. Then you must pick someone who goes to bed early and gets up at the same time. Someone who'll start the fire and cook breakfast. Get someone who's got a four-wheel-drive and isn't afraid to use it, a good boat, a better dog, and a relative who owns a sporting goods store; someone who's a no-good, lazy bum who doesn't worry about jobs or day-to-day responsibilities.

Say, pal, you got a minute?

Notes

12 The scene is an often-repeated one—an early, moonless night, in a remote area, along a river's edge; lanterns cast eerie glows; people speak in whispers.

A drug deal going down? A plot unfolding to overthrow the government? Folks making dark play with the devil? Naaah. It's catfishers. Catfishing—hooking up good fishing with good sport with good taste and good friends.

Whole families, lunches packed, coolers filled and sometimes frying pans hot, go catfishing. They use cane poles or throw lines or the expensive stuff they use for bass. And for bait? Name it: worms, chubs, suckers, limburger cheese, rotten chicken guts, congealed cow blood, very old liver soaked in stale beer—you know, the usual stuff.

They fish at night, because then cats move out of deep pockets of daytime protection to shallow riffles and shorelines to feed—even now in the heat of summer.

Like most anglers, catfishers need perseverance and patience—hence the lunch, the cooler, and the wonderful company—of childhood memories.

Young toads—toadlets?—emerge now and must be careful lest they be chewed on by snakes. Honeysuckles perfume the countryside and make it look nice, too. And sad calls of mourning doves sound over hay fields. Nettle stings unwary berry-picking fingers. Some shorebirds seriously consider moving south again. The heck with them. And each big maple tree in big, busy cities each day sucks up airborne lead from a thousand gallons of car-burned gasoline.

Notes

July

Field crickets fill the night air with songs. Rain we didn't want in May and June, we're praying for now. Painted turtles hatch, at least those the raccoons didn't get as eggs. Orange, black-veined monarch butterflies float over meadows, weedy fields, and watercourses, especially where milkweeds are found. Most pheasant eggs have hatched.

13 Ever wonder why some people work so hard acquiring a comfortable home with all the gadgets imaginable to make living easy, then at the drop of a sunset (or a weekend) leave it all to sleep on the hard ground under the stars and to eat bacon burned over a campfire?

Some things, I imagine, are best just done, and the motives not too closely examined.

Actually, camping doesn't have to be a particular hardship at all. With a bit of planning, some practice, and a clue or two, camping can be downright comfortable. For instance, no camp should be without baking soda. Besides its many other uses, some mixed with enough water to make a paste soothes insect bites, poison ivy, heat rash, and sun burn.

If someone oversalts the soup, a peeled potato dropped in for ten minutes or so will soak up the excess salt. And to give camp gravy a special kick, add a cup of leftover coffee.

See?

Notes

14 A time comes, here in July, when we unlock our souls from the duties of summer, from fishing, from mowing and hoeing, from hay making and corn cultivating. We untangle ourselves from the streets and highways that cut our lives into thin slices and follow the roads that lead us to our deer camp. We go to mop, to clean, to cut wood, to scout, to plan, to remember. It's also a time for the Professor's potato pancake breakfasts.

For each eight cakes, the Professor puts three tablespoons milk, one egg, one and two-thirds cup raw potato chunks, one-half onion, two tablespoons flour, one-half teaspoon salt, and one-eighth teaspoon baking powder into a blender and runs it half a dozen seconds at high speed. Then onto a hot, greasy griddle he spoons it. Those of us who have some left bring along venison sausage. Those with maple trees provide the syrup, and everybody else chips in good company and good stories of hunts past and hopeful hunts of the future. Then, of course, too soon it's time to go, to wind our way back to the maze of our lives. Before we do though, we're sure to leave just enough mess and just enough uncut wood, so we'll have to come back in a couple of weeks to finish the job.

Now that thistledown is becoming available, goldfinches finally get around to building cuplike two-inch-diameter nests of grass and thistledown in bushes and saplings. Since they're seed eaters, they have to wait until weed seeds become available before they can have their three to five little ones. Green frogs sound like banjo pickers. Weeds gain the upper hand on hoers by sneaking back to carrot rows when the coast is clear.

Notes

July

15 Dewy cool mornings of hot July days are the berry best times of the year for those who hunt the wily blueberry or who brave pokes and scratches fishing around for raspberries and their black cousins.

Some berry hunters savagely store their trophies in hidden corners of freezers—to be baked into holiday pies. Others, as the heat of the day settles in, enjoy the fruits of their labors piled high atop slabs of ice cream.

Yet others get fancier—mixing together two cups of freshly washed blueberries, one-half cup sugar, one-half cup water, and a teaspoon nutmeg. This they boil for five minutes and spoon, still warm, over individual servings of vanilla ice cream. Or they fix them like my neighbor does; she creams a stick of softened butter with a cup of powdered sugar. Into this she beats one-half cup mashed raspberries or blackberries flavored with one-half teaspoon vanilla. She refrigerates this as she would plain old butter and uses it the same way, especially on saltines.

Around here, those who don't pick don't eat—which means it's been years since I've tasted wild berries. Except for midnight raids on the fridge.

Notes

16 Barefoot kids armed with cane poles, heavy lines, hooks, and cork bobbers might have, a long time ago, been any of us. But times change. Kids grow up and trade, among other things, cane poles for technically correct rods and reels, and heavy lines for monofilament.

And bobbers go the way of pimples, shy kisses, and giggles, or are relegated to amateurs and lazybones. Such grown-up attitudes, though, can cost us some mighty fine fishing, for what a bobber does so very well is to put a bait at a precise depth.

Bluegills, bass, and northerns, for example, change levels at a whim. With a bobber, we can cast, drift, or troll, altering our fishing depths until we hit the jackpot. We have control—whether we want to go to the bottom, reach just above the weeds, or suspend in the middle of nowhere.

And bobbers, like us, have changed considerably. Today, bobbers are of such shapes, sizes, uses, and colors as to keep even the most gadget-conscious among us busy for weeks and weeks and weeks.

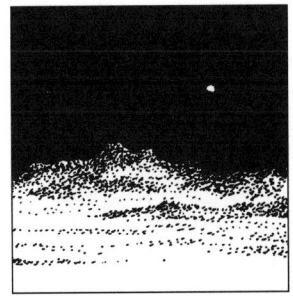

Hot little Mercury, only 36 million miles from the sun and only three thousand miles through the middle, is an evening star tonight. Some gooseberries are ripe. Cattails are brown. Grasshoppers hop and call from grassy spots. Tiger swallowtails hotfoot it over the countryside. Wood ticks are less obnoxious; deerflies are not. Bats play hide and seek with falling darkness. City folks head into the country for vacations; country folks go the other way.

Notes

July

Blueberries are good and ripe. Or is that ripe and good? Most duck eggs have hatched. The young of the great blue heron fledge. Pincherries ripen. Snakes shed their skins. Baby beavers, within their mounds, beg for food. Spring peepers hunt for insects on the floors of swamps and in thickets. And somewhere, a female moth, the cecropia, sends out a perfume that carries three miles to attract matable males.

Notes

17 The destruction of wildlife habitat has been steady and relentless. And too often farmers and ranchers shoulder the blame for it. But we're all sinners in the crimes against our environment and the loss of habitat.

We all drive on miles of paved roads, shop in acres of malls, and build homes where deer once roamed and antelope once played.

The fact is that many farms and ranches provide improved habitat and a greater abundance of food for much of our wildlife—which thrive on fields of hay and grain and waterholes, pastures and shelterbelts. Indeed, most farmers and ranchers don't begrudge giving wildlife a share. They are, after all, in the business because they enjoy nature, the out-of-doors, and wildlife.

Management and cooperation are the keys. For the better that land is managed, the more it will profit all concerned. We—wildlife managers, sportsmen, ecologists, and just plain folks—should not look upon those who make their living from the land as antagonists but as partners in schemes to benefit the lives of wildlife and, thereby, ours as well.

18 It doesn't matter much—snooty brookies, classy walleyes, channel cats, bullheads, bass, panfish, or lumbering carp—grasshoppers bring them all to bay. Grasshoppers, plentiful (oh so plentiful), are also so versatile that there's virtually no limit to the ways they can be fished or to the fish that take to them. And the catching of hoppers provides almost as much fun as the fishing of them.

One way to nab them is to put a person at either end of a stretched-out minnow seine, and walk at a pretty fast clip through areas of low vegetation, keeping the top of the seine a little ahead of the bottom, raking down into the foliage, without putting too much drag on the seine, causing hoppers to hop in foolish attempts to flee. When they hit the seine they cling to it, at which point the two ends are brought together, trapping these hapless cousins of crickets and katydids.

Stalking hoppers, however, one on one, is perhaps more sporting. They can be caught at night with the aid of flashlights as they cling to tall grasses, or in early mornings when they're sluggish with the cool of the night and the damp of the dew. Like you and me.

Canada geese have regrown their flight feathers and regained their confidence and begin to fly once again. Cedar waxwings regurgitate berries and small fruits into the mouths of hungry babes. Baby shrews follow their mothers single-file, nose to tail, in endless search for insects. Crab spiders make their appearance on new-blooming goldenrods.

Notes

July

Half-grown raccoons shuffle along behind mother— snagging crayfish, insects, birds, eggs, small rodents, fruit, berries, and leftovers from garbage cans. Headwaters of small streams dry up. Silver-haired bats right-side-up themselves from daytime sleeps in trees to gobble up to one hundred fifty insects an hour. Each. Trout rise to stream surfaces, gently inhaling mayflies—real McCoy mayflies—and ignoring my phonies.

19 Whitetails have learned to cope with the spreading influence of humans, thriving often at the edges of cities; mule deer, unless forced by weather conditions to do so, are not quite as tolerant, and have become creatures of deserts, prairies, and mountains— the big country.

Mule deer are more sedentary than whitetails, more placid by nature, larger, heavier—averaging a hundred pounds heavier. And mulies don't wave the traditional white-flag farewells of their more northern cousins either, but run with their tails flat—perhaps embarrassed at such a stringy little thing. It's the only thing they have to be embarrassed about, though. They can stand forty inches at the shoulder and measure six feet in length, have been known to make horizontal jumps of twenty-five feet, and can jump eight feet high.

When more puzzled than alarmed, mulies bounce into the air and land stiff-legged in a kind of pogo-stick Tigger fashion. They've been clocked at thirty-five miles per hour. They travel extensively and usually drift, in minor migrations, between summer and winter ranges.

They have big ears.

20 There's nothing more downright disappointing to a hunter than driving down a country lane abloom with "No Trespassing" signs. Actually, it makes us mad.

Yet, most rural folks post their lands merely to protect themselves from thieves, pranksters, n'er-do-wells, slick talkers, con men, and boneheads cleverly disguised as hunters.

And who can blame them? I don't know a farm family whose members don't work their tails off, who're not involved in constant, bitter struggles for survival; they don't need heavily armed hombres roaming the land that is their home and what's left of their livelihood.

Yet, most rural folks are regular folks and don't mind if another regular person moseys up and offers a hand in exchange for a couple of days of hunting—a person who doesn't need the biggest buck or the most pheasants on the place, a person who might just share or bring a box of candy for the kids once in a while.

A couple of regular folks can come to a heap of understanding in a short time and reap a lifetime of friendship in the process.

From bird apartment houses, four or five young purple martins per apartment are ready to fly and join other purple martins in chatty purple martin conversations. Hot summer wildflower colors of red-orange, flaming yellow, and orange-yellow dominate the countryside landscape. Thistles show off their purple blossoms. Here in mid-July things are changing. It's not something to put a finger on or anything, but . . .

Notes

July

21 Good bowhunters, if they hunt from trees, try to practice from trees too, because practicing from a solid-ground, standing position is as different from shooting from a tiny platform a dozen feet in the air as making hay is from making whoopie.

Good bowhunters practice from tree stands in order to hit from tree stands. And from their stands they try all the angles and all the shooting positions—to the right, to the left, down the center, from the awkward to the straight on. They shoot standing up. They shoot sitting down, up close and far away, so when the real thing comes along, they'll have the experience to do what they came to do. And sometimes they practice in full gear, the stuff they'll be using on opening day—camouflage, boots, jacket. If there's going to be any scraping or scratching they want to find out about it now. They tune their bow and each of its components—sight, release, rest, stabilizer—for use in the woods.

When the season rolls around, good bowhunters don't want any loose screws—on their bows or between their ears.

Notes

22

Men and women become hunters and anglers so that they might find excuses to walk through meadows and forests, to wander where wildflowers grow and birds sing. They become people of the out-of-doors so they might witness fishing lines curving through foam and rapids, rod tips jumping like something alive, amid the companionship of oaks and pines and rocks and clouds and shimmering sunlight.

In their hearts these men and women are poets, perhaps not aware of it nor able to put it down on paper, but theirs is a world of motion, of color, of sound, of silence; a world of dreams and anticipation. In their world the greatest rewards come from doing well those things that present the greatest challenge—to those who have the desire, the will, to accept that challenge.

And if they come home with no fish, no bird, no deer, perhaps they will do better next time. And since they have experienced the freedom and the pleasure of doing what they want to do, they feel no shame at an empty creel or featherless game bag, and only hope and pray that such moments and more might be stretched into eternities.

White water lilies, those "Queens of the North," open their flowers. Sumac comes to fruit in woods and waysides. Wine makers open the season on elderberries and chokecherries, in anticipation of holiday cheering. Luna moths, stiff with dewy mornings, patiently wait for the warming sun to pep them up.

Notes

July

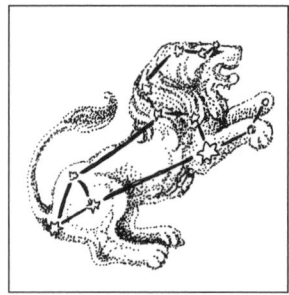

23 If there's an almost absolute in fishing for summertime walleyes, it's fishing them deep. Off the bottom.

Not too long ago, my Uncle Jake caught a nice one just as the sun rested a moment, as it always does in July, atop the pines on the west end of Lost Lake before sliding out of sight.

I was along. Jake anchored over about the deepest hole in the lake, pretty close to a weedbed, and hooked a lively crawler just once through its nose on a #8 hook tied directly to his six-pound test line. He put a small split shot about a foot and a half above the crawler, cast long, and let the thing settle to the bottom.

After a couple of minutes, he began to reel in very slowly. Verrry slowly. Until he felt the tiniest bit of resistance. He stopped reeling at once and opened the bail. "Weeds," I thought. But the line slowly peeled off the reel. At the slow count of twenty, Jake set the hook hard, and a few minutes later I nervously slipped the net under the beauty and hauled it aboard.

It's a good thing, too. If I had missed that fish, I would have had to swim to shore.

Notes

24 Against a dazzling display of a sundown drama, an eagle lands atop lightning-scarred branches of a giant pine; a derelict rowboat slowly melts into a sandy beach; a doe stops to nurse a pair of eager fawns; a half dozen mergansers follow the leader among cattails.

Sigh. If only I had a camera. On an expedition. An outing. A hike. A walk. Of all the ways to collect souvenirs, to gather memories, to tuck away forever the wonderful wonders of the out-of-doors—a spiderweb, a honeysuckle, an oak leaf, close-up trophies of the perfect fragments of nature—a camera does it best.

What better way to spend rainy, snow-filled, flu-struck, or sprained-ankle days than pulling out the special album and reliving better times. What better way to introduce little ones to outside mysteries. What better way to develop patience, stalking skills, an eye for detail, for beauty. It takes practice and a bit of equipment to become a fair photographer—but the fun comes in the getting there, and the payoff is that every day's a payday.

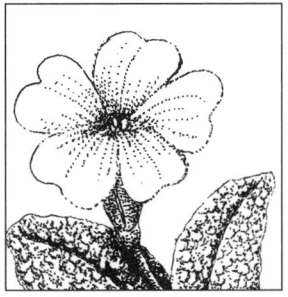

Primroses, here-today, gone-tomorrow, four-petaled yellow flowers, continue to open one evening and wilt by the next wherever it's dry. Otter families, six or seven strong, play follow-the-leader on lakes and rivers, especially at dawn and sunset. Wood turtles slowly roam hardwood forests and meadows, hunting insects and mushrooms.

Notes

July

Along swamp borders, mountain ash display orange-red clusters of berries prized by thrushes, waxwings, and grosbeaks. Bitterns, solitary skulkers of the marsh, pump their heads and sound like coughers, gutterally doing just that. Muskrats have it easy, picnicking on cattails, grasses, and mussels. And fish move so smoothly, so gracefully through water that is 780 times thicker than the air that we sometimes so clumsily navigate in.

25 Whereas we make elaborate efforts to approach deer stands and duck blinds silently, stealthily, we too often roar into favorite fishing spots with wide-open throttles—splash anchors overboard, drop thermoses to boat bottoms, scrape tackle boxes against gunwales, slide oars out of the way.

But midseason's low, clear waters require us to exercise more caution than that, to be more alert to the disturbances we create on or near the water.

Low, clear water means fish can see and hear us much more easily, much better than they can when high water keeps us farther above them and when it is filled with the debris of melting snows and spring rains.

Now's the time for us to be goose-hunter sneaky, moving quietly in and out of boats, staying out of sight as we check out dark pockets and deep holes.

Now's the time to use lures of delicate, natural colors and try for longer casts.

Now's the time to put the wits to work and catch some fish.

Notes

26 Consider the porcupine—that craver of salt, the salt on canoe paddles, ax handles, and saddles—that critter equipped with a coating of thirty thousand needle-sharp quills.

A newborn porky weighs more than a newborn bear cub and comes complete with its first eight teeth in place, and its eyes wide open, and within a half hour it has quills ready to do a job.

In the wild, porcupines live to be six years old. Their eyesight is poor, they can't smell very well, and their hearing isn't good either.

They're good climbers, though, and pretty good swimmers, and they were born to chew.

Their eyes don't shine in the dark. And they're too tough, too ornery, or too lazy to hibernate, chewing leisurely upon treetops at twenty degrees below, during full-blown blizzards.

Porcupines are difficult to cozy up to—especially the brutes that chew each night on the corner of our house, gnaw away at our maples and the sugar bush, and poke holes in the noses of our curious puppies.

It seems a bit early, but katydids make some music. In bogs and marshy areas bloom pitcher plants, those sneaky, meat-eating little devils that lure insects in on a one-way trip into hairy, water-filled, tubelike leaves. Sphinx moths fly over flower gardens, sipping nectar as they go, clothed in quiet beauty. And most of the butterflies in our lives, when they rest, rest with their wings straight up, while moths spread theirs flat.

Notes

July

Snow geese in the Arctic tundra get ready to come back. Painted turtles are picked up by kids and imprisoned in five-gallon buckets until the kids get tired of the game—about a day and a half. Possum babies, up to fifteen or so of them, hang on to their mother's pouch for seventy days. Moss grows nicely thick and soft.

27 Serious bowhunters, who hunt from trees, scout from trees, too. When they find a likely looking tree they sit in it a few evenings to study the place from this height advantage. And they do it early. They do it now.

Really serious hunters get high-flying friends to take aerial photographs, which show incredible details of hills, gullies, streams, fence lines, trails, beds, and pockets of thick growth.

Actually, serious hunters do it all more than once, planning on at least a couple of stands and planning on using them both. They figure that going and coming from the same stand, sometimes a couple of times a day, day after day, might busy-up the place just too much, so they alternate. They further figure that more than one stand gives them options in case the wind or the weather changes.

And serious bowhunters get in shape, limber up, to take the creaks and squeaks out of poor old bones in case they have to draw down on a great big one come next fall.

Notes

28 Interrupt a gray squirrel going about its business, and it'll hightail it up a tree. Right now. But trip up a fox squirrel at its daily duties, and it'll stick to the ground whenever it can, and more than likely get home free in a quick game of hide-and-seek.

Some claim the squirrel is the slyest critter in the woods and the ultimate in small game hunting. The fox squirrel is a charming fellow, with majestic movements. It doesn't, for instance, flick its tail like the gray, but waves it, and the fox squirrel's not as nervous or quick or fidgety as its smaller cousin. It's bigger and heavier than the gray, which may be why it likes to keep its feet on solid ground.

The fox comes in a variety of colors, ranging from light gray through several shades of red and yellow to midnight black. It likes open hardwood woodlots in the north and pine forests in the south—with plenty of sun-splotched spaces in both. And if the morning's wet and chilly, it likes to sleep in until the sun comes out.

Something we have in common.

Pin cherries are ripe and jam-ready. Red squirrels continue their noisy, ratchetlike scoldings in the great North Woods. Honeybees continue to visit hundreds and hundreds of blossoms a day in a constant quest for honey-making nectar—making their lives short but sweet. Kids of all ages build sand castles in late July, some on the beach and some in the air.

Notes

July

Mink pups, usually a half dozen to a litter, leave dens of rocks or natural cavities to follow their mothers in single file along riverbanks and shorelines, hunting for small mammals, birds, frogs, and fish. Gutsy red fox pups, four or five to a litter, go yap-yap-yapping after mice and half-grown rabbits. Testy yellow jackets, themselves living mostly on flower pollen, kill many insects to feed to their larvae-children in underground paper nests.

29 Enjoyment of the out-of-doors need not be limited to those times when we carry guns or pack rods or make weekend rendezvous with tents and campfires and red squirrels. Enjoyment of the outdoors includes being part of such epic scenes as snow-covered mountain peaks, pastel sunsets, the changing leaves of autumn, and the fury of a summer storm.

It can also include observing the little dramas that occupy the outdoor stage, and our ability to see, hear, and smell what's out there and interpret what we're seeing, hearing, and smelling. It can include developing keen perceptions, as we pussyfoot through forests or meadows, studying our surroundings for the hundreds of unseen eyes watching us and being accepted as part of the community. It can be, as we drift along as silently as we can, learning the wild words, songs, tones, rustlings, rattlings, and flutterings that are the sounds of the out-of-doors. Or enjoying the perfumes of flowers and pines, ripe marshlands, spongy mosses, and sandy beaches.

It can include thoroughly relishing our allotted times in the out-of-doors, sometimes armed with nothing more serious than a peanut butter and jelly sandwich.

Notes

30 "Take a hike," they told me.

So I did, and took the whole family along. We've been hiking ever since. Walking is putting one foot before the other on the way to the mailbox or corner grocery for milk and lottery tickets. But hiking, though achieved in like manner, involves adventure, excitement, intrigue, and a whole lot more. You can take over-the-mountain hikes, and hikes over vast stretches of tundra, and hikes into jungles fraught with lump-in-the-throat monsters of the imagination. But they all require special boots and overnight stays.

No. We're talking of hikes hiked on Sunday afternoons with the kids and Grandma—leisurely stuff in tenners and sweat pants or packs and parkas—that get us back for supper. We don't cover much ground, but travel on trails in parks, along waters' edges, or on country roads. We all, even the little ones, take turns at being leader, and we pick out themes for the day, like birds or leaves or insects or rocks or tracks. Grandma really knows her stuff, but the kids are catching up, and to everyone's surprise, so am I.

Say, why don't you come along next time? We'd like your company.

Notes

Bald-faced hornets are busy at their nearly football-sized nests high up under the eaves of garages, which seems more honest of them than those yellow jackets, who live in underground paper houses and wait and wait and wait in ambush. Deserted woodchuck dens shelter rabbits, skunks, foxes, and coons who need a place to hole up for a while. And in the garden, without noticeable signs of struggle, a morning glory quietly strangles a petunia.

July

Pairs of barn swallows, who fed up to a thousand leaf hoppers a day to their young, must be pleased that the little tykes can do it on their own now. The special magic of warm July nights, lit by fireflies, gives way to nights of August with special magic all their own. And yet, we approach August with some apprehension; once we turn the corner from this month into this next one, there is no turning back.

31 The two of you in a canoe soar with eagles; you are one with wild wolves howling against a moon and with trout shuffling into a current.

But the two of you in a canoe joined by a child or two in the middle of the canoe are up a creek.

Oh, children love the canoe; they adore canoeing—for the first four minutes and thirty-six seconds into the watery, downhill slide—after which they begin to suffer severe behavioral disorders, and you become candidates for loonie bins.

But not necessarily. Not if the two of you have outthunk that kid or two. Not if you supply them with kiddie paddles (never the big ones). Not if you furnish them with bathtub boats and fishies to troll on fishing lines. Not if you have gathered a handful of pebbles for them to kerplunk into the passing waters. Not if you provide them with the 25-cent activity books you have used to keep yourselves together on automobile trips, or have taught them knitting, or given them scorecards to tally moose and loons and turtles. Then you and the kid or two in your canoe will float blissfully through infinite fields of peace and quiet.

Notes

August

August

August is like middle age. We look wistfully back at what we had hoped to accomplish by this time, shake our heads at what little we have done, of fish not caught, of camps not made, of rivers not paddled, of gardens not hoed, and resolutely forge on toward autumn through August, the month of the Sturgeon Moon, the Blueberry Moon, and the Moon of Green Corn.

1 Omigosh! Here's August already. And you know what that means. It's time to pick tomatoes. Time to make sauerkraut and dill pickles. Time to walk through the woods, eliminating a few mosquitoes along the way and cussing out those damnable deerflies, for which there is no cure but time. It's time to visit duck blinds, sit an evening upon deer stands, clean deer camps, shoot some clay pigeons, and fire up deer rifles—for practice.

There's time yet for careful fishing with old friends, sundown porch sitting with old folks, one-on-one camping trips with kids, and moonlight strolls with whoever will have us.

It's time to can peaches. Time for suppers of fried catfish (trout will do), corn on the cob, and baking powder biscuits with blueberries in them.

It's still time to rev up canoe paddles, catch summer bass, and sharpen the hooks on muskie plugs and blades on lawnmowers and get new line for weed cutters. There's time for one last summer fling, and then it's time again to gas up school buses.

Notes

2 Not enough ways exist to count the joys of hunting, and not nearly enough to count those of hunting over a good dog. But the road from pup to dog to hunting dog to great hunting dog can be a long, potholed one, for experts probably hold as many theories about raising and training puppies as they do about raising and training kids. Kids, though, just show up at the dinner table one day with the announcement that we are all theirs. But the pup? We get to pick out the pup.

This picking-out business offers a great challenge, a very real responsibility. Before choosing a pup, we should determine, without qualification, just what exactly we'll expect from the dog this pup will become. We should know precisely what its duties and chores will be, and only then choose a pup from a breed with those potentials.

While we'd like a dog that "does it all," such an animal probably doesn't exist. We'll have to specialize. Though sometimes mutts make, and have made, the best of hunting dogs, it can only be considered a wise thing to check a pup's credentials, its pedigree, its heritage. And be grateful it cannot do the same with us.

Now, as a sign of things to come, bobolinks molt from the brightness of their summer jackets into the heavier dullness of winter coats. Crickets play raspy violins. Soon they'll turn over the microphone to fiddle-playing katydids. Brilliant sunflowers track the course of August's harvest-making sun.

Notes

August

In wooded areas—or open areas for that matter—near sphagnum ponds, swamps, and bogs, salamanders live under stones and logs and conveniently drop their tails behind them if someone or something takes hold of one with a salamander sandwich in mind. Queen Anne's lace, called wild carrot, grows thickly at roadsides. Bracket fungi, looking like big oyster shells, suck the juice and the life from the trees they call home.

3 Generally speaking, diving ducks fly with faster wing beats than do puddle ducks; given their druthers, beavers prefer a diet of aspen, or popple, trees; when fish jump and tail-dance on the water to shake plugs, we try not to give slack if we can help it, but keep our lines tight; chucker partridge were introduced to this country from Western Europe and Asia; old-timers sometimes call lake trout Mackinaws.

Badgers prefer small mammals at mealtimes; pines, larches, spruce, hemlocks, and balsam fir belong to the pine family, but cedar, yew, and junipers do not; cones of firs grow upright on branches, but those of spruces hang down.

Redhorse, carpsuckers, and buffalo are members of the sucker family, while brown trout, brook trout, and lake trout belong to the salmon family; muddler minnows are favorite artificial lures for browns, and June bugs (tipped with worms) are spinners that catch walleyes.

Woodchucks' best protection from hunters lies in their keen eyesight; and are the fish ever going to start biting?

Notes

4 Muskies, those awesome, toothsome creatures that are more hunted for than fished for, bring me out here with my pretty-good muskie fisherman, er, hunter, Uncle Jake.

Jake takes me out a lot—to run the boat, pour the coffee, and net his fish—if you know what I mean. And since so many of his old fishing buddies have passed on, to fish the big ones in the sky (it is true that good anglers, when they leave this life, go up and not down), I'm about all he's got.

See, I have a college education, so Old Jake figures I'm not too bright. And I don't argue the fact, since I've wondered about that myself from time to time.

Anyway, I sort of mentally tune Jake out, now and then, the way you do a baseball game on the radio when neither team is yours. But I learn a lot from him and file it away for later to share with you, so we'll do okay, too.

Like today. He's cross because I can't find water at seventy-five degrees, which he says is where muskies always feed the heaviest. That's pretty important, so keep it in mind in case I forget.

The last wild rose blossoms of summer are gone, around here, at least, and in their steads have come good jelly-making hips. Listen for the katydids. Some believe that the first frost will come six weeks to the day after the first of those little critters sounds off. When in September would that be? August winds, in search of windmills, must settle for oak leaves and frolicking, shadow-chasing clouds as playthings.

Notes

August

Gentle little smooth green snakes—bright green above and off-white below—breed now. Red-eyed vireos set plans to leave their thick thickets of summer homes for far-away winter ones in South America. Shore birds from the Arctic tundra migrate through. White snakeroot blooms in its flat-topped cluster way.

5 Most of us guys who call ourselves outdoorsmen could not, probably, in our personal habits and inclinations, be considered to be on the cutting edge of cool. For instance, for whatever our reasons, most of us would rather not carry a purse on our person. Indeed. Most of us would not be caught dead carrying a purse. If we were at the grocery with our wife, and at the checkout she said, "Honey, I forgot my purse. Go to the pickup and fetch it," we would decline the opportunity. We carry instead, or keep close to us at all times, a manly ditty bag. And in this ditty bag we carry such essential equipment as needles and thread, tape, rope, string, rubber bands, lip balm, Band-Aids, safety pins, bug dope, sunglasses, spare change, matches, candle, flashlight, compass, jackknife that is also an opener, corkscrew, and screwdriver, and one of those flimsy raincoats that fold to nearly nothing. A little of this, a little of that, the stuff that gets lost or forgot and that makes us Boy Scout prepared. It's a ditty bag, and anyone who says different is looking for a fight.

Notes

6 They weigh, on the average a pound, or maybe two, and grow, again on the average, to a foot long. But smallmouth bass are not average fish, by any means. Pound for pound, inch for inch, they're probably the scrappiest of all freshwater game fishes. And the most sought after.

Smaller than their largemouth cousins, they have jaws whose corners do not extend past their eyes—eyes that are red.

They're most active in water sixty to seventy degrees Fahrenheit. Early mornings and late evenings often provide the best times for fishing smallmouth bass. Then, feeding, they move toward edges of riffles in search of insects, helgramites, crayfish, frogs.

During the daytime they move back into deeper holes or seek sheltering rocks, logs, or brush.

Anglers looking to clear their arteries by getting their hearts pumping really good use fly rods or very light spinning outfits on these little fighters.

They keep rod tips up and lines tight, or they'll kiss that smallmouth, and all hopes for supper, good-bye.

Thornless high-climbing wild grapes begin to ripen in thickets and at the edges of woods. Good, good stuff, these grapes. Milkweed pods are big and ripe and green. Where it's cool and wet, jewelweeds snap, crackle, and pop, and touch-me-nots blossom. So do pearly everlastings, where it's dry. And joe-pye weeds. Goldenrods answer the call to donate color to the beginning brownness sprouting here and there.

Notes

August

Because they're among the most obvious of weeds blooming now, at the height of hay fever season, goldenrods take a lot of the heat for causing this seasonal malady. But goldenrod pollen is basically too heavy to blow in the wind. Blame the ragweeds. Black bears dissect old logs and stumps looking for grubs and ants in the rotting wood. Finding some, they gobble them up and then settle on roots, berries, mushrooms, and insects.

7 An angler, a hunter, a hiker, in your self-imposed isolation you're startled at a nearby growling—in this case, your stomach. As hunger, like a drooling beast, rumbles about your belly, do you forsake stream or blind or tree for the golden arches, do you retreat? Do you reach into your pocket for a sugary, chocolatey lump of candy? You do not. Rather, you dip into your ditty bag and retrieve a wax-papered bit of goodness about the size of a polish sausage, a bit of something so rich it's a complete meal, a bit of something strong enough to carry you for hours, a bit of something you made yourself.

In a bowl big enough to mean business, you mixed a cup each of dried peaches, apples, and prunes, and raisins, shredded coconut, and chopped nuts. You dumped it all in a blender, gave it a couple of shots, poured it all on a cookie sheet, and mixed in one-half cup each of margarine, honey, and peanut butter, formed it into sausage configurations, rolled it in powdered sugar, and wrapped and froze it.

And now the only growls you hear in the bush are big hairy things made up mostly of claws and teeth and ugly dispositions.

Notes

8 Jackrabbits aren't rabbits at all, but hares—their young are born fully furred and open-eyed. Jacks come in two basic types, white-tailed and black-tailed. They get to twenty-six inches long and ten pounds.

Most jacks live out their lives within a four-square-mile area, their basic coloration matching their background well enough to provide some camouflage—even turning white (or whitish) against snow.

Jackrabbits don't drink much water, but they eat plenty, often competing with cattle and sheep for range. They waste about as much as they eat. They're breeding machines, with gestation periods of six weeks, producing an average three to four little hoppers at a time.

Living their lives in open country, they do most of their moving about at night, allowing them temporary safety from the bobcats, badgers, foxes, bears, mountain lions, dogs, cats, hawks, eagles, owls, snakes, and people who try to do them in. None will die of old age. Boy, can they run—usually cruising, holding ears up and taking big look-see hops every fourth or fifth bound at around twenty-five miles an hour; but they lay out at top speed, with ears flat, up to forty.

Goldfinches eat the first ripe bull thistle seeds. Dragonflies and damselflies still skim over ponds for mosquitoes. Prickly ash fruit turns red. Wild plums are ripe for the picking. Which we do. In old fields and borders of woodlands, sumacs boast thick clusters of dark red, hairy seeds. On these dew-heavy mornings, the early sunlight catches and sets aglow silken strands of spider homes. The round, unbelievably delicate webs are those of orb spiders.

Notes

_____

_____

_____

_____

_____

_____

August

Wild raspberries keep coming and coming and coming. We can certainly live with that. Busy goldfinches still feed a hungry brood many thousands of weed seeds a day for a couple of weeks. Whew! And in this heat. Bonesets bloom on edges of lakes and ponds. Many baby snakes are born. Young osprey tentatively test new wings. In the quiet, well-oiled perfection of August, muskie anglers gear up for action.

9 Unlike other diving ducks, buffleheads can get from water to air without a running head start. Males wear black and white glossy feathers and have pie-shaped heads that seem too big for their bodies. Their heads, black-purplish, have triangular white patches from below the eyes around to the back—without the black edging that characterizes hooded mergansers. They carry white patches on each wing—easily seen in flight. Females are gray-brown, with smaller wing patches and small white patches behind each eye.

These small, chunky, stubby, puffy-looking ducks have short necks and blue-gray bills. On the water, they are our whitest-looking ducks and they float feather-light high. They're called butterballs, dippers, didappers, doppers, marionettes, Scotchmen, shotbags, spirit ducks, and woolheads.

They eat fish, aquatic insects, plants, and crustaceans, and nest in tree holes along lakes, rivers, bays, and oceans, remaining as far north as open water permits. They feed in small flocks of five or six birds and, except for peeps or weak quacks, are silent.

Notes

10 Snapping turtles have been around for some two hundred million years. They were here before dinosaurs and lived through whatever it was that did those big things in. Snappers can be aggressively tough customers when caught or cornered—well equipped to defend themselves.

They have surprisingly long necks, and they strike with the speed of rattlesnakes. Snappers don't have teeth, but rather sharp beaklike bony jaws, so that "Once one gets a hold on you," some old-timers contend, "it won't let go until it thunders or you hold a match under its tail." Which must seem like a painfully long time.

Snapping turtles start out as small eggs and end up as "the orneriest, ugliest, most dangerous critters in the marsh." (That said probably by some guy hunting hurriedly for a book of matches.) They average from ten to twenty pounds and measure around two feet from stem to stern.

Duck hunters don't like their habit of slipping up under baby ducks while doing lunch; but snappers deserve to continue their long record of survival and to occupy their niche in nature.

Grasshoppers sing, if you don't mind using the term loosely, in the afternoon. Up until nearly sunset, actually. Fireweeds begin blooming their four roundish, purplish blossoms. Night crawlers get picked for catfish bait. Gray squirrels have second litters. Spring-born, half-grown young of the year—from rabbits to weasels, from squirrels to muskrats—carve out cubbyholes of living space where they can. A tricky time for them.

Notes

August

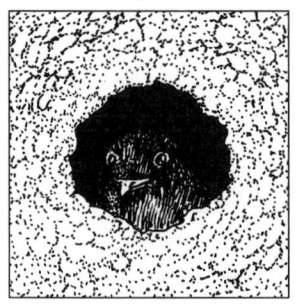

A second batch of barn swallows are fledged in mud nests attached to the rafters or under the eaves of barns or houses. If any of those little-flowered fleabanes still hang around the garden, go get them now. Each one will scatter a quarter of a million seeds, enough to keep you hoeing all next summer. Sugar maples, ash, and box elder trees let go their seeds, which flip and flutter to the ground to await the cover of leaves.

11 It's summertime. Do you know where your cat is? That lively, lovely little ball of fun and frolic? That purring chunk of milk-lapping catnipping, kitty-littering son-of-a-gun? Tabby? Muffin? Buttons?

Well, if it's outside, it's killing something.

It is so. Free-roaming household cats are probably the most deadly predators in the country, inflicting incredible damage on wildlife, having a devastating effect on ground-nesting birds and young out wing testing.

Cats kill more rabbits than hunters do. Like their lion and tiger cousins, cats are efficient killers; but unlike their relatives, cats kill not for food, but for the sheer joy of it. Cats don't fit into the scheme of things in the wild. They are human-introduced aliens, upsetting the delicate balance of things. Even the mice they catch were meant for foxes and owls.

Walk through a park. Drive down a country road. How many cats do you see? Out for a stroll? Not a chance. They're hunting. They have no choice. It's what they do. If each of the millions and millions of kitty-cats out there kills once each day or once every other day . . .

Notes

12 "Look!" one of the kids shouts, pointing to a small pile of sticks and mud as we whiz by a swampy-looking place, our minds on other things. "A muskrat house."

Sure enough. Such a plain, unpretty thing, built by industrious little rodents, this small island in the midst of so much muck serves them as home, pantry, day-care center, school, town hall, dance hall, pool hall, and nursery.

But muskrat lodges are more than that. These wondrous essential parts of nature's scheme of things provide homes and resting places for countless other critters as well. Redheads, ruddy ducks, mallards, Canada geese, and loons use them as resting and nesting sites and havens during molting times, when these birds are particularly vulnerable and cannot fly. Turtles, snakes, toads, and frogs make themselves quite welcome. So do herons, bitterns, blackbirds, and who knows how many insects. Mink and coon frequently visit. Meadow mice can spend entire lives here as freeloading guests, like nonfishing second cousins who come for a short visit, and never go home.

Purple martins, our largest swallows, gather in big flocks in groves prior to migration. Their combined voices are said to sound like escaping steam. I guess it does. We can't really blame them for their early departure—they have to get out before the bug supply gives out. Gray jays steal food from careless campers. Vireos, wood thrushes, and bobolinks quietly take their leave.

Notes

August

Chipmunks gobble up pin cherries, pantry-storing some underground for winter desserts. Weasels begin mating. Ring-billed gulls are about to migrate. Maples begin to show surprising, shocking streaks of red, and occasional birches and ashes, splashes of yellow. Some purple martins head for Brazil. Black-eyed Susans look droopy. Berry pickers get nettle-stung. Moonlight shines on dying fires and sleepy campers.

13 I'm not cheap, but I can be had. In this case it's my aunt buying me off—with one half of one of her apple pies now, and the other half when the job's done.

Here's the deal. Seems like my fishing Uncle Jake has just gone to one more final send-off for one more old fishing buddy and just doesn't have the heart to go out anymore.

"He's not himself," she says. "He's got to go fishing, and you've got to take him."

It's been a while since I've caught a walleye and it's good apple pie, so we shake on it and I eat my advance.

We have a still, clear August day, just awful for walleye fishing, but about sundown, I get a grumbling uncle on the lake, and like I figure, the master fisherman in him takes over. He casts long into deep water and waits for a crawler hooked to a #8 by the nose, weighed with a small split shot, to settle to the bottom. He reels it in very, very slowly, and sure enough, at the eighth or ninth cast he hooks a nice one, and I net it the first time.

Well, Jake gently takes the hook out, lays the fish on the water, and to no one I can see, says, "This one's for you," and he lets it go.

Notes

14 You can always tell an experienced camper by how much gear he or she takes, or doesn't take, on a campout. Now I've been camping a time or two myself, and I have this packing business about down to a science, so I'll pass along what I've learned to you.

You may take notes: Pot. Pan. Frying pan. Lids. Pot scrubbers. Hot-pad. Turner. Cup. Bowl. Plate. Fork. Knife. Spoon. Toilet paper. Stove. Fuel. Funnel. Matches. Foil. Grill. Plastic bags. Extra underwear. Pants. T-shirt. More toilet paper. Sweater. More matches. Extra socks. Hat. Rain gear. Bandanna. Towel and washcloth. Rain fly. Tent. Ground cloth. Sleeping bag. Toothbrush. Wool shirt. Soap. First aid kit. Aspirin. Shovel. Ax. Rope. More rope. More toilet paper and matches. Tape. Candle. Rod. Reel. License. Map. Flashlight. Compass. Tackle box.

Weiners. Marshmallows. Bread. Catsup. Canteen. And big bag of gorp.

Now, if you plan on staying overnight, you must more or less multiply accordingly. To save space, stuff extra underwear and socks in toilet paper rolls.

More asters bloom. Hummingbirds hover over feeders at two hundred wing beats a second. Squirrels sample green acorns. Hazelnuts are getting ripe. Giant puffballs appear to the delight of just about everyone—human and animal. Little raccoons follow mothers fairly far afield. More sandpipers and yellowlegs pass through.

Notes

August

Some burr oaks drop acorns. Restless red-orange and black redstarts begin to leave over woodlots, swamps and shrubs, suburbs, and parks for South America. Gardeners surreptitiously leave baskets of zucchini on doorsteps of unsuspecting nongardeners. Country folks climb from the daylight into the night armed with fishing pole and worm can to go catfishing.

15 Don't do without a bit of dessert on the trail or at camp, especially one the kids can make while you're getting the rest of the meal ready.

Have them drop into a large plastic bag two sticks of butter, a half cup of powdered sugar, two cups of flour, and a half teaspoon each of baking powder and salt.

The kid with the cleanest hands should get right in there and mix it all together until the dough is smooth. Others can gather berries to mix into this if they like.

On the bottom of the canoe or boat (or on waxed paper) they can all form large cookies from the dough. Then they place them on a cookie sheet leaning against rocks—sharply toward and close to the fire, with a sheet of foil umbrellaed over it to reflect the heat of the coals onto the pan.

These shortbread cookies should turn a very light straw color and must be watched so they don't overbake. This will probably work at home, too, if you can get a canoe into the kitchen.

Notes

16 All athletes worthy of the game must undergo lengthy periods of preseason training to force themselves into condition, to build muscles on top of muscles, to develop stamina, to get the old blood pumping like crazy without their ever having to breathe too deeply or too fast.

Dogs—true athletes of hunting teams—must therefore get into shape now, must make the change from sedentary kennel keepers to rugged jocks, before the starting whistle of opening day blows—so they do not poop out, get stiff and sore, thus becoming inefficient, wearied members of the hunting team. Goodness knows, one of us is enough.

Running, as it is with all athletes, is a good way for dogs to get into shape. So is swimming. Lots of it.

Now, we live in a busy world, so what we do, see, is to let the kids, bored by now with summer anyway, work the heck out of the dogs. And vice versa. They'll give each other plenty of exercise and, with any kind of luck at all, wear each other out.

We talked, back in June, of mighty Jupiter being an evening star. It's back; it never really left, only now it's a just-before-dawn shiner. Many birds molt, exchanging bright summer colors for those more subdued for winter. Big bluegills bite and muskies hit on crankbaits, though you couldn't prove it by me. Fluffy, white-flowered Queen Anne's lace graces roadside ditches.

Notes

August

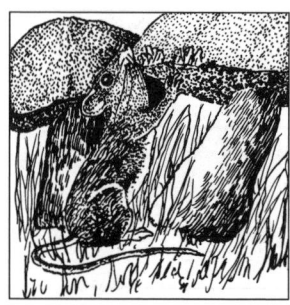

Many mushrooms grow now in damp places, being eaten by mice, deer, bears, chipmunks, and red squirrels, who sometimes dry them on tree branches. And now is the time of the Perseids, those meteors, falling stars that migrate from the constellation Perseus in the northeast. Though that could be stardust. Evening bird songs are, to some extent at least, being replaced by insect songs—mating songs as old as life.

17 You get the idea just how tough this stuff can be when you get a package in the mail trussed up in it. Without a doubt it held the package together. Without a doubt, despite your best efforts, it intends to keep doing so.

It's called strapping tape, and it makes a handy in-the-field substitute for rope, wire, cable, string, glue—an emergency repair kit that'll handle anything but a dose of poison ivy.

It won't stretch, so when something's tied down with it, it stays down. Use it to mend a split canoe paddle, a cracked gun stock, a fishing net, a mooring line, an anchor chain, or snowshoe webbing.

Use it as a belt, as a packstrap, as legging straps, as a gun or gamebird sling, or as a boot lace, or use it to reinforce canvas and leather, to hang food caches from trees, to close off boot tops to keep snow out, to secure rod guides, or to drag a deer out.

Care, I suppose, should be taken in the handling of the stuff, lest we get so tangled in it we'll never get out, and all they'll find will be our bones—neatly packaged.

Notes

18 Black bears aren't always black, but chocolate- or cinnamon- or even vanilla-colored. Black bears weigh anywhere from a naked eight ounces at birth to five hundred pounds plus at the peak of their prosperity. They'll eat darn near anything—berries, grass, gophers, squirrels, mice, grubs, bees, pigs, ants, fawns, carrion, and garbage.

Mostly, they don't eat people, but they should, none the less, be given the respect due to any five-hundred-pound fast, well-armed, heavily muscled, unpredictable, predatory beast with a nasty temper and an appetite that won't quit.

Bears can't see too well, but make up for it with excellent hearing and an unbelievable sense of smell. They're good swimmers, can stroll along at around three miles an hour and move out at thirty or more, in great leaps and bounds, when in a hurry, and can climb a tree just a little slower than they can fall out of one.

We can't outrun or outclimb a bear, so when it's absolutely necessary it's probably best to try to scare it off, which is kind of chancy too, since we're more than likely doing in our pants what bears usually do in the woods.

Bunches of creamy white elderberry blossoms have become purple-black berries for wine-making purposes, the second blessing of this plant. The first is its easily hollowed out twigs for whistle making. Warblers— all kinds of them—edge southward. Swallows consider doing the same. Yellow jackets are late-summer karate-tough and pushy. There is no shortage of mosquitoes—the little zingers that waste no time in sabre-rattling tactics.

Notes

August

Robins gather in premigration get-togethers. Mayflies still hatch, of course. Algae scums over ponds. Shining semibrightly tonight is the dog star in Canis Major, companion to the great hunter Orion, blamed by the Romans for causing the hot, still weather and poisoning the water, causing animals, two-legged as well as four-, to run amuck—hence the "dog days." Crab apples ripen in the misty dawn.

19 None of us should die of skin cancer, yet each year, many of us do. As outdoor men and women, we expose ourselves to the sun for long periods of time, and among us the general tendency is to dismiss skin cancer as a minor possibility—no real threat. We are wrong about that. For our skin never forgets any exposure to the sun. Each day in its light, each hour, each minute adds to the cumulative total; and though it's different for each of us, when a certain critical level is reached, bingo. That's it.

Especially dangerous to us are ultraviolet rays that bounce from the water, sand, or snow. Clouds offer little protection, nor do tanning lotions help.

Since staying out of the sun is unthinkable, our only alternative is to wise up, to protect ourselves as best we can. We wear hats (not baseball or seed-corn caps). We use a sun block with a ton of block to it. We dress with more good sense than good taste. If you, like me, don't want your wife's next husband (or husband's next wife) to inherit your fishing boat and fishing tackle, then you, like me, had better start taking better care of yourself.

Notes

20 The sun is rising up in the black timber country, up in the breathtaking heights of the lofty reaches of the Rocky Mountains and down in the valleys below them.

The sun is rising on a summer dissolving into the burnt gold, the glowing gold of a grandmother's worn wedding ring. And with the silence of a baby's yawn, elk begin drifting into lonely meadows.

And then the rising of the sun is interrupted by a chill wind blowing, by a shrill whistle blowing, and no longer lonely, the meadows become busy, sometimes bloody battlefields, for the bulls of the elk are in full rut and proud of it.

And as the sun rises in the camps and ranches in the valleys far below, hunters pack guns and grub and camping gear, and they saddle horses to ride up and up into the sky-scraping high country where the buglings of bull elk make big holes in the quiet.

Slowly ride the hunters, searching for dreams to slide into the not quite believable compartments of their memories. In the here and now, there is probably no place on earth quite as good as this.

A cricket's a cricket, but it's the snowy crickets making all that noise. Bobolinks are ready to leave fields and meadows, farmlands, and marshes for South America. Red-winged blackbirds come out of molt-hiding retirement just in time to head south. Cottontails have new families, as usually usual. Early mornings come a little later, and we pinch ourselves to remind us that it's still good old summertime.

Notes

August

Young red squirrels now leave their mothers' sides to strike out on their own. They feed on acorns, chestnuts, and seeds of spruce cones, burying into storage what they can't eat—scolding as they go about their business. And ours. Plovers keep moving through. Sulfur butterflies flit all over the place. Raccoons eye what's left of sweet corn crops; pheasants, so pleasantly brilliant, clean up on small grains spilt by combines.

21 In the heavy half-light, the sound of a snapping twig breaks the silence. Two heads, that of the hunter and that of the hunted, jerk to attention, and in a micro-moment atremble with excitement and anticipation, an arrow leaps, splitting the dewy stillness in search of blood.

It is a moment of truth. That razor-tipped arrow is as deadly as any bullet, can kill as cleanly as any bullet, and, carelessly placed, can maim and cripple as surely as any bullet.

Bowhunting is an ancient, honorable sport, and the vast majority of bowhunters are noble men and women. But too often we bowhunters forget that in that crucial moment before we loose an arrow, we must not merely hope for the best.

We must be as certain as we are humanly possible of being that the arrow's flight will carry it exactly to the point where it belongs, exactly to a vital area where it will kill quickly and cleanly an equally noble animal.

Or we must hold the arrow for another day. Another time. Another deer. Another chance.

Notes

22 Borrow a magnifying glass from one of the kids or from Grandmother and take a good look at the business end of a favorite lure—even a new one. Unless you're the one angler in a zillion who consistently checks for and sharpens dull hooks, you will be surprised at what you see.

Hook-sharpening devices are available on the market, with instructions on how to use them, though you've probably got something in the kitchen that'll do the job. With a file, it's important to remember to push the hook forward only, and not back and forth. Many who do this job right leave the curved inside of the barb looking somewhat like one angle of a triangle, facing back to the shank. They don't do much at all to the outside of the point.

Don't worry. Experience will tell. Any fairly sharp point is better than a dull one and will increase your catch.

We put such time, energy, and money into the fine art of fishing, we ought to take a few minutes to fine-tune our hooks to do what they are designed to do. I, for one, intend to mend my ways and get right to the job—as soon as Grandma finds her magnifying glass.

With few little birds and fewer eggs around, skunks eat grasshoppers and beetles and larvae of bees and whatever else they can find. The young ones, born this spring, must disperse now to make it on their own. They've never been taught not to cross highways at night. Daisies fade and katydids scratch itches in the night. Where not much else wants to grow, grow mulleins, tall as a tall man, tall as a small tree, in plain, simple isolation.

Notes

_____

_____

_____

_____

_____

August

Walnuts drop from trees. The store-bought English ones are easier to open. These are impossible. Goldfinches continue to feed on thistle seeds—providing the only decent reason for the existence of thistles. Putting hummingbirds to shame in the I'm-faster-than-you department, mosquitoes—and plenty of them are still around—beat their wings six hundred times a second. Is that possible?

23 For the sheer excitement of it, for the heart-pumping, blood-rushing, palm-sweating fun of it, top water fishing for bass is just about the most fun a person can have that is legal, moral, and nonfattening.

Top water anglers don't need any special gear, and a wide variety of lures are available to them. They can try floating minnows, which make little noise but make up for it with tantalizing little twitches with help from the angler. Or they can try propeller baits, noisy and full of action, casting them, letting them rest a bit, then giving them a twitch or two, retrieving in jerks and starts, alternating the retrieve.

Or for night fishing they can try poppers and gurglers, which bring bass in from far away to investigate the commotion. Or they can try buzzing baits—metal things with revolving blades on a wire shaft in front of the lead body of the lure. These anglers must retrieve fairly rapidly, or the baits will sink, which violates the spirit of things.

There are more, and the daring fishing folks might try them all, if they've got all summer and think their hearts can stand the excitement.

Notes

24 When for some mysterious reason the pickup is not where we left it, when streams mysteriously change courses from one day to the next, when mountain ranges get moved from their traditional locations, and nobody tells us, we are not lost, we are but temporarily direction-confused.

Since we do not get lost, it is not necessary for us to carry a compass. And we do not, for time is on our side. Or more specifically, a timepiece. A watch.

Try this. Hold your watch flat and rotate it until the hour hand points to the sun. A line half the distance between the hour hand and the number twelve is true south. Do an about face, and you're looking straight north.

And suddenly the world is right again. Pickups return to where they were. Streams flow between their own banks. And mountain ranges return to old moorings.

We must remember, however, if we're to travel cross-country without a compass, to travel only on clear days, from 7:00 A.M. to 7:00 P.M. central daylight time, and never but never to wear a digital watch.

The first monarch butterflies begin to head down to somewhere in and around Mexico. Bobolinks head south any day now. So do ovenbirds, with their ringing, "teacher, teacher, teacher, teacher" calls. Some sumacs, rushing the season, break out in rashes of bright red.

Notes

August

25 Around 1878, a gent named Mr. Orvis asked a New York fly tier, Mr. Haily, to tie him up some coachmen. Now Mr. Orvis didn't want just any old coachmen; he wanted some extra strong ones.

So, the agreeable Mr. Haily tied a most handsome fly, coachman-like, but with a little band of silk in the middle to prevent the peacock bodies from fraying out. And he added a tail of the barred feathers of the wood duck. Nobody knew what to call it. "Well," said Mr. Orvis to a gathering of fishermen, "that is easy enough; call it the Royal Coachman, it is so finely dressed." And they did.

No one has the slightest idea what insect the Royal Coachman is supposed to represent—though many have attempted to match it up with something flying, crawling, or swimming. It doesn't matter. Other fly patterns have come and gone as quickly as rock and roll groups, but the Royal Coachman has been around for all these years since, and will be, as long as there are trout in streams and men and women to fish them.

Notes

26 The life cycle of a tree is never-ending, for even as its leaves fall for the last time from bone-brittle branches, the old monarch that once provided home and haven for so many birds and animals begins life anew as a wildlife hotel for over eighty species of birds and nearly fifty mammals, which use cavities in standing dead timber for nesting sites.

Pileated woodpeckers hammer holes for nests in these old giants; foxes and gray squirrels give birth to and raise their litters in such holes and gather inside them for protection in severe weather.

Great horned owls use larger cavities to hatch and home their downy offspring. Chickadees, titmice, wrens, screech owls, mergansers, and downy, hairy, red-headed and red-bellied woodpeckers, flickers, kestrels, and saw-whet owls seek out, indeed must have, such trees as homes.

Bears, raccoons, woodchucks, and opossums use them.

Eagles rest on their gnarled branches. Ruffed grouse nest against the protection of their roots.

Often cut down as eyesores, as waste, these old dead trees can stand for decades as places of excitement, teeming with life.

Those born these days are born under the sign of Virgo, the Virgin, usually pictured seated, holding an ear of corn or a branch. The great blue star Spica, giving off the light of 2440 suns, but so far away that its light takes three hundred years to reach us, is at Virgo's left hand. Sunsets are noticeably cooler, casting shadows yet and yet earlier. Mourning doves call in sounds we never tire of.

Notes

August

Large flocks of sandpipers continue their migrations from the tundra to winter on the coasts. Young flying squirrels, like migrating college students, leave homes to seek their own apartments—in woodpecker holes in old trees. Ground squirrels fatten up for a hibernation that'll last seven or eight months. We've lost over an hour and a half of sunlight since that longest day back in June, which seems like only yesterday.

27 Call it "Hawg."

It's on most everyone's most-wanted list. Look for it when the water reaches the low seventies. Then it goes on the prowl, moving silently through the dark underworld, cruising from one bit of cover to another, seeking yet another victim.

It's suppertime for the largemouth bass, so-called because, unlike its smaller-mouthed cousin, its mouth extends past its eyes.

Without apparent table manners, the largemouth gulps its food, piglike, and if that food should be at the end of your line, set the hook hard. That big mouth is mostly bone.

The largemouth, when it's biting, will often hit on anything—live or artificial—worms, minnows, poppers, streamers, plugs. But when it's not biting—well, it just won't.

It must have cover—weeds, lots of weeds, or brush piles, piers. And warm water—where it waits and grows, up to ten or eleven pounds—whatever it takes to bust your tackle.

Notes

28 Reference books have so much to do and so little space in which to do it. When they describe an animal, they must reduce it to bare-bones cold facts: raccoons—family Procyonidae. Length, to 33"; tail to 10". Young: usually four, born in hollow tree; Habitat: etc; Habits: etc; Voice: etc.

No personality there. No character. Such references can't take the time, for instance, to tell that the coon is doing just fine in the space age, that it's a fearsome creature when cornered; that it has a higher IQ than a pretty-smart house cat; that it is, along with skunks and cats, probably the greatest threat to ground-nesting birds and their eggs; that a full-grown twenty-five-pounder can drop fifty feet from a treetop and hit the ground at a full gallop; that the trash can doing a tumble at 3:00 A.M. may be a coon and not the neighborhood dog; and that I've given up growing sweet corn because coons ruin it all the night before I plan to pick it even if I plan to pick it the day before I planned to.

And all of that is pretty bare-bones too, but with so much to write and so little space in which to do it, what can I do?

Lines of swallows gather on telephone wires to continue discussing migration routes and to prepare for the long journey, which they'll make during daytimes, to as far away as Brazil. Most of the chokecherries are gone or soon will be, but high-flying highbush cranberries are ripening. So are crab apples. Arctic terns will soon become Antarctic terns. Blackberries are ripe. Joe-pye weed is in full magenta-red blossom.

Notes

August

Tall and graceful on broom-like branches, slender wild rice seeds, encased in papery, bristle-tipped husks, are ready for the blessing of a harvest. Most all the warblers, depending upon insects for a living and finding fewer and fewer, have taken off. Pumpkins have turned yellow-orangish. If you listen to the news, you'll swear the world has gone to pot; if you go outside, this early-autumn day, you'll see that it's gone to seed.

29 For many, the last days of August slam shut the doors of summer as surely as football pads come out of mothballs and the janitor dusts off the desks and props open the schoolhouse door.

But before we rush into the good things of fall, we take the time to clean and loosely roll or fold tents, sleeping bags, and backpacks, and store them in dry, ventilated places.

We clean stoves and lanterns, repair them, and empty them of fuel. (Though I keep mine handy in case we get a blizzard that knocks out the electricity for days, and I can heroically save my family with "all that expensive camping junk." Of course it never happens.)

We wash coolers and wipe them with vinegar-soaked cloth. We stash ropes and tie-downs, and we wash all cooking and eating utensils in the kitchen sink for a change.

Yep, we must put it all away for another season. Except, of course, for the memories.

Notes

30 What happens when a kid shows up for a baseball game without ever having shown up for practice?

The kid gets the boot, that's what. It should be that simple for the bow shooter.

How much practice is enough practice for us? For each of us it's different.

Some of us need more; some need less. But whether our goal is to hit bull's-eyes in cardboard or the lungs of a dream of a twelve-pointer, each of us who nocks an arrow must through trial and error and common sense, arrive at the amount of practice time that gives us the mental and physical characteristics to perform our best—whether on the firing line or perched ten feet up in the branches of an old oak tree.

There are those, too busy or too lazy, who never have practiced and never will practice as much as they should, but are satisfied with the mere flinging of arrows—which might be okay, I guess, if they're flinging at cardboard, but is unforgivable at live targets.

Once fat and green, thumbs of milkweed pods turn a warm reddish brown and open into piles of fluffy stuff to be carried by winds, eaten by birds, and shaken loose by little kids. Adolescent muskrats, who must now leave the family home, are sent packing and go poking about for wet places of their own. At night the moon hangs in the west and the pole star shines in the north; beneath it and a bit west is the Big Dipper.

Notes

August

Velvet still camouflages antlers. The few blackberries left are still guarded by a few heartless deerflies. Mink leave tracks in soft mud. And young-of-the-year ruffed grouse look almost like mother. August slowly cools and slips into September, and across the land are heard the cries of summer-spoiled children preparing for the annual flights back to school.

31 Even before the bright skies and southerly breezes of late summer give way to leaden skies and nippy winds out of the northwest, a restlessness takes hold of them. Then on the wings of cold fronts they begin— just a few at first, perhaps last night as we slept, then a few more today and tomorrow.

Some go by day, some by night, until the entire summering bird population joins the exodus. Into major flight lanes and minor ones they stream south over river valleys, seacoasts, prairie potholes, cornfields and mountain ranges, traveling in short hops or for thousands of miles at a crack.

Beginning first with shorebirds, swallows and nighthawks in August, birds on the wing build up in number through September, reach a peak in October, and diminish to a few stragglers in late November.

What makes them want to go? What guides them so surely across states and countries and continents and oceans? And what brings them back?

They will come back, won't they?

Notes

September

September

September begins like the dawn of a busy day, with living things not quite ready to rise from the soft bed of a lazy summer and not quite ready to face the busy business on tap, as each in its own way must prepare for what lies ahead. It is good to be alive in September. Mornings are cool, though the sun still has the power to warm our bones and make us feel very good in this beautiful month of the Harvest Moon, the Wild Rice Moon.

1 It's September already and again, and you know what that means. Summer's over. It's time to clean the furnace, order fuel, and stack firewood. It's time to reload shells and get our shooting eye in gear. It's time for bird hunting—pheasants, partridge, woodcock—with a good old dog who's waited a long time for this and good old friends who understand us and what it all means.

It's time for long walks through ankle-deep leaves with the kids and the older folks before the weather turns. It's canning time, with the chuga-chuga sounds of pressure cookers. It's time to dig potatoes. Time to check deer stands, clean up and out hunting shacks, and ready duck blinds.

It's time to remind the kids that school is great and friends are nice, but home is where the heart is, and prove it to them. It's time to read stories and help with homework. There's still time, in some of the best times, for a campout—a weekender—and a slow canoe trip to nowhere in particular. It's time to let those we love know it—by telling them, if we can, amidst a September sunset, and showing them if we can't.

Notes

2 Indian legends tell us that the creator made the woodcock from leftover parts of other birds. Others maintain the Virgin Mary took pity on a small outcast bird and transformed it into an elegant loner, with a bill long enough to reach deeply for worms, its favorite food, gave its plumage a golden hue, and taught it to fly erratically to escape its pursuers.

The Virgin, it is said, laid three fingers on the little bird's head, leaving three brown imprints called "Virgin's fingers," still visible today.

As the first north winds chill the nights, and forests deep begin to slide from green to brilliant reds and yellows, the woodcock, following rivers, stars, and instinct, drops gracefully out of the skies to eat and rest before moving on.

If we're lucky, we can hear its nasal "peent" as the sun sets and the harvest moon lights the night.

Some of us will hunt the woodcock. We might kill it and eat it. The riddle of it all is that we will love it all the more.

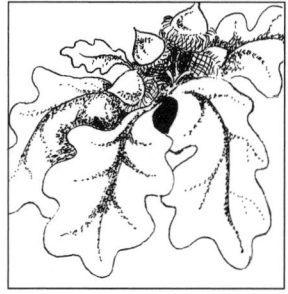

Warblers leave now for warmer winter homes. In September Mother Earth dresses in some of her finest clothes and beadwork and dances one last dance, which lasts well into October, sometimes, before winter stops the music, flips off the lights, and closes the doors on such frivolity.

Notes

September

Monarch butterflies begin to drift to a faraway south. Tree swallows gather to discuss the upcoming move from these places where they built their nests, laid their eggs, raised their young, and generally had a good time. Mercury turns over its watch of the evening sky to Saturn. Ruffed grouse families begin to break up, and whitetails begin to exchange summer coats for those that will shield them from the bite of what's ahead.

3 As a lad, I steeled myself and took the truth of Santa Claus with some degree of composure, and when an older cousin claimed to have hunted down the Easter bunny, I accepted the reality of it. By the time I discovered the identity of the tooth fairy, I was hardened to the point of indifference.

But I can't quite accept the notion that it's not Jack Frost, after all, who's responsible for the magnificent colorings of autumn's leaves.

The cold truth of it is that the pretty colors are there all the time—camouflaged by so much green. This green stuff—chlorophyll—captures the sun's energy to supply food for the tree, but as the year wears on and the sun shines less, the green just can't cut it anymore and fades away, leaving what's left—reds, oranges, and yellows.

The tree is then faced with a starvation diet, and protects itself against the evaporation of precious liquids by cutting its leaves off without so much as a thank-you. Kicking them out, banishing them to the forest floor.

It is true though, and it's a proven fact, that Jack Frost is in charge of painting windowpanes and windshields.

Notes

4 Take bass, for example. Now, in early autumn, bass inaugurate a protracted feeding rampage in preparation for the long, cold months ahead. And take my Uncle Jake, a fisherman who takes advantage of the situation.

Jake says sure bass feed heavy now, but where they do it in these slowly cooling, slowly changing lake waters of fall can and does shift and switch on a daily basis—making it tough on bassin' folks. Of course Jake's been around awhile, and he figures the fish have to be somewhere, so he doesn't take any chances and fishes the whole thing from top to bottom—whenever there's good cover.

Especially in early fall, Jake starts out with top water lures, which he long-casts into and beyond the good cover he intends to fish. He retrieves them as fast as he can. If that doesn't get him any action, the old guy goes down to middepth with a chunk of pork rind on a spinnerbait, changing colors every so often. If that still doesn't do the trick, he knows the big pot-guts are down deep. He goes there with wicked, bottom-bumping lures. It might take a while, but Jake's going to get him some bass. Big bass.

Though leaves of poison ivy turn from their waxy green prettiness to just-as-tempting red, yellow, and orange, they do not lose their sting. Giant puffballs of mushrooms seem to appear magically in the cool, damp woods. The six-ounce bear cubs, born back when snow was deep and ice was thick, weigh half a hundred pounds now and join their mothers, brothers, and sisters in zealous pursuits of calories.

Notes

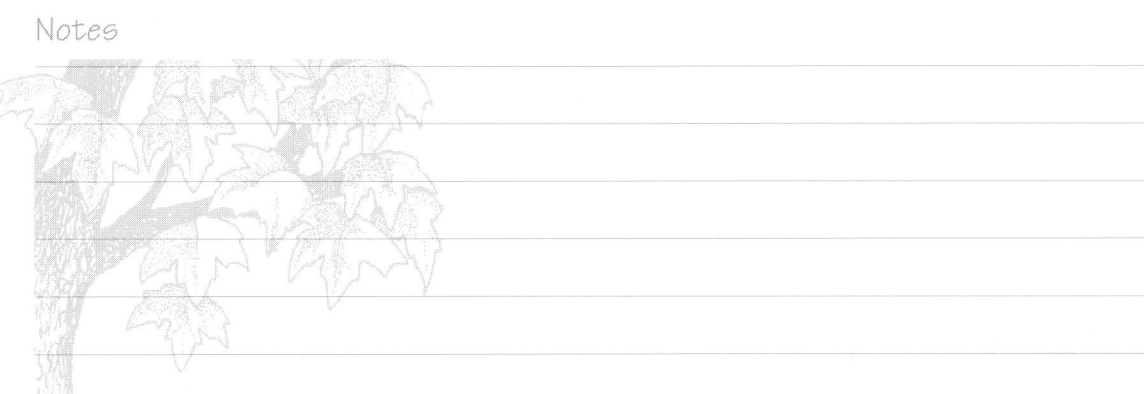

September

Cabbage butterflies are up and about. Spotted touch-me-nots bloom, to explode at a touch. As this perfect season progresses, more songbirds, their supplies of insect-food dwindling, leave. They move out mostly at night, spending their days resting and feeding. Bird hunters add smells of gun oil and old hunting vests to those of pickling cucumbers and pressure-cooked string beans in the kitchen.

5 When we weekend shooters miss a shot, we blame it on everything from the gun to the shell to the wind and to the basic state of world affairs.

Actually any number of blamable possibilities for our misses exist: one could be that we don't mount the gun correctly—that we don't, as a matter of habit, push it forward with our front hand and then bring it back to the very same spot on our shoulder each time as we should.

Here's how one shooter eliminates inconsistent shooting. He stands in front of a mirror with his eyes closed, and he quickly brings his unloaded shotgun up and aims it. He opens his eyes and hopes to be looking straight down the barrel, seeing the sight and a bit of the rib.

He wants his reflection to show his head straight forward on the stock. He practices this a couple dozen times a day, while wearing his hunting coat.

It's hardly an exciting pastime, but it can help us shoot-when-we-can folks shoot a little better, when a little better is all we need.

Notes

6 Let us say it is a Saturday morning; you, eager to shake the dust of a week's work from your body and soul, roll out of bed, wrap yourself in hunting clothes against the crisp morning, case a favorite shotgun, and head to where the grouse are, or might be.

This bread-and-butter game bird for many hunters will probably flush when least expected (more than one set of dentures has been dropped, and more than one heart has skipped half a dozen beats when an innocent-looking snowbank or brush pile exploded in a hunter's face), or sit tight when it should take flight, or make a getaway on foot.

You are a pretty good wing shot, but you know that even with luck you'll hit only one in six, seven, or eight shots. Some young birds, not-too-bright adolescents, will come easier to your game bag, but the sly old veterans will more often than not keep you heading out to the woods and fields whenever you can get out into a September day in the country.

Highbush cranberries, *mashkigimin*—child of the marsh—to the Ojibwa, turn bright red. Their leaves, too, will turn. In the low, eastern morning twilight, Venus shines brightly in the "sickle" of the constellation Leo. Hanging just below it, nice, but not so nice as Venus, is the star Regulus. Mountain ash trees are loaded with pea-sized red and orange berries that ward off, as the story goes, evil spirits.

Notes

September

Third-year needles on red pines turn to brown and will soon drop to carpet the forest floor. More hummingbirds begin to leave September's flowers and back-porch feeders of sugar water in retreat. More noticeably, the sun now slips out of sight earlier and earlier. On these first cool nights of September, smells of wood smoke come to the quiet places of our souls like reflections of loved ones no longer with us.

7 The gadwall's flecked brown back and head beg comparison with its close cousin, the mallard, but the fluid black and white markings of its breast and belly lend it a graceful continuity with the water, and set it apart.

Gadwalls make fair table fare, but cannot compare with other well-known species. Since they are usually found only sparsely mixed with larger flocks of other waterfowl, they seldom reach the dinner table anyway, and remain an enigma to both hunters and researchers.

Gadwalls are usually paired before they reach their breeding and nesting grounds, but not uncommonly an unattached drake shows up and tries to muscle in. Perhaps the frequency of such practice indicates a chronic shortage of female gadwalls.

Whatever the reason, the mated drake will not easily be ousted from its happy home, and a fierce competition of ritual courtship occurs. The loser, usually the interloper, is cast out into the cruel waterfowl world, where he must be content to live the life of a lonely, wandering Ishmael.

Notes

8 It is one thing to own a bow and consistently hit bull's-eyes of backyard targets, and it is quite another to be a bowhunter.

The challenge confronting hunters is that the odds are stacked against them, and the evening up of those odds a bit makes bowhunting the sport it is and bowhunters the kind of people they are.

Bowhunters must be woods-smart, capable of moving through rough terrain like shadows, able and prepared to kill from extremely short ranges.

They must stalk with the stealth of frontier scouts and acquire the patience of Job. They must be equipped with a smattering of Indian lore, mixed with a thorough knowledge of the country and game hunted. They must be able to take full advantage of snow, or lack of it, ground topography, wind, sign, and camouflage.

For bowhunters to be successful they get little room for error, and they wouldn't have it any other way.

Far to the north, young Canada geese stretch and preen new feathers and flex untried wings, responding to a silent, mysterious call to go. Dewy orb spider webs shine and twinkle in early morning sunlight. Great globs of red and orange explode on our sugar maple trees.

Notes

September

The funeral procession that is September begins. Shedding ragweeds pack noses of hay fever victims. Birches drop yellow-gold coins of leaves on shriveled creeks. Along with Mars and Venus, Jupiter lights the morning sky. Mercury is on its way. Milkweeds toss their seeds to the wind. Bumblebees still sail along at 240 strokes a second, feasting on late-blooming zinnias. Flickers, usually loners, get together in premigration gatherings.

9 I've never been turkey hunting, and by the looks of things, I'm not about to start. I've been outsmarted by trout, walleye, muskie, partridge, squirrel, rabbit, pheasant, and deer, and what I've read about this big-game bird suggests it's the smartest, quickest bird or beast ever invented, so I see no sense in setting myself up to be made a fool of one more time.

Besides, I've heard it's dangerously addictive, that good, solid, hardworking family men, after exposure to this gobble-gobble cat-and-mouse game of turkey hunting, go goofy over the sport, neglecting family and careers in a never-ending pursuit of ol' Tom.

And worse. One fellow of my acquaintance had the terrible misfortune of shooting one on his first time out; now he's so hooked that he's decided to give up trout fishing and deer hunting to devote his life to conning turkeys within shooting range.

It's my opinion that anything capable of so completely taking over a man's body and soul must be the work of the devil.

Notes

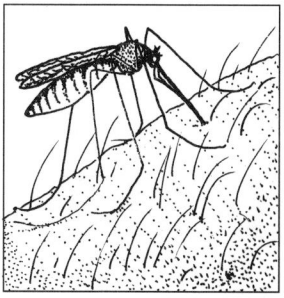

10 Though it filled some teenage hours very, very well and most enjoyably, many of us put squirrel hunting away with our last high school hop, last drag race, and final pimples.

We were, perhaps, too hasty. Squirrel season is among the first to open and offers great opportunities. What a chance to stretch legs too long cramped under desks or pushing at gas pedals or on shovels.

What a chance to rest the ears. Squirrel hunting is quiet business.

What a chance to carry a gun again, to put on the old hunting shirt, to get into the woods for an afternoon, to sharpen the old shooting eye.

What an excuse to scout for deer, for partridge, for a hidden little trout stream. What an opportunity to be reminded that squirrels in the wild are quite unlike the cutesy pets of parks.

What a chance to remember back to the junior prom and burning some rubber when we beat the heck out of old what's-his-name in the quarter-mile stretch just out-side of town.

With hardly the enthusiasm they once had, katydids, grasshoppers, and crickets serenade the night. Though there's got to be a better word than "serenade" to describe what they do. Red maples become fluorescently so. White-footed mice fill their root cellars. Straggling monarchs gamble on the weather. Hearty mosquitoes get good meals from evening porch sitters and anglers. Many birds have become fall-quiet, but not blue jays.

Notes

September

Having had enough of summer, tiger salamanders find creases in walks and abandoned gopher holes in which to spend the winter. Three or four will settle in the dark corners of my basement. Garter snakes hunt for rockpile winter homes. White-tailed bucks begin to feel the weight of their antlers and the weight of the responsibilities they bring. Does stalk windfall apples, building fat reserves to sustain them during winter shortfalls.

11 Pheasant hunting, as it was in the good old days, just doesn't exist any more. I don't know, maybe it never did, but the classic pose of a pair of glittering, gleaming cocks rising at the end of a good dog's nose over honest, straightforward rows of corn seems to be more the stuff of calendars than the down-to-earth real thing.

That's okay, of course, because ringnecks have survived, in good part, because they're flexible and have adapted to a tremendous diversity of habitat. As pheasant hunters, we can do no less.

These birds thrive in timber-choked river bottoms. They love overgrown cattle-country fence lines. Weedy railroad rights-of-way are heavens on earth. Where grow thick thickets of wild roses and leg-biting blackberries, there grow modern pheasants. A fallen-down farmstead is a paradise. Wetlands suit them nicely. Postage-sized weed patches, too skimpy to hide a mouse, hide a nestful of pheasants.

Yes, those pheasant hunters of us who pass up such birdie covers as these on the way to Grandpa's cornfields are leaving them to those of us whose Grandpas have moved to town.

Notes

12 Hunting from canoes opens up new worlds, new hunting lands, and new opportunities. To make the good even better, a paint job on the canoe might be in order.

I suppose the owner of one of those new, very expensive canoes might be loath to point a can of spray paint at it and pull the trigger or slap a brush dripping with paint against it, and so might I. But if you've got a canoe like mine, it really doesn't matter, and by camouflaging it, we can turn it into a floating blind. It's an easy thing to do.

First, we spray the entire craft with a flat deep green paint. After that dries, we spray patches of black or dark brown in no particular pattern.

Then we get a leafy branch or a handful of cattail rushes as a mask and spray paint a mustard or dull yellow color over the black.

The results are impressive, though if you'd like to practice on a friend's canoe first, I would understand.

I've even thought of camouflaging my wife's car like this. But don't tell her. I want it to be a surprise.

Rafts of coots blow in with cold-promising winds, playing tag with September. They float darkly and low. Maple leaves become extravagantly orange and red and yellow. The last of the wild grapes are ready for picking. Ferns at the forest's edge turn brown. The praying mantis has laid her eggs on weed stems, insulating them with airy masses of bubbles. Then, the very reason for her existence satisfied, she's done for.

Notes

September

Red-bellied snakes slide into big ant hills in which to spend the winter. Milkweed pods keep busting open, throwing parachuting seeds to afternoon breezes. Woodchucks eat with real meaning, storing fat for the long winter's sleep. Trees in the woodlots, set to chattering by September's basically housebroken winds, argue the pros and cons of their immediate future—of turning over a new leaf, you might say.

13 Well, we've been waiting for partridge season for a long time and we're all set to go. We're getting our guns and gear and heading out to our favorite partridge hot spots, which, incidentally, seem to be the favorite partridge hot spots of everybody else.

Let's face it. Our favorite hot spots have cooled considerably. It is the fly in the oatmeal of partridge hunting.

Whereas we are otherwise daring folks, we can be such timid mice of habit when it comes to cool hunting spots and the changing thereof. It's too bad, too, because the changing thereof is as sweetly simple as proceeding to the county courthouse and procuring a plat book.

The pages of plat books illustrate in fine detail nearly every inch of the county—every logging road, right-of-way, crick, creek, pothole, pond, and trail. The drawings clearly note public lands and private.

Armed with a plat book, a compass we trust, and a fanny pack of possibles, we'll tiptoe into new territory, into new hot spots; we'll tread where maybe no partridge hunter has trod in years, and you know what that means.

Notes

14 What some folks love most about fall is not the coolness. Nor is it the transfiguration of leaves, nor the evacuation of pilgrim-birds to greener pastures. No. It is the brown trout—beautiful, feisty brown trout, migrating now from summer waters to spawning waters.

These folks love the pleasant business of calculating where in the water that migration is taking place (we call it "reading the river") and what exactly to do about it. These anglers appreciate the fact that browns must sometimes settle for what they can get, but when they can get it, they'd rather gather in straight, heavy runs with rock and gravel bottoms.

Spawning browns are bottom-feeding browns, so flycasters cast substantial streamers upstream and at an angle, trying to make the bait look like a hurting minnow. Sometimes they fish weighted nymphs the same way. Spincasters go with jigs and spinners, up and across, too, retrieving slowly as the lure spins by.

Female browns, those with an inward curve to the anal fin, lack the hooked lower jaw and carry a bellyful of eggs. For sure, we let those go.

Cattails are brown. Jumping mice, fat and sleepy, settle down for a long, long winter's night—up to eight months of long. Needles of tamaracks mellow to golden green. Though the days are often gentle, warm, and sunny, the evenings just as often carry a cool snap. A warning. Against the turning browns of the in-between summer, in-between fall season, goldenrods shine, keeping the bees in business.

Notes

September

Snapping turtle eggs, laid at the end of May, begin to hatch, sending motherless babies scooting to the relative safety of open water. Pin cherry trees are as gloriously red as they'll get. White oaks drop their acorns, to feed nearly every wild thing out there and to sow, of course, the seeds of their own tomorrows. September has soft, dreamy, lazy afternoons. But not today. Today there's wood to stack.

15 Standard thermos bottle fare for us out-of-doors people is coffee or hot chocolate—good enough stuff all right. But when enough coffee is enough and more hot chocolate is too much, I switch to this tomato whatchamacallit, from a recipe we found when we were hunting for something to do with yet another bucket of tomatoes from a garden that refused to quit.

First, we slowly cook, for about fifteen minutes, around twenty cups of cut-up tomatoes, stirring quite a bit. Then we press the stuff through the food mill to extract the juice. To the juice we add one cup of chopped onions and boil for a half hour, keeping up with the stirring. Then in goes a quarter cup of lemon juice, one tablespoon sugar, two teaspoons each of salt, horseradish, and Worcestershire sauce, and one-half teaspoon hot pepper sauce—more or less of each to suit you. We simmer all that about ten minutes, pour into pint jars, and seal and process in a hot water bath for another ten.

We serve it hot if it's cold out or cold if it's hot.

I suppose I should point out that the "we" here is actually "she," though I did help hoe the tomatoes a time or two.

Notes

16 All things considered, the mourning dove is probably the American hunter's favorite game bird. Hunted by thousands, the bird thrives, its numbers growing marvelously each year.

Doves breed in all of the lower forty-eight states, Mexico, and Canada. A parenting pair builds a nest, lays two eggs, and incubates them within thirty days. Two weeks later, the young leave the nest, and the pair begins another family, and another, and maybe yet one more in a season.

Pass shooting at dipping, rising, zigzagging, fifty-mile-per-hour flying doves provides one of the grandest, most challenging of all shooting sports. States that refuse the hunting of this migratory game bird merely pass it down to those in other states that do.

Despite sometimes passionate pleas to the contrary, mourning doves, taxonomically speaking, are not songbirds, though the song of a dove, rising with a rising sun or a summer sun reluctantly setting, is a wonderful song indeed.

Ash leaves turn golden yellow. Aspen leaves—popple—getting the idea, follow suit. Sumac-red leaves, among the first to have changed color, begin to fall. Red squirrels spread out to establish small territories of their own. Nearly a third will not see spring. Late this afternoon a woodcock called. Nighthawks, running out of insects, migrate through to where bug hunting is better.

Notes

September

Pelicans gather. Franklin gulls pass through. Maple trees spread colors—glowing with ghostly iridescence in the harvest moon. Streams of birds without benefit of road sign or map become silent rivers of migration in a sky-high adventure along routes established forever ago. Spots of frost spatter the front yard, the work of last night's moon. This morning's sun, rising blood red, will erase it before the coffee's hot.

17 Coming through a morning mist or disappearing into a sunset is the unmistakable silhouette—long neck, elegant graceful lines, and long, pointed tail—distinctive trademarks of the pintail.

There are, I suppose, prettier, and certainly there are more colorful, ducks, but none is more formally clad than the pintail in its tuxedolike attire of long coat, tails, and a white cummerbund.

Pintails, shooting and eating favorites of western hunters, are among the most widely traveled of waterfowl—summering as far north as the Arctic and Siberia, wintering as far south as the South Pacific. They are hunter-wary birds, preferring vast, open waters and grassland habitat, where they feed on seeds and grains.

Greyhound, longneck, picket duck, sea or water pheasant, spindle tail, spike tail, chocolate bird, and the often-used sprig—they're all nicknames of this classy fellow. Unlike most dabbling ducks, pintails ride high in the water.

And they ride high in the hearts of bird watchers and waterfowlers.

Notes

18 Here's how bowhunting is for me. And probably for you, too.

I sit for long hours waiting for a deer that I've met on several occasions. So I know him pretty well. And I like him.

I know, for instance, that he's a ladies' man. I see his girlfriends all the time. And some of his offspring. I know that he's so careful he'll insist another deer cross a road or a trail ahead of him to check that the coast is clear. I know that he's a bully, that he chews his food with his mouth open, that he drools, that he's not as young as he used to be.

I know the look in his eye when he senses that I'm around; I know the twitch of his tail, the flick of his ears, his great speed, the length of his leap.

I know each tine in his rack. I know how ghostlike he appears and how he disappears without seeming to move.

I know that if he should just once get careless and I should get lucky, then I know that I would be a happy man. And I know that I would miss him very much.

Muskrats build mounds from cattails, bulrushes, mud, and not just a bit of determination. Butternut trees cut loose shriveled leaves, and what purple martens remain go, though bothersome mosquitoes enough for many meals stay. Beavers, able to hold their breath for as long as fifteen minutes, engage in a frenzy of industry as they cut aspen, willow, and cotton-wood to store in underwater pantries for winter's use.

Notes

September

Winterberry shrubs show clusters of orange-red berries. Banded woolly bear caterpillars forecast to some the strength of coming winter. Highbush cranberries turn red. Chipmunks, squirrels, and waxwings eat them up. Blue herons feed in shallow waters. Crows seem particularly raucous in their morning flights, but crows seem particularly raucous all the time.

19 Duck hunters, by the nature of our hunt, seem to face more hazards than do other hunters. Ironically, much of it is of our own making, for duck-hunting casualties more often than not have nothing to do with guns or gunning, but drowning. Too many of us are more concerned with camouflaging our duck-hunting boats than with equipping them with what we need to save our lives. Basically, we do not stock them with life jackets—even the comfortable, camouflaged "float coats," which not only keep us up in the water but keep us warm in icy waters, too. And too often we load our boats to the sinking point with guns, shells, decoys, and the great paraphernalia of duck hunting. And we forget that waders and hip boots on our legs, even full of water, can help keep us afloat and warm in hypothermic waters. We don't secure our gear to prevent sudden shifting. And though we expect no bluebird days in duck season, we forget to watch the weather and heed its warnings.

Duck-hunting season is some time off yet. But the planning is not. We duck hunters are a special breed. We ought to take better care of ourselves.

Notes

20 Hunting down long miles of old trails, over hills that get steeper from one year to the next, into acres of brush that get thicker and thicker certainly has its moments. Wonderful, wonderful moments. But after the first couple of hundred miles or so, our legs don't want to go anymore and we poop out.

It's not necessary—the pooping out, I mean—if we follow the lead of duck hunters who fill game bags by hunting along rivers and streams from canoes. Floating down streams not only saves the legs, but it takes us off the beaten path to areas rarely hunted, to places where the only trails are game trails and where the partridge, squirrels, and deer view hunters as curiosities rather than threats.

We'll need two of us for this kind of hunting, dropping your vehicle at a downstream take-out point and taking mine with the canoe up to the put-in place. Only the up-front one of us hunts; the other paddles, but we'll take turns often. And if we get tired we'll stop, eat a lunch, soak our toes in the cool wetness of a babbling brook, and take a nap.

Asters and goldenrods bloom all over the place. Hummingbird moths feed on the last garden flowers. Those animals that will hibernate continue to add layers of insulating fat as their temperatures begin to drop and their heart rates begin to slow. Rose hips turn red-orange. We generally treat all of September as fall, but now the calendar makes it legal. It's fall, or about to be. Leaves are falling and so are temperatures.

Notes

September

Tree crickets fill evening hours with froglike chirping. Swallowtail butterflies sip last suppers from remaining flowers. Shy flying squirrels feast on acorns. Animals planning to stay up and about all winter stash caches of cold-weather snacks. Frosty mornings are not necessarily a novelty any more, and northern lights practice dances for grand performances in October.

21 Without the aspen (we call it popple), the ruffed grouse of the north (here called partridge) would be a hurting bird, indeed, and the North Country bird hunter, a hurting hunter. For the popple, through the various stages of development, provides for the bird's every need through all the stages of its development.

As a tree is cut, dozens of root suckers spring up around the stump. This thick growth makes cover for partridge chicks and cover for the insects on which they feed. As a tree passes through its youth and teenage years, it gives food and cover to partridge passing through theirs. And as it matures, at about twenty-five years, until it is harvested, blown down, or dies of old age, the popple becomes the supermarket, pizza parlor, and hamburger stand to the bird, as male trees produce a constant supply of flower buds, a primary food. Fallen trees become drumming logs.

Yes, the seasoned partridge hunter who wants a bird, or needs one, heads for the trees, a mixed-age stand of popple trees.

Notes

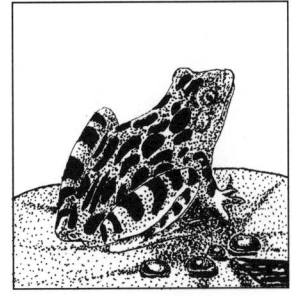

22 For survival, each animal and bird in the wild depends upon living space uniquely suited to its specific needs of food, water, protective cover, and nesting and birthing sites. Among other things then, a key element in locating game is to determine which critter needs what and then to find such a place to hunt it in.

For example, rabbits, pheasants, squirrels, and deer gravitate to cluttered and overgrown fence rows and windbreaks that border on open fields. Here they find cover, food, and safe travel routes. On the other hand (and depending on the trees), wooded areas with definite edges adjoining fields provide what squirrels, grouse, rabbits, pheasants, and deer need to thrive. Ponds and waterways within these woods act as magnets to all who live there.

Overgrown railroad right-of-ways provide homes to grouse, cottontails, deer, and pheasants.

Open fields of high grasses, marshes, clear-cuttings, hardwoods, cedar swamps, bottomlands, ridges, ravines, grainfield stubble, and pines: each different, each exclusive, each stomping grounds for one game-bag-filling critter or another. We just do our homework and then put the puzzle pieces together.

Leopard frogs go on the move. Ironwood trees join leafy associates in color-changing yellows. Sapsuckers, out of sap for the season, head south. Breeding mudpuppies gather in shallow, moving water. Starch-heavy, pond-floating duckweed sinks to the bottom to await spring. Theoretically, day and night are equal today and tonight. The score is tied, but we've seen this game before; night will win, overcome, conquer, overwhelm, triumph. For now.

Notes

September

Hawks migrate, passing through strict, narrow corridors. Beavers add sticks and mud to lodges in thick or thin insulating layers, depending on the severity of the upcoming winter. They continue to cache winter's food. A beaver family might need up to a ton of twigs and bark to survive the frozen months. Cassiopeia is off to the east of the pole star.

23 Like most hunters, I make up my mind to kill long before the hunt begins, before the pheasant flies above the corn rows, before the partridge leaps for pine tree protection, before the deer shadow looms into my sights, before the duck sets its wings to my decoys. I am fully aware that I am about to take the life of a beautiful wild creature, a creature I care about, and I do so anyway.

Why? To feed an empty belly? It is not so for me. My freezer is full. To satisfy leftover animal instincts of tooth and claw? I am born and bred no later than good people who choose not to hunt, so that is not so for me either. Am I then a demented fellow who must inflict pain? I have seen enough pain in my life, so that is not so for me. Is it sexual? No. Do I need the space? I like sharing my life and land with wild things.

I do know that when I go out to hunt I can meet myself coming back, that as I pull a trigger or release an arrow, I am taking a life as I must some day give mine.

It gives me pleasure. That is all I know and all I need to know.

Notes

24 I suppose we can argue the point until the cows come home, but it's probably closer to the truth than not: the truth being that ten percent of the anglers catch ninety percent of the fish.

If it is so, it's because those ten percenters understand that ninety percent of the fish live in maybe ten percent of the water.

In order to live, each fish must have food to its taste, water temperature to fit its needs, and some degree of safe cover—and an entire body of water won't meet all those needs for all fish at all times.

Now I don't believe for a minute that turning a fishing rig into an electronic, fad-gadgeted warship will automatically elevate us average folks to the ranks of the ten percenters.

No. That'll happen only when we understand the fish—what it likes, what it does, where it does it, and why—and when we can tie that together with the makeup and temperament of the water we're fishing in.

And that takes study, and it takes a lot of hands-on experience—experience we should go get some of right now. I'll drive.

Yellowed, pie-plate-sized basswood leaves layer forest floors. Red and gray squirrels feed on ripening acorns, not always waiting for them to drop. Clouds of bank swallows flee the coming winter. The two coats of the raccoon—one a bristly overcoat, the other a dense, furry undercoat— thicken in the latest fall fashion. Sumac is afire with flames of red. Barred owls hoot from within the dark corners of pine trees.

Notes

September

Flotillas of coots on their way through continue to pause in area lakes. Coats of whitetails change from reddish-brown to grayish, thickening with the growth of long, hollow, heat-holding hairs. Fawns lose their spots because they cease to offer camouflage. Red-winged blackbirds sing farewells from tops of cattails. Asters—stars that grow from stems—twinkle just as neatly as do those that dangle from the moon.

25 A guy in our gang we call the Professor, because he knows more about white-tailed deer than the rest of us together and doesn't mind sharing it, imparted this information at a recent get-together to discuss the coming season.

Since he's pretty long on reliability, I hereby pass it on to you.

"A whitetail's home range is limited to about one and one-half square miles, but within this area is a forty-acre core in which it spends ninety percent of its time." And "Whitetails seldom spend much time near noisy running water because the sound mars their ability to hear approaching danger. They take a quick drink and a bite to eat at such places, then get the heck out."

And "Whitetails probably can't see as well as some of us think. They're color blind and lack three-dimensional sight, so if a hunter stands perfectly still, a deer might look right at him and think he belongs, but they do see very well in dim-light conditions and can detect the slightest motion."

It was a long meeting.

Notes

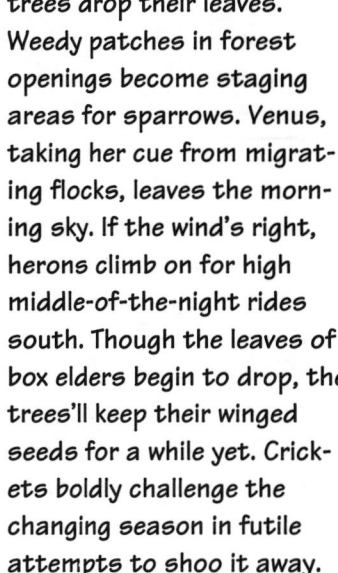

26 Within the next few days and weeks some backyard robin will tap her mate on the wing and inform him that the time has come to pack up and move out. Later a mallard will do the same, and a red-winged blackbird, and then more and yet more. Winter is coming; they're heading south.

No one has figured out all the whys and hows of this fascinating phenomenon—migration. Even the birds don't agree, each species doing it a bit differently.

Woodcocks, coots, and warblers, for instance, sneak out after dark, migrating only between sunrise and sunset. Herons, falcons, and eagles, wanting to see where they're going, do so only during daylight hours. Ducks, gulls, and some shorebirds don't care. Day or night—it makes no difference.

Snow geese fly nonstop for some sixty hours from summer to winter homes. Robins, orioles, and sparrows mosey along at up to twenty-five miles per hour, while ducks really move at up to fifty miles an hour.

And the tough little chickadee just sticks it out here with us.

And we appreciate it.

Cottonwoods and cherry trees drop their leaves. Weedy patches in forest openings become staging areas for sparrows. Venus, taking her cue from migrating flocks, leaves the morning sky. If the wind's right, herons climb on for high middle-of-the-night rides south. Though the leaves of box elders begin to drop, the trees'll keep their winged seeds for a while yet. Crickets boldly challenge the changing season in futile attempts to shoo it away.

Notes

September

Though many, many leaves have yet to fall, it is not uncommon to see snowfall, too. Frost becomes quite common, though not quite commonplace. Hibernating cattails reroute nutrients from dying upper stalks to mud-rooted rhizomes, where they stay very much alive under the coming ice. Black and red-brown woolly bear caterpillars gorge on last meals before rumbling off to hiding places to spend winter, Popsicle-stiff.

27 For some bird hunters, hunting without a dog is as exciting as eating an apple pie without the apples. Pity then, temporarily, this fellow whose young dog brought shame to its mile-long pedigree by bolting for cover with each boom of his 12-gauge. The desperate lad tried everything he and anyone else could think of, but the pup continued to carry the curse. He couldn't get rid of the dog because his family had taken a shine to it, and it wasn't yet paid for.

Then an old-timer came to his rescue. The old guy tied a fifty-foot cord from the coward's collar to the guy's waist, gave him a .22, and sent the two of them into butt-deep water—deep enough so the dog had to swim. Then, all the time sweet-talking the dog, the guy fired the little rifle. He continued talking and firing (at one-minute intervals) for twenty minutes—repeating the lesson three times in as many days. Then he did the same thing with a .410—being in no hurry; then with a 20-gauge, and finally with a 12-gauge.

Today, the guy wouldn't part with his dog for a million bucks, and he thanks his lucky stars it wasn't afraid of the water, too.

Notes

28 On paper and in theory, pheasants are easy. They only run around fifteen miles per hour—not so fast. They fly about forty, but it takes them a while to reach that speed. They can't smell us. They see well, but they can't see much from the thick cover of their ground-floor homes. They're reasonably large targets.

So then, why haven't you invited me over for pheasant supper lately and vice versa? I'll tell you why.

It's because pheasants disappear under a mere half-dozen blades of grass. That's why. And because pheasants know their turf—every rock, bush, dip, and doodle of it. It's because they slide along the ground like low-down slippery snakes. They run wildly and flush at great distances. Or not at all. It's because they run with the wind or against it. You never know. They live in wild wood areas, the thickest of tangles, or wherever there's a mess. And pheasants don't play fair.

So pheasant hunting isn't exactly pheasant shooting and pheasant shooting isn't exactly pheasant eating, so let's neither of us send invitations nor fire up the cookbook until we have got the feathers in the bag and the guts in the garbage. If you'll excuse the expression.

Nighthawks who haven't done so do so—catching up with migrated relatives. White-throated sparrows come to feeders. Bittersweet vines show orange berry clusters. In rainbow-balance, wild grapevine leaves turn yellow. En route out, flickers briefly flock to roadsides, food searching. Squirrels stow nuts and acorns by the bushel. The sun, still not quite used to fall, still rises almost due east, and still sets almost due west.

Notes

September

Notes

29 Some fine muskie fishermen use only artificial baits—big classy things that are a pleasure to land in and of themselves. While my Uncle Jake has a suitcase full of them himself, here in the early fall he uses big sucker minnows—eight- to ten-inchers, hooked through the lips with a single hook.

Mostly, he lets them swim free and clear, and when a muskie hits, he gives it line, slack even.

And then comes the hard part. Each muskie is different. But if he sees a jump or a swirl or feels a strong run he sets the hook right now.

Otherwise, contrary to his nature, Jake becomes the most patient man in the world. He waits.

Jake takes no chances. He says a slow-moving muskie is still carrying the groceries home, and one that stops and goes and stops and goes is just taking the scenic route to the supper table, so he waits—a half hour, an hour.

Old Jake says that only a muskie who's really moving out is engaging in an after-dinner stroll, so only when that happens does he go into action himself.

30 To the background music of a fiddler perched on a rooftop, a man and a woman ask themselves, "Is this the little girl I carried? Is this the little boy at play? I don't remember growing older. When did they?"

Among the greatest gifts we can give to our children before they quickly grow away from us is a love, an appreciation, of the out-of-doors. A child who experiences the fine tradition of the hunt and the great joys of wresting fish from the water need never taste the poison of boredom.

A child who enjoys the companionship of campfires and waves washing shorelines, and who can trace Orion's travels across night skies, will know no lasting loneliness. One who learns the discipline of handling firearms responsibly, whose heart can leap at an eagle's flight, who can set an efficient camp and leave it without a sign, will leave the world a better place than he or she found it.

One who can wax philosophic at waning moons and rising suns will resist the beckonings of false prophets, and one who can be equally at peace with windsongs and raging rainbows will grow into adulthood with the calm and confidence that all men and women need but so many lack.

And through it all, through changes and comings and goings, through silent leaf fallings, through glorious flights against setting suns, through wonderful stillnesses of putting to bed, September, as much as any other, is the time of wood smoke and quiet places. And as shadows lengthen and cool sunlight brushes ever barer tree tops, like a slow, gentle river, September flows lazily into a wider, more dramatic October.

Notes

October

October

Ah-h-h-h-h-October. Surely not the suns and skies and clouds, not the singing birds, not the flowers of summer can rival for one hour the splendor that is October. But with the passing of September, so passes all chance of that summer. And we are promised glorious days and cool, good-sleeping nights in October, the month of the Falling Leaves Moon and, finally, the Hunter's Moon.

1 It's October already. It's time for cider making. It's mourning dove and timber doodle time and time for sighting in and loading up. It's time to wade through ankle-deep leaves and time to thank our lucky stars for those who fill the quiet places of our hearts. It's time to thrill to a crying line of geese V-ing into a setting sun. Time to rise and shine for a good duck hunt. Time to put up storm windows. Time to punch time clocks at bow-hunting tree stands (no overtime, though). Time to mulch strawberries and sneak out for a go at pheasants. Time to pull out the snowblower. Change the oil and grease it up. No? Some other time then.

Time for Grandpa to tell us how many ducks there useta be. Time for wild rice and partridge and fresh bread and apple butter. Time out for touchdowns. Time yet for a well-dressed picnic. Good time for good fishing. Time for a paddle down a river steep enough to last a long time. Time to gut a pumpkin and chisel in a pair of eyes and a crooked grin to greet giggling goblins who come with jumpy hearts and open bags.

Notes

2 The gales of autumn—the cold, the wet, the wind—that is duck hunting weather, and we like it like that. But as bad luck would have it, weather turns sometimes on the men and women who hunt ducks. Skies clear, suns shine, temperatures rise, and winds die. These are called bluebird days, and on such days hunters cannot nudge a duck loose with a crowbar. Or can we?

Yes, we can. Early in the season, ducks haven't completely reached the brilliance of their breeding plumage; therefore, newly painted, brightly colored decoys, no matter how artfully arranged, scare off incoming ducks, especially on lets-have-a-picnic days.

We use, instead, our most unpainted blocks, and make at least three-quarters of them drab hens. And we mix up our decoys so they don't all look alike and so they appeal to a wide variety of ducks. And when we call, in the stillness of fair-weather days, we softly chirr and croak and grunt and cluck and whistle in the sounds of contented birds, creating the same mixture of songs as our decoys represent. And finally, we station our decoys so as to draw attention away from the shoreline, where we sit and wait.

October days are punctuated by later sunrises and earlier sunsets and skies that daily empty of birds fleeing south. And those that haven't, except the ducks and geese, of course, had best get about it, for time, having its own way as always, is running out. Winter squash comes in from the cold to hibernate in root cellars.

Notes

October

Love-hungry rutting moose bulls stomp through the woods, bellowing, fighting, shadowboxing, stalking lady moose, anxious for the tryst. More flocks of robins and yellow-rumped warblers hurry through. Tamaracks splash gold-needled richness in swamp and bog marshes. And early-morning renegade ice forms on bird bath and dog dishes.

3 "Kuk-kuk-kuk," warns the sharp-eyed sharptail, first spotting the hunter. And the others in the flock answer, "kuk-kuk-kuk," passing the word.

Then comes an explosion of wings, astonishing in their split-second, up-and-away acceleration, wings that'll cup and carry the soaring birds (at forty miles per hour) half a mile or more away. Yep. A sharptail hunter is a hunter willing to wear out a lot of boot leather.

This grouse, looking like a cross between a prairie chicken and a hen pheasant, is a bird of the distinct transition zone between prairie and forest; it is a bird of the grass and the brush.

Oh, the sharptail's mating dance is something to see. From March through May the male puts on a marvelous display that includes considerable foot stomping, strutting, and running with wings outstretched and tail high, all the while cooing and cackling sweet nothings in a vain-glorious attempt to impress the object of his affections.

Not long ago, at a party, a friend of mine demonstrated the procedure. I saw the guys in white coats coming. "Kuk-kuk-kuk," I said. Too late.

Notes

4 When the "red leaves hit the water," so does my Uncle Jake. As the nights and days cool, maple leaves come raining down, and at the same time, water temperatures here in Lost Lake begin to drop, triggering a definite change in the heretofore solitary lifestyle of muskies and an equal reaction from my uncle.

Jake claims that when water temperatures hit the high fifties and low sixties weed-oriented panfish commence to bunch up, and no longer then do muskies need to play cat-and-mouse games with scattered, weed-hiding, peewee perch and bluegills. Now the big fish leave the deep water en masse to gorge themselves on easy pickings.

This is hurry-up time for Jake, not a time for slow fishing or careful. He goes aggressively, checking out all the deepest weedbeds. Either they're there or they're not—he says—and he doesn't tolerate any slowpoke tactics from fishing partners (meaning me). He uses his conventional muskie bait casting gear (if there is such a thing as conventional muskie anything).

This red-hot, red-leaf action only lasts a few days, before temperatures sink out of sight; so quick, tell the boss you've got the fever and let's go muskie fishing.

Highbush cranberries are ripe. Birches show bright golden yellow. Hemlock seeds fall from cones to lie dormant until the coming snows leave them to sprout and grow in the faraway spring. For now, only the feet and ear tips of snowshoe hares are white. Ruffed grouse feed on birch leaves and aspen buds. In the half-light of dawn, we note, in the stillness, how autumn never struggles, never cries in alarm, but murmurs, sighs.

Notes

October

Juncos return to bird feeders. Hunters take time from gunning and anglers take breaks from some of the best walleye fishing of the season to lay in the last of the firewood and secure final harvests from fields and gardens. Young beavers must now strike out on their own. It is a tough time for young beavers. Procrastinating robins perk up things around noontime with a not-too enthusiastic peep or two.

5 Let's say we're walking through a pretty, birdy-looking piece of cover, and we're trying to think like a partridge, which is mostly a very useful thing to do. And we're thinking about the World Series, and we're thinking that if we were in the batter's box and a bird got up between the pitcher and us we wouldn't shoot (it'd be too close), but we would if it got up between the pitcher and the second baseman, (that'd be just right) and wouldn't again between him and the center fielder (which is too far).

And we're thinking if a bird flushes and is slanting down on a straightaway, we'll hold under it, but if it's rising on the same flight plan, we'll swing the barrel up past it and pull the trigger just as the muzzle covers it, because if we see a rising bird over the barrel, we'll miss it low again for sure. And we're thinking that partridge in a hurry fly fifty feet a second, but the shot can hit around fourteen hundred. And right about then a for-real partridge really gets up in an explosion of leaves and in a flurry of sounds, and by the time we get our thoughts together, it's gone—though we shoot anyway.

And then we're thinking that we think too much, and that it's a good thing we don't count our shells.

Notes

6 On one camping trip, you might throw a meal together in about twenty minutes—only to find you must sleep outside the tent, it being unsafe to spend the night in an enclosed area with those you fed.

You will not be lonely out there, though, for soon you will be joined (and perhaps pursued) by your fellow campers.

Then on another you can spend hours and hours preparing the same meal, alas, only to discover that much of it must be thrown away, your comrades having starved to death with the waiting and passed on into that great chow line in the sky. Somewhere there's a happy medium.

Every outdoor-lover worth a spice rack must learn how to cook. You don't have to like it, but when the bottom line is cook or go hungry, and you've got your life in your own hands, you ought to be able to do something about it.

For what is cooking anyway, but the exposing of assorted foods in an assortment of pots and kettles to an assortment of fires for various lengths of time.

I ask you. What could be simpler than that?

By the way, pal, make mine medium rare.

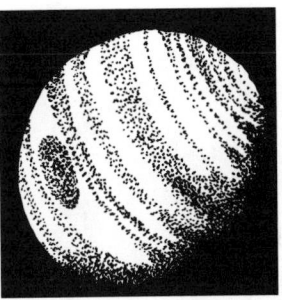

Jupiter continues to shine in the morning sky. No rush now for him to flee before a later-sleeping sun. Hummingbirds right about now fly up to five hundred miles nonstop across the Gulf of Mexico. Mice explore attics and pantries for suitable winter homes. From the garden comes more of the last of the harvest, popcorn, to hang near the furnace to dry even more and prompt us to wonder what would happen if every kernel in a pot popped at once.

Notes

October

Young ravens become independent of their parents and join other youngsters for wild, noisy sunset parties. Elms let loose their leaves. Poky, deliberate oaks, any day, will follow suit. The scientific name for beggar ticks is translated as "having two teeth." Two teeth they have, and beggars they are, as they chomp a toothy hold on passing hikers and hunters for free rides from meadows and woods.

7 Sitting down on the job isn't so bad. For the rifle shooter, in fact, the sitting position is perhaps the most effective of all in most hunting situations.

We've read the stories and heard the boasts of hunters slapping rifles to shoulders, firing away at racing targets, and putting bullets where they'd hoped they could.

But the shoot-from-the-shoulder shooter is firing from the chanciest of positions; whereas with butt on the ground and elbows braced on knees, you can hold around five times closer. And with a tight sling on the upper part of the left arm (for right-handers) the wobble is cut again in half. Though it takes some practice, shooting from the sitting position isn't difficult and, oddly, doesn't take any longer.

With legs angled in front of you and knees raised, put your left arm between the rifle and sling, cross your left forearm between the sling and rifle again, take hold of the gun's fore end, raise it to your shoulder, rest elbows on knees, slide your left hand to the rear, increasing the sling's bracing effect, and pull the trigger—in an eternity of around half a dozen seconds.

Notes

8 Canoes and johnboats are ideal hunting-from-water craft, because they are lightweight and maneuverable and draw little water—important on these low-water rivers of autumn. And they are easy to transport. What they are not, however, is quiet.

Aluminum water vehicles are noisy, and as any out-of-place noise frightens fish from anglers, so does it alert game to a hunter's approach—what should appear to be no more than a floating log becomes a threat.

So here's where hunters who hunt from the water take a clue from their fall fishing buddies—which is to line the floor and the seats of their boats with carpeting. A layer of carpeting quiets things down real nicely.

And just as important, carpeting serves as an insulation against the coldness of the water transferred so completely through the metal to the feet and behind of a hunter.

Hunting from the water is sneak-hunting, and there's nothing sneaky about a shivering, shaking hunter dropping a #4 to the bottom of the boat and kicking over the thermos trying to retrieve it.

Yellow jackets flock to any sweetness available and seem testier than usual. Butternut, black walnut, and hickory trees are golden, butter yellow. Hoarding chipmunks emphatically gather every bit of food they can get ahold of against the long winter—most of which they'll sleep through anyway. Tippling partridges get potted on fermented grapes and berries, sometimes mistaking picture windows for wide open spaces in short but sweet flights.

Notes

October

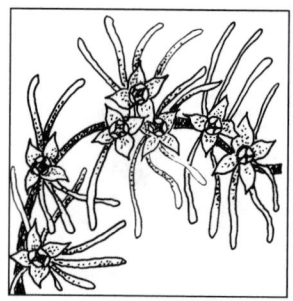

Just as most plants call it quits for the season, scraggly witch hazels, in the bottom lands and on stream banks, turn out their curious yellow flowers. Later, just as curiously, when their woody fruits turn brown and hard, they'll spit out a seed—up to fifteen feet or more. Woodchucks are winter-fat and ready for hibernation. And fallen leaves, like fields of milkless cornflakes, make sneaking up on anything all but impossible.

9 After the opening day excitement has come with the dreadful slowness of a long-awaited holiday and gone with an awful suddenness, after the young dumb-of-the-year have become pleasant pheasant dinners, toothpicked away for another season, after the old, hunter-wise ringnecks have disappeared, evaporated, then some hunters put up their guns, satisfied that a little bit was a bit better than nothing.

But some folks just love the hunt too much to give up, give in, so easily, so early. Some study the ways of the wary what's-left birds with the same care they give to an elk hunt. They know where the wise old birds feed (cornfields) and when and where they hide out (cattails, weed patches, and willows). And they know the routes the slippery cusses take to get from one to the other, and they blind-hide themselves, well-camouflaged, and wait for the birds to come to them—never underestimating pheasants' hearing ability (up to a mile) or their eyesight (as good as a turkey's).

Does it sound, as a matter of fact, like a turkey hunt? A dry duck hunt? A bowhunter's deer hunt? It does! And a sure-fire way to hunt late-season pheasants too.

Notes

10 In October no time, at any time, is better spent than the time spent fishing for brook trout. In October leaves of trees lining narrow little streams singing so sweetly become reds and golds and yellows and browns. And leaves of trees ringing radiant sky-colored ponds and pools become reds and golds and yellows and browns.

And in October, male brookies, hook-jawed and tooth-studded, already the handsomest of fish, explode into colors of their own, colors that outdo even those of the brilliant leaves. In October, while the females busy themselves on gravelly bottoms, trenching nests in which to drop their eggs, the males become aggressively, territorially bold. Greedy, selfish, grasping bullies, they dart and dash all over the place, driving off predators and warring on other males with ruffian schemes of fertilizing those eggs with milky clouds of their own sperm. In October, in such a state, male brookies recklessly, impetuously mistake the flashings of silver blades, the buzzings of spinners, and the gay stripes of streamers for such interlopers and take ready whacks at them.

Yes, indeed, this is a time like no other time to answer to the calls of October.

Tamaracks (some folks call them larches), having changed their bluish green wispy needles into soft sprays of gold, now drop them entirely to the forest floor. Raccoons begin exploring for winter dens in hollow trees, in culverts, or under abandoned buildings, not to hibernate, really, but to do some very sound sleeping. The reds and browns on red oaks are an unmistakable, understated gorgeous.

Notes

October

Some bears head for their interpretation of what hibernation is all about. Mothers will, of course, take this year's cub along for the long winter's nap. Sandhill cranes flock in premigration gatherings. On saplings, whitetail bucks, big and small, rub mossy coats from antlers. Basswood trees launch tiny seeds on only slightly larger sails to ride October's winds to ports of growth and industry.

11 Pinecones are such sexy little things, each and every one representing a promise of the future, each holding in its nutty little self a pledge of new life, of rebirth. For it is from these small, seed-bearing forms that pines, spruces, firs, and hemlocks sprout.

Most familiar to us, of course, are the pretty female cones, composed of numerous hard scales, each of which holds a seed or two. Prepubescent, pollen-producing males are smaller, rakishly if not macho-ly resembling flowers. Seeds from pinecones rank high on the menu list of partridge, turkeys, pheasants, rabbits, squirrels, chipmunks, and even coyotes and bears and deer, too, when the going gets tough.

White pine cones grow to a skinny eight inches, while Norways get to be a plump, round two inches. Each fall, each cone releases pairs of winged seeds that sensuously float and spin to the forest floor in search of cradle space, into which to take root and grow. Spruce cones are petite and oblong; hemlocks are among the tiniest. Some, like the jack pine, let loose their seeds only when forced to do so by fire, which pops them free of their waxy pods.

Such great drama from such ordinary things.

Notes

12 A hunter experiences many thrills in a hunting, but few can compare, I think, to that of talking a flock of geese into swinging your way and skudding over your head into a set of your decoys, or that of calling in to you a dozen mallards out of a morning mist.

Hunters, usually and obviously, hunt for their game, but a wildfowler tries to put a flip onto that coin by conning the birds into coming to him or her. It is fine entertainment, but becoming good at it is a long, laborious process, begun perhaps like a kid at a first violin lesson.

Like that kid, you must choose your instrument with care, and in turn give it good care. And you must be willing to practice though you become the object of head shaking and finger pointing. Duck-calling books and duck tapes can help with the lessons, and fine callers can give sound advice on the science of waterfowl solicitation. And you can attend calling contests—recitals if you will—which provide arenas for novices and virtuosos alike. And like the kid who sticks with the instrument, you can, for a lifetime, experience the satisfactions and reap the rewards of mastering a true art form. Except you can eat yours.

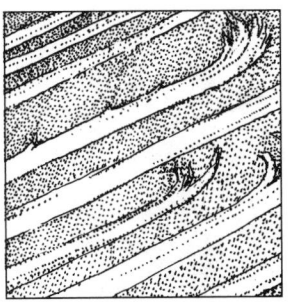

Silky, wispy cirrus clouds tell tales of sky doings. Surface waters on lakes sink to noticeably cooler temperatures. There'll be no more swimming for me. Bucks leave scrapes in the woods, personalized with hoof signatures and deer-peculiar invitations. Leaves of cottonwoods add their yellows to the splash of October's colors. And maple leaves, single-bladed helicopters, whirl lazily on one-way drops to the ground floor.

Notes

October

Cattail heads puff inside out, sending into the winds thousands—some say 250,000—of tiny seeds on tiny parachutes. On warm, sunny days red-bellied and garter snakes and painted turtles soak up what rays they can. Scaups, ringnecks, buffleheads, and goldeneyes flock to large bodies of water to rest from their migrating labors. And the ax-songs of woodchoppers split the evening air in presupper ceremonies.

13 It can be a long time between ducks for a hunter in a blind, a long time between deer for a hunter in a stand, and to an angler up to the neck in trout waters, it can be a long time between strikes. Hungry times, sometimes fidgety times. Unwrapping a sandwich is a noisy, two-handed, time-consuming job. Opening a bag of chips is a noisier three-handed job requiring special tools. Cousin Ken has the answer. It's jerky. Not the commercial, recapped tire stuff, but the down-home, homemade kind that softly, efficiently, silently satisfies his need to fill an empty corner of his stomach, to occupy nervous fingers.

He mixes up one-half cup teriyaki sauce, one-half cup water (or wine), a tablespoon each ground red pepper and allspice, three teaspoons each of salt and brown sugar, a few dashes of Worcestershire and tabasco. To this he adds long, thin strips of top round steak, and he lets it all sit for four to six hours. Then, sometimes using toothpicks, he lays the strips on an oven rack at 150°, with the door ajar, for two or three hours. After which he puts them in plastic bags and hides them in dark corners of the refrigerator, to keep them from me.

Notes

14 My Uncle Jake maintains that fall walleye fishing is up-and-down walleye fishing—bottom-bouncing, jig-fishing fishing. And he works hard so he can dangle the jigs right down at the tip of a walleye's nose.

Jake likes to fish for them now near shore areas situated close to deep water, fishing anywhere from ten to thirty feet. To locate fall walleyes, Jake puts his electric motor in reverse and runs it as slow as it goes. If it's windy, he runs it against the wind to slow it down even more. Sometimes he'll run for a dozen or two yards, shut off, jig for a bit, and then go again and stop and jig and on and on. And sometimes, in a small wind, he just drifts with it.

Jake says the bait's got to be right at the bottom, and he expects his constant up and down jigging to aggravate a fish into action. The second his line twitches or seems to hesitate in its fall, Jake slams the hook home.

When he takes a fish, Jake isn't so daft as to drop his anchor right in the middle of a school. No. He right away throws out a marker and calmly floats on by a ways. Then he anchors, and then he lets out enough rope to set him right over the honey hole, and he's open for business.

Crickets are still at it. Some straggling sparrows, thrushes, and robins continue to play cat-and-mouse games with the weather. Sometimes they lose. Red squirrels cache what pine and spruce seeds they do not eat on the spot. Cedar waxwings, grosbeaks, slowpoke robins and thrushes, bear, moose, and snowshoe rabbits dine on mountain ash berries, if they can. Does and fawns still feed on the windfalls in the orchard.

Notes

October

Now's the time, when so much foliage has dried up along roadsides, ditches, and fence rows, to locate and map dry stalks of asparagus for good eating come next spring. They say the fluffy stuff of each frayed thistle holds about four thousand seeds, each taking ten seconds or so to float six feet, where they'll settle till spring and then begin to send taproots down and down and down.

15 It has come to my mother's attention that some of you out there plan to go deer hunting and to shoot a nice buck, but that you do not now, nor did you ever, plan to eat the liver. This upsets my mother, and it will upset yours, too, if she finds out about it. Sure, as kids we did not like the stuff; but nowadays it's different, partly because we are grown up, partly because Ma's still the boss, and partly because since we fix it the way she taught us, the liver is about the first part of the animal that gets eaten at camp.

We (meaning the guy with the short straw) fix it like this: first, we soak it a couple of hours in cold water and half a cup of vinegar. Then we wipe it dry and cut it into half-inch slices and trim away all fat and gristle. Then we pour boiling water over the slices, stirring for a couple of minutes, and then chill it once more in cold water, and finally wipe it dry again, dip it in seasoned flour, and fry it with onions in hot fat.

And even though it ain't steak, it ain't bad, so eat hearty. It'll make your mother happy and keep mine off my back.

Notes

16 Are there any among us who get more out of fall than the squirrel hunters?

Their passion is autumn and a game bag bulgy with a wary prey they consider to be among the most challenging and demanding in all of the out-of-doors.

In their true sport of hunting, to be successful means calling into play all the wood sense they possess and to be at home enough in the woods to move ghostlike through thick carpets of crunchy tree droppings.

Some still-hunt, in a slow, observant hunt where looking and listening are more important than covering ground and steps are measured by the inches per hour, where the stopping is as important as the stepping.

Some hunt from a stand, content to sit and wait for the curious, scooting, scampering busybodies to show themselves.

Some use .22's, some shotguns; some go by themselves, some use partners or dogs; some use calls, some are silent.

And all answer the call of autumn—as pure and simple a call as there is.

Though October is much more fall than winter, it is hardly above reminding us who's boss, now and then, with a few snowflakes—a taste of what's to come, or a downright dumping-on. Muskrats fatten up on starch-rich cattail tubers, a favorite food. Hunting boots and waders rustle impatiently in hall closets and, to the duty-bound men and women who own them, whisper sweet promises of good times, come the weekends.

Notes

October

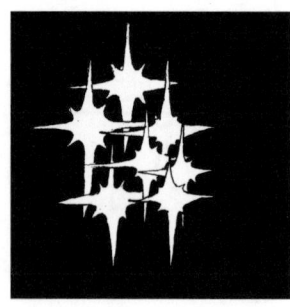

17 Timing, they say, is everything. And if "they" is talking about bowhunters, "they" has never been more on target. For the bowhunter will get, as the deer comes into sight, only one moment that will offer the best chance for a shot. One split second of time that will be the best time to release the arrow.

The selection of that moment will mean the difference between filling a tag or putting in for another try on another day.

Such a decision. Should I shoot at forty yards when the animal might come to within twenty? Or spook at thirty-five? Should I shoot at a little doe within spitting distance or wait for the big buck that might be right behind her? Or maybe not.

And when a deer magically appears so close to me it can hear my whiskers growing, do I risk any movement to shoot then?

Experience, hard-won, cues us to when the right time is at hand—mostly. Experience. The sun. The wind. The capriciousness of the deer.

And not just a little bit of luck.

Notes

18 If you should see a kind of a grayish brown goose that looks just shy of a yard long from the tip of its pinkish bill to the end of its dark brown, trimmed-in-white tail and appears to have a wingspan of, say, fifty inches and likely weighs between five and six pounds . . .

If you should see a kind of a goose that sports a bright white badge on the front of its face and has an off-white breast and an off-white belly that's dappled, blotched with spots . . .

If you should see a kind of a goose that travels, sometimes at least, on migration flights with Canadas, that flies in the same kind of V formations as Canadas, that feeds with Canadas, that can be lured into the same kind of decoy spreads . . .

If you should hear a kind of a loud, rollicking wah-wah kind of a laughter from a goose far off, or a chattering kind of kow-kow from one contentedly feeding up close . . .

If you should see such a noisy, strong, fast-flying, sharp-eyed goose, then you've come upon a white-fronted goose, a specklebelly—one of the wisest, most alert animals in the world—a challenge, a trophy.

Purple finches wander, rather aimlessly it seems, heading to nowhere in particular other than to feeders full of sunflower and thistle seeds. Floating atop pond waters, match-head-sized duckweed, now starch heavy, sinks to the bottom to await spring. Some woodcocks migrate. And the sun gives up to the moon more and more of the responsibility for dividing our time and measuring our lives.

Notes

October

The once-fat green pods of milkweeds have become reddish brown and have burst open, spilling tiny parachuting seeds into the winds. Streams run heavy with loads of October's leaves. Woolly bear caterpillars parade for winter weather forecasters. With so many leaves down and out, oaks light up the place with deep reds, purples, and browns, and we appreciate it.

19 I was going to call this "phenseline pheasants," but the editor threatened to confiscate my stubby pencil and my ragged thesaurus, so I won't and here goes: When the corn's been picked and the oats combined, when cover's sparse and leaves have fallen and weed patches and swales have been hunted a dozen times or two, then's when pheasant hunters who haven't yet given up the game walk the fence lines.

These thin weedy ribbons of cover offer sly old ringnecks ideal napping places in between feeding forays and offer hunters grand opportunities to provide the wake-up calls.

This is not for the lone hunter, though. No, hunting fence lines takes about five. Two walk on either side of the fence, moving slowly to keep the birds on the line. Two others take wing positions, ten to twenty feet out and slightly ahead, to get a crack at birds sneaking off or flushing to the side. The fifth cools his heels at the end of the line to get at those slippery birds staying on to the last minute. That'll be my spot. This was my idea, remember.

Notes

20 There is no right way, sure way, easy way to hunt woodcocks. There is only the hard way. For to find woodcocks, we must find woodcock cover, which is wet cover, cover saturated with worms blindly groping just below the dirty surface, multitudinous cover dense enough, snaggily enough, prickly enough to shred the clothes from our bodies and the skins from our backs.

We must find that cover and then get into it. And we need not just one such cover either, but must have plenty of them in our arsenal of birdy beds, and move from one to the other in gamey checkmate chases—especially when the moon is full and the weathervane swings around to the north.

For then, in heavy flights the woodcocks come; pushed by the wind and guided by waterways, hitching rides, perhaps, on witches' broomsticks, they come to plucky hunters who'll hack their ways into make-it-do ports in the storm that were dry of birds the day before. And we love them for it, for though we couldn't live long on the meat of a woodcock, the pure pleasurable satisfaction we get from a brace in the game bag can carry us halfway into winter.

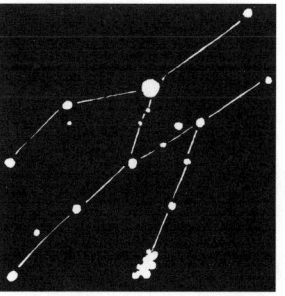

Taurus the bull, in constellation form, wades silently through the night sky. The bright, reddish star Aldebaran is the right eye of Taurus—really Zeus, who changed himself into a bull to be near a lady he liked—and Pleiades rides on his shoulder. Fox sparrows report to bird feeders. Beavers vigorously lop off trees to store for winter food. Tiny, web-riding spiders float on silken strands in midmorning breezes.

Notes

October

Cedar waxwings, the here-today-gone-tomorrow birds, are gone today. Quite a few of them. Box elder trees dangle seed tufts. With the coming of winter, and no longer worth a hill of beans to the hive, drone bees are kicked out. If they come back they'll be kicked out again and again until they get the point.

21 It gets downright touchy, at times, to justify to our kids, too young to go along with us, that we want to spend free time away from them with a musty old dog in a duck blind, or in a deer camp, or thigh-deep in a trout stream.

If your kids are like mine and are feeling left out, you might try something like this: for each day you'll be gone (even if it's only an afternoon), send them a letter.

For real young ones use large colored markers. Keep it simple. Ask how they're doing. Tell them what you're doing and when you will be home. Let them know you love them. Cut pictures from an outdoors magazine and include them. Someone can read your letter to the very young. Plan ahead so your letter will arrive on time. On weekends or holidays, leave the notes with the person taking care of them, who might also need a note if it's your spouse.

Once you start, though, you'll have to keep it up. Miss just once and those big, hurt eyes that greet you at the door will haunt you for a week.

Notes

22 Way back, when Grandpa caught more fish than the family could eat at one dinner time, Grandma didn't have the luxury of wrapping the fillets in white, waxy paper and storing them in the freezer. She canned them: an alternative still worth consideration, since canning fish offers some practical advantages, not the least of which is freeing up valuable freezer space.

Most frozen fish, especially oily trout and salmon, must be eaten within a couple of months, but canned fish have a shelf life of a year or more. And canned fish, when the time comes to use it, is already cooked and ready for such dishes as fish cakes, quiche, fish loaf, sandwiches, salads, or appetizers. There is no shortage of available recipes. Bones no longer present a problem with canned fish—larger ones are removed in the process, smaller ones soften and become edible. The special equipment of appropriate jars and lids is necessary, as is a steam pressure cooker. Instructions come with the cooker and abound in cookbooks, and though the process might sound complex and time-consuming, you can can if you think you can. Just ask your grandma. Or somebody else's.

The second crop of chipmunks looks about full grown. They eagerly, voraciously add to underground pantries that can hold up to half a bushel of groceries. They'll wake up now and then this winter to nibble. Wasp and hornet drones, too, are forced to leave the nest or be stung to death.

Notes

October

Popple trees continue shutting down for the winter, though some still neonize the woods with bright clumps of golden leaves. Hundreds of migrating wood ducks follow strictly defined waterways to wintering quarters, pausing at early evenings to roost, en masse, on lakeside trees. Frogs, quite seriously, begin hibernating. Mostly, since for now at least we don't have to shovel it, we don't complain too much about the cold rains of October.

23 None of us enter into the woods planning to get lost, so when we do—and we do—it always comes as something of a surprise.

Oh, we might be a little prepared, with matches and chocolate bar riding in the bottom of a coat pocket, but we're caught off guard.

Our first impulse is denial; our second is to chuck that thought and get the heck unlost. We hurry over a ridge where the pickup might be. Hurry over through a bog, a shortcut to the road, and then another.

This impulse to hurry complicates the getting out. Of the survival gear we carry, the best is our common sense. We should use it to overcome the sinking feeling of desperation that hits us.

We tell the kids to stop and hug a tree when they get lost. Stop. Hug a tree. It's good advice for us, too. Stop! Don't move until the feeling of panic subsides. Stop! Until we can coldly assess our situation. Check the wind, the sun, the stars.

All's basically all right with the world. We'll be okay. Just like last time.

Notes

24 Steelheading in the glow of spring, when, after a snowbound winter, fish-needy fishermen are hungry for fish to fish, is wonderful.

But steelheading in the nose-nipping days of autumn drives outdoorsmen like my Uncle Jake to put away grouse guns, hang up deer rifles, and leave wives and children and bosses to fend for themselves.

According to Uncle, these migrating rainbows in the fall are made of "rawhide and whalebone, are explosive as TNT, and are capable of licking their weight in wildcats."

Always hit-or-miss unpredictable, these fall-running steelheads become even more so, hitting fast and furious one day and sulking the next. Wary and spooky, they have to be hunted like deer, stalked like turkey.

Jake uses tough, sparsely dressed flies that readily sink to the bottom.

In-the-fall steelheaders don't measure success by the size of their catch—Jake, not necessarily a man of few words, says just one of these jumpin', rollin', rampagin', line-snappin' son-of-a-guns is cause for celebration.

Two is downright braggin' material.

Some hanging-low leaves of weeping willows drift down in brief golden showers. Ants continue hoarding with antlike industry. Night frosts kill mosquitoes by the millions. Let them go. Chimney sweepers climb to house tops in autumn rituals of a stitch-in-time. Orion is visible in the east, and traveling. Cassiopeia rides high above. And down below here, the virtues of October wane as our little corner of the universe diminishes in ever-earlier sunsets.

Notes

October

Blue jays come and go. Many of them, along with white-breasted nuthatches and chickadees, store seeds they'll need this winter against the times we, heaven forbid, let the feeder run dry. Muskrats continue active campaigns of repairing old homes and building new ones. On-the-go, hurry-up redheads and canvasbacks say hello and good-bye in nearly the same flap of the wing.

25 They are native to China, domesticated there between 800 and 300 B.C.

Then the Romans took a strong fancy to them sometime during the first century A.D. During the Middle Ages they became fashionably famous, a diet delicacy throughout Europe.

Treatises extolling their virtues were written about them. They have long figured in Asian art. In Japan they are used as symbols of strength, and to some Buddhists they represent devotees who succeed in reaching enlightenment. Aristotle compared them to the goddess of love, and Isaac Walton raved that they were "queen of rivers, a stately, a good, and very subtle fish."

They were brought to North America as soon as a strong wind blew a ship here fast enough. The U.S. Fish Commission decided they were the ideal sports and game fish, rearing some in special ponds at the foot of the Washington Monument. Congressmen hurried them to their anxiously waiting constituents.

To this day, they are prized and in great demand by a goodly number of citizens. To most of us, though, they're just lousy carp.

Notes

26 When we're goose hunting, what raises the little bumps on our skin is geese coming in. If they do come in.

When geese come in, if they do, it's because we set our decoys facing into the wind—even the heads-up sentries—because geese feed into the wind, and everything looks okay.

When geese come in, if they do, they'll usually set down in front of the feeding ground, so we strategically lay out our spread, leaving an opening in front of the blind to ensure good gunning.

When they come in, if they do, we try to remember that geese have slow wing beats and appear to be flying slower than they really are. When they come, if they do, we won't do anything. We won't call. We won't move. We won't blink. We won't fire until they set their wings, or until we can see their feet, leaving the long shots to the sky-busting, bird-crippling duffers.

When these great birds come, if they do, our skin'll start to crawl, for those little lumps growing under the long johns aren't called goose bumps for nothing.

It has been written that of all the wild creatures, the loon seems to best typify the stark wildness of nature. Flocks of fifteen or twenty of them gather on lakes now before migrating to the Atlantic coast. Tamaracks dust off the last of their needles, taking a little bit of our hearts with them. Nowhere is there a more golden gold than the gold of October's tamaracks.

Notes

October

27 Ducks migrate, geese migrate, elk migrate. Tweety birds migrate. And so, in their own way, do big northerns—as they make their annual fall movement from summertime deep-water haunts up to shallower hunting grounds—in a gesture that gladdens the hearts of anglers, who, like my Uncle Jake, need a last shot of some good fishing before the open-water season ends. We're not talking mere northerns, and though many fishermen claim great and understandable success in tying their baits directly onto monofilament line, Jake, who's lost a few nice fish that way, uses fine wire leaders. As the waters become colder and colder, Jake replaces his deep-diving plugs and spinners with minnows, sucker chubs, and golden shiners and works them in and around weedbeds and over deep-water structures. And sometimes, as the water gets colder still, he switches to spoons and trolls very slowly over deep-growing vegetation and around areas of rocks at moderate depths—moving just fast enough to give the spoon a slow, steady swimming action, trailing the lure twenty-five to thirty yards behind his boat and two or three feet below the surface. I do what Jake does.

Notes

28 Rarely does a deer drop at the shot, so tracking a wounded animal emerges as a routine necessity, no less a part of the hunt than writing a check for the license or pulling on long underwear. And following a blood trail to its logical and moral conclusion becomes as important as squeezing a trigger or releasing an arrow.

If we can recall exactly where we hit a deer, it allows us to anticipate its movements, to better understand the task ahead of us, to more directly and surely pursue the wounded animal.

But most of the time, in the heart-racing, blood-pounding explosion that occurs with the shot, it is tough to know for certain or remember exactly if the bullet or the arrow went where we wanted it to go, where we meant for it to go. So if we know that wounded deer react differently to different wounds, and that wounds from different parts of the body produce blood of different colors and textures, then it helps us hunter-trackers to understand what must be done.

A deer can lose one to two pints of blood before dying—at a drop a time, that's a lot of blood trail, a lot of tracking.

Piled high, cumulus clouds climb the October sky. Is the wood bin full, is the kindling split? The Great Bear, the Big Dipper to some of us, is on the northern horizon to wash his paws in northern lakes before freeze-up. Woodchucks drop into the deep sleep of hibernation, breathing only once every five minutes. Dotted pencil lines of geese gobble and gossip in the too-distant V formations, closing behind them the curtain on anything left of summer and October.

Notes

October

Raccoons settle into winter quarters—not to hibernate really, but to enter into fitful sleeps. They'll wake long enough to mate. In the night, Pegasus gallops high overhead. What isn't food storing, migrating, or seed releasing seems ready for bed. Late-leaving birds hunt for late-deep-diving worms. And porcupines snuff along without a care, to the tune of an early snowflake falling in the night.

29 The retractable claws of bobcats rarely show in the tracks they leave. Raccoon tracks look like those of infants: they are plantigrade—the heel put down before the toes. A walking deer places each hind foot in (or nearly in) the track of the front hoof on the same side.

Just as nearly everyone can learn to read words on the printed page, so too can we learn to read the fascinating manuscripts written in the snow, on sandy beaches or muddy shorelines or forest floors or on the paths of city parks—where wild signatures leave detailed records and often complex stories.

Whenever wild animals move over the land, they leave some evidence of their passing to those who would read of it. Was the animal alone? Or in the company of others? Was its young with it? Was it frightened? Or feeding? Or merely passing through? Was it hunting? Or being hunted? Did it leave its blood upon the trail?

The ability to read sign adds greatly to an appreciation of the out-of-doors, for the readers witness firsthand the stories written there for them to find, interpret, and imagine.

Notes

30 We're all out at the deer shack to talk about our favorite four-legged, white-tailed animal. The Professor is winded, having just completed an annual push-up, his conditioning regimen for the coming-up season. Of course he's not so winded he can't continue to educate the rest of us.

He says that in 1905 only about 350,000 whitetails lived in the entire lower forty-eight, and today that number is over 16 million. He goes on to say that a doe usually has a single fawn her first year, and every year thereafter, twins. If four does and a couple of bucks are put in a protected enclosure, within six years those six will become 356. Proving that the whitetail is often its own worst enemy and that without a well-planned harvest of surplus animals each season, the deer will reproduce to the extent that they'll literally eat themselves into starvation.

The Professor ho-hummed his Saturday night lecture by informing those of us still alert that each mature animal needs about ten pounds of food each day and that the average buck weighs around 165 pounds—25 to 30 of which is lost in field dressing. With that, he corked his bottle and dozed off.

Gregarious, wandering grosbeaks gather at food trays loaded with sunflower seeds. Pine siskins, flocking with redpolls, do the same. Canada geese continue to arrive for very short visits from Hudson Bay way. Snowshoe hares are all white now. And weasels are now ermines. Some two-bit-sized snapping turtles hatch and head for water, and some don't.

Notes

October

Muskrats make last-minute house repairs and last-chance additions to pantries. Brook trout move to spawning beds. Antlers of whitetails are sleek and shiny. Deer are rutting or wish they were. Clouds thicken, winds rattle bare branches, days shorten, wolves cry to what's left of the Harvest Moon, witches glide low, ghosts and goblins giggle in pumpkin patches.

31 When our kids first tell us they want to become hunters "just like the old man," it's okay to right away let our hearts skip a beat or two at the pleasure of it, but then we ought to get down to business. We ought to tell the kids to read everything they can about hunting, about shooting, about sportsmanship, about game birds and animals. It is good advice.

But we also ought to tell them not to quite believe all they read, nor to quite believe all they hear, either. We ought to tell them that when they are told an animal will "always" do something under a certain set of circumstances, or will "never" do something, or will "only" do this or that, well, then they should be on their guard.

It is true, we ought to tell them, that an animal might "usually" or "often" or "quite likely," but never "for sure"—that there are "always" exceptions to all rules. And that while gathering background information and consulting experts are most necessarily important, ultimately the best place to learn is in the field, and that with hunters, the learning process is an ongoing, never-ending, wonderful process.

Notes

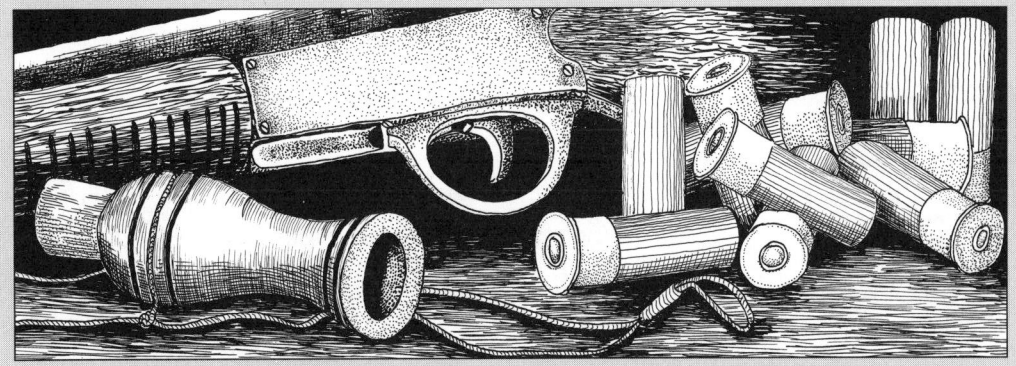

November

November

November is the month of infinite variety. We hunt for partridge and pheasants. It's deer hunting season. We have rabbits to chase. And squirrels. And geese to fill holiday platters. Fishing has not been better all year. And though we should do it more often, in November we set aside a special day to give thanks for it all, in this the month of the Beaver Moon and the Moon of Ice Forming.

1 Uffda. It's November already. It's time to put up the storm windows, and no buts about it. It's time to clean bluebird houses and wood duck nests. Time to mold tiny jigs for ice fishing. Time to reload more shotgun shells and time to sight in deer rifles. It's time to insulate the dog house, time to add antifreeze, time to get new plugs for the snowblower, and change the oil. Yes, it is.

It's time to drain the outboard and put the old friend away for a while. Time to sharpen skinning knives. Time to read a good book. Time to cook the last of last year's venison. Time to put away the tent and clean the sleeping bags. Time to shovel out the hunting shack and dust it off. Time to drop Christmas-shopping hints and then time to be more attentive around the house.

It's a great time for duck hunting and pheasant hunting and partridge hunting.

It's time to hug the kids, to take them fishing yet or hunting or hiking. Time to break in new boots, to dig gladiolus bulbs, to get off a backside and do someone some good. It's time to put the canoe to bed, time to watch a sunset with someone you love, time to smoke a turkey, and time to give thanks.

Notes

2 As deer spring from shadows of pines or pheasants explode from tangles of grasses or geese release themselves from morning fogs, hunters throw butts of guns to shoulders, slide hands to fore-ends, and pull triggers with index fingers of the other.

If these hunters fire, say, #2 shot, it is possible that the BBs will travel the length of three football fields and a couple of first downs before dropping into the dirt. Fours might quit at the end of three football fields. Sixes will go to two fields and an eighty-yard run, and eights only slightly less.

If, on the other hand, the hunters are firing .22 long rifles, they'll be sending out chunks of lead up to a mile and a half. Thirty-thirties'll go up to two and a half miles, and 7 mm's and 30-06s three-quarters of a mile farther than that. And they all go fast; bullets from .45s travel around 880 feet a second—or six hundred miles per hour.

Now this is old stuff to old shooters, and the figures are arguably arguable, but in the glorious heartbeat of a shot, the old rule about not shooting unless we're absolutely sure of our targets and what's beyond them is worth reminding ourselves of.

Big as crows, pileated woodpeckers, sounding like woodcutters working at firewood, carve great holes into tree trunks infested with carpenter ants. They pick them out as we do the chocolate-covered cherries in a box of candy. Foxes yip, yip in the starlight—mouse hunting. Some tough weeping willows still hang on to golden leaves. And into the winter coats of blue jays has gone the blue of summer's skies.

Notes

November

3 When they finally do come in from their northern breeding grounds, they ride in on blasts of frigid, finger-numbing cold, whispering their arrival in the dark predawn with a whistle of wings.

Officially they are lesser scaup. Some folks call them little blackjacks, or raft ducks, broadbills, river bluebills, cove bluebills, or bluebill coots. To us they're bluebills.

The males have purplish black heads, necks, and rear ends. Their backs and scapulars are white mixed with black. These are diving ducks, related to canvasbacks, redheads, and their cousins of the "greater" variety.

In tight formations of forty or more, they streak out of a morning sun, sweep across decoys, and rocket over blinds as half-frozen camo-clad hunters shiver-wait for these two-pound bundles of feathered dynamite.

Clouds of drakes and drab-colored mates hopscotch from pond to pond, preferring, often, the big, big waters where the rapid-fire piccolo hum of their wings turns them into distant specks and takes them out of sight in the time it takes to sneeze.

Notes

4 I just don't know of a single solitary soul whose heart doesn't skip a little beat at the sight of a deer track. Of course I only associate with the highest order of folks and, admittedly, do not know everybody.

Anyway, a couple of us are debating a set of tracks we'd come across when the Professor hears us and jumps right in. And though he has said it before, it doesn't bother him a bit to say it again.

"Tracks," he sighs, looking his most profound, "don't tell us if the deer that makes them is a buck or a doe. A big set of prints, punched deep into the ground, or marks of dragging hoofs or dew claws just shows us the deer is a big one, whatever its sexual persuasion." (Of course we knew that, but here's where we might have learned something.)

"Does tend to walk more pigeon-toed, and meander more than bucks, which tend to turn their hoofs more outward as they travel, and walk in a more straightaway fashion as though they had a definite destination in mind.

"Which is," he suggested somewhat unnecessarily, we thought, "something more of us ought to do."

October is a big spender, blowing its paycheck on color and fluff and the great migrations, and November picks up the change of returning juncos, stay-at-home chickadees, and feeder-feeding purple finches. Occasional dandelions with short stems and shorter memories stick their yellow heads up for a quick look-see. Pushed by November's winds, birds' empty nests swing on leaf-empty limbs.

Notes

November

Lying on their sides, patting out nests of gravel with their tails, brightly, beautifully colored female brook trout lay tapioca-sized eggs immediately fertilized with the spawn of equally colorful males. A glance at the browns and grays of November and the fallen leaves and brittle branches is a glimpse at a year growing old.

5 Goose hunting is often thought of in terms of permanent pits and traditional hunting grounds, because that's what puts a goose on the holiday dinner table. But sometimes a goose, because of the wind or the weather or the hunting pressure, basically goes someplace else, and then it's the hunter who goes where the wild goose goes that gets the job done.

This is the hunter who is wise to the bird. Who watches and understands goose-feeding patterns; who anticipates; who scouts. Who goes to the goose. This hunter is mobile. Travels light. Changes game plans readily. This hunter lies down in a combined wheat field under a camouflage of straw, or on snow, just as comfortably rolls up in an old bed sheet. This hunter might wade through ooze or belly-crawl through the same stuff, placing decoys close by so heading-this-way birds will think the calls are coming from them, and doesn't overcall migrating geese (they're not used to it), but chatters away to refuge birds (they're gossips).

This hunter's head never goes up to look at circling birds, and so can bow at the blessing over mashed potatoes and a Christmas goose.

Notes

6 The nitty—no nonsense—gritty is this. If we truly wish to preserve the wild places, we will take our kids camping.

If we are sincere in our efforts to make and keep the rivers and lakes clean, we will take the kids paddling and fishing upon them. If we want to keep the wild animals forever bountiful, we will take our sons and daughters hunting. If we want the memories to roll on, the traditions to continue past our generation—our humiliating, me-first, selfish generation—we cannot rely upon the fickle nature of politics and politicians.

We cannot lay the responsibility of conservation entirely at the feet of the schools. In the great American tradition of rugged individualism, the duty is ours. The hope, the salvation of our children—all children, wherever they live, from whatever background they come—lies with us.

We must teach them, lead them. For the hope, the salvation of the wildlife, the trees, the waters, the sky-blue skies, lies with our kids, our greatest, after all, renewable resource.

We cannot fail them. We cannot fail the universe.

Coats of fighting little weasels, triggered by short days, long nights, and cold temperatures, have turned, except for the black tip of their tails, all white. On clean snow, if it weren't for their shadows, we probably wouldn't see them at all. Slugs and snails that haven't done so burrow into the dampness of swamps and marshes. Slowly, I suppose.

Notes

November

7 My Uncle Jake doesn't hunt in the fall. He's too busy. Too busy fishing. Too busy fishing all kinds of fish. Too busy fishing walleyes.

Jake uses various methods to take walleyes this time of year, though his favorite daytime rig is probably the standard jig and minnow combination—deadly on autumn-hungry walleyes. In early fall, while the fish are still in shallower water, Jake employs lighter, one-eighth-ounce jigs; later, as the fish move to deeper waters, he'll switch to the heavier stuff.

Though he usually lip-hooks three- to four-inch chubs to his jigs and catches big and small walleyes with them, when he's after the lunkers he baits up with five-inchers. Or longer.

He trolls where he can, or casts the jig and minnow, working it very slowly, frequently pausing during the retrieve in case some fish wants to catch up, but not too badly. With the water skiers hibernating, hot weather history, and bugs part of the temporary past, Old Jake, surrounded by changing leaves and near-perfect solitude, gets into some of the best fishing of the year and once again becomes my favorite uncle.

Notes

_____

_____

_____

_____

_____

_____

8 With the gun-toting deer season approaching at the speed of the due date on a ninety-day note, things picked up at the hunting shack this week.

The Professor took time out from making what-to-do lists for everybody else to straighten out a couple of youngsters who were having a rousing discussion/disagreement about the rut, which they both correctly figured was about to start, but couldn't quite agree on just why. This kind of stuff is the meat of the Professor's sausage grinder.

"The rut," he sighed, looking particularly scientific and tolerant, "isn't triggered by cold air as you two seem to think, but a postautumnal equinox event" (giving the kids a shot of more syllables than they truly cared for). "As the days begin to shorten, decreasing levels of daily sunlight coming through the eyes of the deer have a reverse stimulation effect upon the pituitary gland near the brain, signaling a temporary slowdown in body growth and simultaneously an increase in the secretion of sexual hormones."

Of course the kids listened politely, and now you know why we call him the Professor.

Large flocks of little scoters migrate from the tundra to either coast. And chunky old squaws leave large lakes and bays for the oceans in erratic, buzzy flights in small flocks. Sometime this week the earliest noon of the year occurs, as the sun reaches its twelve o'clock position about sixteen minutes earlier than its average. Give or take.

Notes

November

Clumps of red cedars, for the season, exchange blue-green summer colors for shades of dull brown-green. The Milky Way grows milkier. Barred owls, with much of the night skies to themselves, make a chorus of their "Who cooks for you? Who cooks for you all?" calls. And more winter birds come out of the woods and pastures and roadside ditches, and out of the cold, for daily rations of store-bought seeds and suet balls.

Notes

9 When my favorite marsh gets jammed with johnboats and so many decoys we can't tell whose are whose, and the competition is as stiff as a hero's upper lip, and not even the dullest duck undertakes an infiltration of the heavily armed perimeters of the place, I pack it in—to lonely, way-out-of-the-way marshy potholes.

That is, after all, where ducks go when they can't get into where they'd like to go.

I find these places with plat books, maps, and aerial photos, and you seem like an okay person, so if you want to, you come along.

I should warn you that it's a little bit of work, but we'll pack light—maybe a dozen small decoys and that many sandwiches.

We'll need a compass so we won't get lost in the dark or turned around on foggy, misty days of good-luck hunting.

We'll camouflage ourselves real well and find, along the edges, a natural upwind blind that gives us good screening cover but not so much we can't see the ducks coming in—which they will, you know—two for you and three for me.

10   When the winds of November blow and the water's a white-capped mess, and the meteorologist on the ten o'clock news points at a cold front moving in, gutsy walleye fishermen go hunting—walleye hunting.

November walleye are feeding walleye, and these anglers take advantage of it. Those cold winds blow little bitty things in the lake all over the place. Those little bitty things are pursued by hungry bigger little bitty things, which are pursued by yet bigger things, and they by bigger still, and they by some pretty big stuff, and they by walleyes. And waiting in the bone-chilling cold for this long procession to arrive are fishermen.

They watch the wind and head for windswept points and flats on the inside curves of structures where everything sort of catches up to everything else. They study maps. They use big boats. They dress warm. Oh, they're tough, all right, the folks who fish for walleye, braving the general gone-to-hell condition of November's weather for a fish. And someday, when I grow up, I'm going to be just like them.

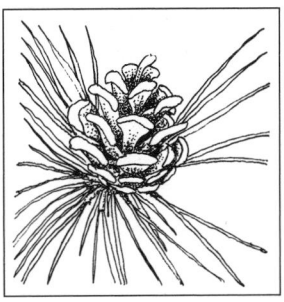

In losing, liquid battles, the edges of small lakes and ponds and quiet bays begin to freeze. Many millions of Christmas trees emigrate from country to city. Storms that sprout way out there or over there on weather maps head this way. And one day, very soon, that spitting snow is going to cough up a big bundle of it, and it's going to stay and stay and stay.

Notes

November

Husky fox sparrows scratch vigorously among fallen leaves for leftovers and visit feeders for long lunches and lengthy conversations. White-tailed bucks, with polished new antlers, move noiselessly through the brush, looking for love, or for a chance to knock heads together. Sleepy, sluggish black bears eat last meals of twigs, grasses, and pine needles to form a series of plugs to keep what's in in during their winter snooze.

11 Stump-sitting deer hunters who at last must get a move on (to reintroduce some feelings back into the behind, to put the old Rh positive back in circulation, to shift the mechanisms of cerebellums into gear), often become still-hunting deer hunters.

As they move, they measure distance in soft slothlike inches, and time not at all.

Still-hunting deer hunters never take a step until they've analyzed each and every potential hideout ahead and to the right and to the left.

Still-hunting deer hunters sniff, quietly, for each fragment of fragrance in the air. They put stethoscopes to everything in earshot. They locomote with the competence of shadows.

At each rustle, at every snap, they glaciate into a deep freeze until there's a guarantee that either what is there is there or what is there is but a figment of a noisy imagination.

Stump-sitting squirrel hunters who at last must get a move on ought to take lessons from our still-hunting deer-hunting friends.

Notes

12 We've all had some exciting moments in our lives. A first kiss. A first automobile. The "I do"-ing of a wedding day or, for some, the undoing of same. The birth of a child. Each sets us in a tizzy and puts us in a dither.

Other things do that too. Like landing an immense muskie. And though the chances, for most of us, of boating a big, big muskie are ever chancy chances, it is in these squalling, nose-numbing, finger-freezing, teeth-chattering times that the dealer slips us a pair of wild cards and the opportunity to draw to a muskie of a lifetime.

Usually sulky and solitary, monster muskies prowl now in search of food to put on fat enough to last them till the sun shines honestly come next spring. They're actively foraging, moving in and out of narrow shelves of sandy shoreline—shallow waters and dead or dying weed beds that drop off quickly into the deep stuff. This is fishing for the determined trophy angler, using big bucktails and bigger round-nosed jerk baits, hunting great fish and the intoxicating thrill of real excitement.

Snowshoe hares (rabbits of our swamps and forests) are about all white now, but for the black tips of their ears and the shadows of their tracks. They'll stay that way till sometime in March or April. Thicker than average, bushier than average, squirrels' tails foretell a winter longer than average, colder than average. So they say.

Notes

November

The last, or nearly the last, of the mallards leave, taking with them their familiar barnyard quacks and much of the fire, the spirit, that is autumn. The deer are fully into the rut. So are the moose—on a much larger scale. And brown bats. And weasels, though weasels are never really out of it, which is not a criticism. The last of the golden kinglets have left for milder central and southeastern states.

Notes

13 Pheasants are truly remarkable birds. Cunning and rugged, they survive where other game birds cannot. As long as they can scratch at a bare piece of ground for a meager seedy living, even the harshest winter weather doesn't faze them over much. Despite heavy gunning, they bounce back year after year in good numbers—as long as they've got the cover. Pheasants can carry more lead than a pencil factory.

Practiced in the art of living pretty close to humans, these birds know, or quickly learn, the tricks of the pheasant trade. As soon as hunters get them figured out, the danged things change the rules of the game. They get around those of us who hunt them on October afternoons by creeping and hunkering, hunkering and creeping, and finally dashing off out of sight, or holding tight, disappearing under a corncob or behind the shady side of a skinny cattail, or flushing with the sound of a tornado beating up on a freight train. And then, when we do get a shot, we're never, ever ready, never cool or calm. I know hunters, and probably you do too, who claim pheasants just don't offer a sporting target. What then should we call all those missed shots? Conservation?

14 The other day the Professor was exactly a year older than he was last year on the same day, so he took the opportunity to enlighten a couple of the boys.

It seems they had lugged some deer antlers into camp with the intention of banging them together to provoke an antsy buck into thinking there was a fight going on over a pretty little doe and maybe he could cut in on the action.

Well, the Professor thought that was a fine idea, and just might work, but pointed out that when bucks duke it out, it's not because they're fighting over a lady fair. And "Whitetails are not territorial," he said, "so they don't feel the need nor the inclination to defend their ranges."

He said the set-tos are basically disputes over ranking in the local pecking order. "Sort of," he editorialized, "like a couple of seventh graders on the playground, and such skirmishes are usually short, and seldom result in injury."

Well, that was too complicated for the boys, who went back to their girlfriend theory, causing the Professor to conclude that great thinkers are never appreciated in their own deer camps.

Or something like that.

Though there's certainly nothing wrong with a picnic in November, it's probably better, and warmer, to take a hike. Hikers, like hunters, smell what there is to smell, feel what there is to feel, and see firsthand what there is to see, like the empty nests in naked trees, giving mute testimony to the birds who once lived in them, and old empty barns and decaying farm houses, once alive. The constellation Aquila, the Eagle, soars tonight low on the western horizon.

Notes

November

15 Aside from the hunting itself and the getting ready for it, hardly anything stirs the hearts of hunters more than sitting down to a supper prepared from the harvest of their skills, the bounty of their labors, the fruit of their good luck.

A wild game feed has to include wild rice. So after the hunt, as the kitchen fills with smells of broiling venison steaks or baking pheasant, or roasting duck or frying squirrel, we get out the heavy skillet and mix in six tablespoons of butter, one-half cup each of chopped parsley and chopped onion, and one cup of sliced celery. We cook that till it's just soft. Then we add one and one-half cups of wild rice, one 10 $\frac{1}{2}$-ounce can of condensed consommé, one and one-half cups of boiling water, one tablespoon salt and one-half teaspoon marjoram or thyme. We put the lid on and cook this for around forty-five minutes over low heat, stirring once in a while with a fork and adding more hot water if we have to. When the rice is tender and the liquid absorbed, we stir in one-half cup of dry sherry and cook, uncovered, for about three more minutes. This is supposed to feed six people, and that's about right, if three don't want any.

Notes

16 Of the whitetail's major defense senses—sight, sound, and smell—smell is the best developed. It plays an important part in the family and social life of the animal.

Does and fawns locate and identify each other by scent. During the rut, bucks seeking romance sniff out does. It is this sense deer most rely on to detect danger. They constantly read the wind with their noses, keeping informed on the goings-on in their communities. Wherever possible, they travel into the wind, approaching feeding and bedding areas from where they can smell what's there before they get there.

Air currents, too, carry news to nosing-about whitetail. These erratic movements of air flow up and down and all around hills and ravines in such a constant shifting and eddying that they can change to and from several directions within a few minutes, bringing malodorous messages of sweating hunters, hunters whose shirts are heavy with the fragrance of morning bacon, whose rifles reek of gun oil, whose cheeks are heady with the aroma of eau de something. Whitetail have good eyes. Their ears are ever alert. But when the heat's on, it's the nose that knows.

Snowy owls, fresh from a lemming-scarce tundra, though generally silent in winter, add icy chills to the night with strangled, angry ravenlike hoots. Nuthatches and brown creepers, with sharp pointed bills, probe beneath corky layers of tree bark for spider eggs. Partridge feed on popple buds, as they will all winter. Those shivering birds on cold days shiver to produce enough heat to keep their body temperatures up around 104 degrees Fahrenheit.

Notes

November

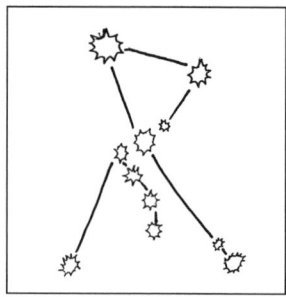

The sky-picture of Orion, the hunter, is seen clearly in the night skies, when night skies show clearly. There stands Orion, with his club raised, facing the charging bull. The Great Dog Sirius, sometimes the brightest star in the sky, follows his master and is in turn followed by a puppy, Procyon, pretty bright itself.

17 "You can't shoot what you can't see," grumbles the frustrated gentleman in the blaze orange cap and coveralls.

And he's right, of course, but the puzzle before the panel, the problem facing him and most of the rest of us, is whether or not he saw what there was to see. And it's not necessarily an easy thing to do, but if we want to see something, we've got to look at it. We've got to be alert, expecting to see, in this case a deer, in other cases a partridge or pheasant, behind every bush, under every rock—though that might be stretching it a bit. But not much. If we can train ourselves to maintain such a frame of mind, we'll spot the slightest movements, note suspicious objects, and hear sounds that could mean we're on to something hot.

It's tough to do in a hurry-up world, but if we go slow, letting as little as possible interfere with our concentration, focusing what attention we can on the business before the court, searching with eyes and ears and noses each and every little bit of cover with a crusading zeal, we'll do okay. At least I hope we do.

Notes

18   Like most deer camps, ours has traditions that we more or less pretty much try to stick to when we can and when we think of it. One of which is the opening ceremonial supper. We got the idea (for the recipe) from the ladies who cook the church supper.

As soon as everyone gets to camp, we cut cards. High card goes out for camp meat. Low card is cook. Everybody else plays five-card draw, nuthin' wild. The cook puts a pound of pinto beans and a teaspoon of salt in plenty of water and boils it.

When the meat comes, he cuts a couple of pounds into half-inch cubes, salts it, and browns it in a big pot in four tablespoons of bacon fat. He adds two cloves chopped garlic, two teaspoons of cumin, one tablespoon of hot chili powder, and one tablespoon of diced onions, and cooks it fifteen minutes. Then he puts in a twenty-eight-ounce can of stewed and one of whole tomatoes and the beans—juice and all—and simmers it three to four hours, while he deals himself in. He'll serve it topped with onions and cheddar cheese.

This'll do for about half a dozen hungry hunters or eight church ladies, so multiply accordingly.

In cozy hibernation chambers, ground squirrels sleep curled in tight balls. The heartbeats of hibernating chipmunks slow from a chattering springtime high of over two hundred beats a minute to but a few, so few that if we were to cut the sleeping animal, it would not, could not, bleed. Snow buntings drift in from over Arctic way. Evergreen trees develop a waxy coating on their needles to reduce the evaporation of winter-precious water.

Notes

November

Already November has taken big bites of neatly stacked firewood, and the pleasant haze of smoke drifts over resting fields and gardens, brushing the bald tops of leafless trees. This is the month when fierce storms of sleet and rain and snow and cold rage without warning against the unsuspecting, the unwary. Wolf tracks in the snow weave stories of soap-opera significance.

19 Discounting just plain dumb luck, probably the single most important secret to successful deer hunting is making the first shot count.

Most of us don't get in all the practice time we'd like; many of us can't even get in the shooting practice we should; but it is the deer hunter who doesn't get out to shoot at all before opening day who has the real handicap.

Somehow practice time must be made. There is no alternative. We must shoot and we must shoot often. For the frequent handling of the gun we hunt with gives us confidence in it and in ourselves. It keeps us calm when things are happening all around us and all at once. It lets us become so familiar with our gun that we will know exactly where the bullets will end up under any and all conditions.

None of us, of course, can prepare for everything afield (no more than we can for life); this is, after all, what makes hunting (and living) an uncertain sport at best. The one factor over which we do have control is the gun we use and how we use it. It takes practice.

Notes

20 Here today. Gone tomorrow. There's just no way to predict partridge hot spots. In a given area, their numbers are high one fall and low the next, depending on the oh-so-many iffy variables that affect bird populations.

About the only thing we can be reasonably certain of, though, this late in the season, is that where they were when the season started, they are basically not there now. And what few do remain in the hot spots of the ancient history of a few weeks ago are on to us.

Nope. Now we partridge hunters must necessarily get to the way-off-the-road places. We must, if we're really into partridge hunting, take the time and make the effort to hunt the unbeaten paths and jungle stuff sane and sensible folks avoid.

Much of November's best shooting is in the lowlands where brush grows thick and in swales bordered by some kind of clearing where the deck is stacked in favor of the birds.

We do, however, have a couple of things going for us. The fields aren't crowded; the birds are bunching up; and none of us is either too sane or too sensible.

Great gray owls, two and a half feet tall, beautiful, solemn, motionless, listen for life, mice-prey, as deep as a foot and a half below the snow. They hoot melancholy hoots tonight, sometimes ten in a row— sometimes many tens in a row. Evening grosbeaks are at the feeders. Cross-country skiers are out and about. Pileated woodpeckers and nuthatches search dead and dying trees for wintering insects.

Notes

November

If I were to watch for falling stars this month, and if I were to find a cloudless sky in which to do it, I would have started a few days ago, and I'd keep it up for a few more, for some mighty fine stargazing activity. Actually, I did, and I am, and I will. And I wish upon every one I see. So should you, if that's your inclination.

21 We're carpooling it to the county wildlife meeting in the Professor's old station wagon, and as usual we are listening to his continuing efforts to educate the rest of us, so we won't embarrass him at the meeting with our ignorance.

He's going on about "body language"—a deer's, and what it means, saying that the animal's ears can tell us what it's thinking.

"For instance, if they're swiveling around independent of one another, it means that it knows something's up, and it's trying to determine the source of its uneasiness, and it would be better for a hunter not to breathe for a while. And," he went on, "a deer's tail tells a story of its own, too. Like when the flag's up and the flared white hairs show, the animal's about to take off (though in the time it takes to say it fast, it's gone). And when a doe holds her tail far to one side, she is ready to be bred by a buck not too far behind, so it's time to put down the sandwich and get ready for Romeo . . ."

We all knew some of that, but since it seemed important to the Professor, we listened anyway. Besides, he was driving fast so none of us could get out.

Notes

22 Hunting deer from a tree can, with a shotgun or rifle, be superior to using a ground blind. It keeps you out of the deer's normal line of vision and offers you a bird's-eye view, and your scent is not so likely to spook a nervous buck.

But a pit blind can be a venison-producing alternative in areas of thick cover—where getting up in the air only makes things thicker. To build this blind, long before opening day, dig a four-foot-by-two-foot bathtub-shaped hole deep enough so that when you stand in it, it comes up to your chin.

As you cut firing lanes, take some brush and pile it in front of the hole and on top of the dirt.

Hunting from a blind like this offers a different experience for the hunter used to shooting from a tree. The earth muffles your noises; you can sit, take a nap, have a cup of coffee.

This puts you on the deer's level, and once you've had a buck come galloping down a firing lane toward you, eyeball-to-eyeball, you've really realized how exciting life can be.

Lake trout breed in the shallows of the Great Lakes and in rivers that feed into them. For each pound of honey, honeybees make fifty thousand trips to flowers, traveling some fifty thousand miles, or twice around the earth. Ten pounds must be a round-trip to the moon.

Notes

November

Rich-colored and ready, cardinals pitch and play at sunflower-seed-filled feeders. Catching sight of them against the browns and grays and sometimes whites of November days is like spotting the first violets back under the similar conditions of last spring. The morning paper reports that the first bow season ever was in Wisconsin in 1934. It was seven days long. One deer was taken.

23 During those magical, mystical half-light couple of hours after daybreak and before sunset, many hunters prefer to still-hunt. Perched on tree stands or hidden behind blinds, they wait just off well-traveled trails, hoping for a shot as deer move to or from feeding areas.

But from midmorning to midafternoon, deer often bed down to rest and generally lie low. It's then hunters climb from stands and begin hunting on foot. Some deer bed in lower elevations or maybe hillside benches. Those that have weathered a hunting season or two, however, often bed higher on hillsides and crests of ridges. For in the absence of winds, thermal air currents rise at midday, carrying any danger scent to them there. From this higher vantage point, the wise old animals can keep tabs on the goings on below. If they see, hear, or smell something they don't like, they simply slip quietly away, and no one will even know they were there.

It's the job of the midday hunter, then, to beat the old boys at their own game. Somehow. Or head back to camp for a nap.

Notes

24 When hunters put their stands where there are deer, the longer they sit in those stands, the better their chances of seeing deer become. But too often, the never-say-die enthusiasm riding with them to their stands fades with each passing cold, wet, long, long minute.

We can, though, besides being well-dressed, prepare ourselves to make our stay more tolerable. We can be in the best physical condition we've been all year. This gives us a tough mental outlook and keeps us warm from the inside out. If we're tough and we know it, it'll take more than a slap across the kisser with a snowflake to chase us home.

We can eat smart and well during hunting season, tossing thoughts of dieting out the window. This, too, keeps us warm from the inside out. Protein makes the fuel that stokes the body's furnace, and salt intake increases the flow of warming blood to cold hands and feet.

We can be well rested, saving the all-night poker sessions and round-the-clock toasting until after we get our deer.

Which we will, you know.

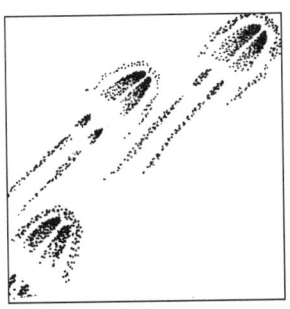

Deer tracks in the snow mark the daily routines of animals adjusting to the seasonal changes in their environment. For some of us, this is tracking snow. Backswimmers, water boatmen, giant water bugs, whirligig beetles, and others of their ilk pass the winter as adults burrowed into the muddy bottoms of streams and ponds, while cicadas and katydids spend theirs as eggs buried under ground.

Notes

November

Some lake ice thickens to the point that some folks venture out with jig sticks and tip-ups for some risky, though excellent, fishing. We are going to make an effort to contain our enthusiasm to do the same until the thickened stuff thickens a bit more. Mice and moles make tunnels under the snow for refuge, even temporary refuge, from hunting, nose-snuffling coyotes and foxes and wolves.

25 For certain, when something's been said often enough, it's taken as the gospel truth, and anyone who doesn't believe it is a heretic or stupid.

Many of us have been taught that when a deer is hit, and wounded, it runs away with its tail down—which is another way of saying that if it runs off with the tail waving high in the typical whitetail good-bye, we clean missed. I've said this myself, and apologize for it.

Setting the record straight is an old deer hunter, an old deer studier, one of the better whitetail-informed gents in the country, and he says it's not necessarily so. And the problem with this mistaken notion, this falsehood, as he calls it, is that it encourages hunters to give up the trail too quickly after the shot. Or to not take up the trail at all.

This, of course, can lead to unnecessary suffering on the part of the deer and needless loss of the animal.

The truth is that in many cases a wounded deer shows no immediate signs of being hit.

Hunters, good hunters, will always follow the trail to its logical, moral, ethical end.

Notes

26 Many folks, by choice or circumstance, are apartment dwellers. As such their only access to the great out-of-doors on a daily basis comes on a balcony at the best or at a window at the least. For them, attracting, providing for, and enjoying any wildlife (except, maybe, for the kookie couple across the hall) might seem impossible.

Of course, it's not. Suet balls, for instance, hung outside even on the innermost city windowsill will bring birds of paradise galore—within minutes.

Small trays of sunflower seeds and cut-in-half oranges set on ledges or balconies do the same, bringing in bundles of feathered color, grace, and energy.

Bookstores and libraries are loaded with all the informational ammunition we need to set up a wildlife sanctuary in a shoe box, if that's all we've got.

Yep. If a bowl of guppies just doesn't do it any more, by accepting limitations as challenges, any of us can change a sterile environment into a vibrant chunk of life, tiny though it may be, providing countless hours of enjoyment and not just a little bit of satisfaction.

Call it a labor of love.

Whirling, swirling snows pushed by great gusts of restless winds put to bed fidgety fallen leaves and still the crunch of hiking hunters. Coats of snow insulate hillsides and swamps and thickets, and next year's crops of countless seeds. Sleds nearly leap at the chance for some action, and snow-excited kids accommodate them. Today's woolly bear caterpillars, hibernating now, will become the pretty pink and yellow Isia moths of late spring and early summer.

Notes

November

Mars joins Jupiter in the evening sky, leaving Saturn in sole possession of the morning twilight—a small responsibility great Saturn handles with ease. The first serious icicles of the year sprout like weeds. Hidden away, filled with eggs, a queen bumblebee snugly sleeps through November, as she will December, January, February, and most of March. She'll rise with the sun of springtime to start things up again.

Notes

27 At no other time is the taking of deer tougher than late in the season, when they are veterans, well wired to the ways of keeping on their toes, and we as hunters have assumed a what's-the-use attitude.

But late-season, last-day deer are taken, and if that's the way it has to be, it might as well be one of us who does the taking.

If we've hunted hard and hunted well, then we've done what we're supposed to have done, and we've no reason to hang our heads.

But while we still can, we must get tough, get out, and find that buck to lay our sights upon.

We must get on with the hunt, do what we know how to do, do what we've been doing—only more so.

Let's check our clothes, our scent, get out earlier, stay later, watch the wind more closely, be more careful, more alert, get off the beaten path, be more of a hunter than we've ever been.

Then if the last frantic seconds of the season tick off and we're faced with a winter of hot dogs and pork chops, maybe we've earned the luxury of crying in our beer.

28 As the days become progressively shorter, as the hours of daylight diminish and the temperatures drop to below zero and snow begins to fall, chemical changes take place in the bodies of white-tailed deer.

Around mid-November, thyroxin, a growth hormone in the deer's body, begins to dissipate and continues to do so until it bottoms out at a very low level, where it remains throughout the winter.

This causes the digestive processes of the animals to switch into low gear, a change that causes them to require less food to maintain their bodies, which causes them to eat less, which means that they move around less in search of food, which means that they change their daily routines, which means that they may no longer take a daily stroll under our tree stand or past our blind, which means that we'd best be willing to do some changing ourselves when the cold, snowy, blowing weather strikes and the deer seem to disappear overnight, or we won't fill our tags, and we'll have to slink around all year like second-class citizens.

Most raccoons have settled in to winter sleeping quarters by now. Damselflies and dobsonflies spend the winter as larvae or nymphs at the bottoms of streams and pools. Frost digs its way into the ground—slowly but surely. Noisy crows, kings and queens of winter's skies, hunt and thieve and scavenge in their wily crow ways. In these mostly birdless skies, it doesn't bother us too much.

Notes

November

In large groups, snapping turtles have settled down and taken up quarters in muddy lake bottoms. Ruffed grouse have grown combs on the sides of their toes— some say to help them walk on snow, some say to help them grip icy branches. Bass sink, for the season, to deeper holes, where they lie in near-dormant, nonbiting states.

29 While the rest of us hustled up supper out at the deer shack, the Professor gave us advice. "The particular attention that goes into the preparation of a deer hunt," he commenced, "and the cautious execution thereof, ought to follow a hunter to the kitchen, in the kettle, and on the plate. Whereas there are countless mouth-watering ways to cook deer meat, the truth is that each and every recipe can be improved upon with a bit of heads-up consideration.

"For instance," he went on as we peeled potatoes, heated the skillet, and washed breakfast dishes so we could set the supper table, "truly thoughtful cooks trim all, and I mean all, the skin fibers and fat from the meat, because to many folks it doesn't taste good. And cuisine-conscious cooks serve all venison steaks, chops, roast, and hamburger on heated plates because venison cools rapidly and becomes tallow-tasting if we don't. And unlike beef steaks, which are better slab-sliced, venison should be cut not more than half an inch thick, nor should they be cooked too well nor too rare—they'll be tough either way."

We sat down, asked a blessing for the deer and the cooks, and dug in.

Notes

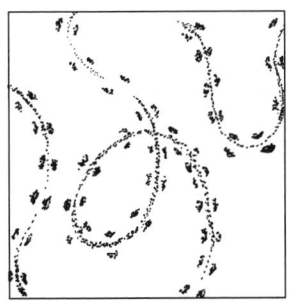

30 It is easier to set down the rifle, put it away for another year, than it is to put aside the golden moment of the hunt—the easing through crisp predawn darkness, along frosty trails lined with too crunchy leaves— the hooting owl—the heart-skipping flight of deer, startled from beds—deer we had hoped to sneak by—the climbing up to stands, feeling out each rung with foot and hand, or settling into brush piles, or sitting on well-sat stumps to wait—the waiting, still, so still, for glowing dawns— the cold seeping up pant legs, sleeves, around collars and ear flaps—the chambering of shells into dear old guns— the switching on and off and on again of well-worn safeties to pass the time—the always breathtaking births of days— the symphonies of birds' songs and squirrels' scoldings— the ghost grays of whispering shadows, which might be deer or might just be vigorous imaginings turning stumps or stones into deer—the careful unwrapping of peanut butter sandwiches or chunks of jerky—the faraway barooming of a neighbor's early shooting . . .

Winds interrogate heavy clouds, which nod agreement, and in collusion (each flake taking about fifteen minutes to form, and each one dropping a couple of miles an hour) they dump snow on us. Under which lives a thriving community of living, breathing, breeding, getting-along inhabitants. Gone is the last warble of the last robin and the last dangle of its last worm, for November has picked up the threads of autumn and turned them into winter.

Notes

December

December

December brings many pleasures to those folks who dare venture out to test its stoutness and who are willing to drift slowly, easily into its long nights and short days. In December much in nature indulges in long sleep-offs, and though at times we might like to follow suit, we instead gird ourselves, buckle up our boots, and make the best of this month of holidays, this month of the Cold Moon— the Moon of Popping Trees.

1 It's December already. And you know what that means. It is time to be good. It's time to sharpen ice augers and change the line on jig sticks and tip-ups.

It's time to dig out snow shovels and write to Santa Claus. Time to reassure the boss that we needed all those days off for hunting season.

It's time to string up decorations. Over the door. Around the outside porch. And up and down the tree in the yard.

Time to find the stepladder. Time to locate the decorations. And to disentangle them. And to lay in supplies of replacement bulbs.

Time to do some rabbit tracking. Time to talk to the kids about the spirit of giving.

Time to drop some cash in bell-ringers' buckets. Time to hunt up a tree that'll fit in the front door.

Time for serious and constant alluding to the need for new rods, reels, guns, waders, boots, shells, tackle boxes, creels, knives, and ohmigoodness, card-sending time and shopping time and time to wish one and all a merry, merry Christmas and mean it.

Notes

2 As winter rampages every which way, and frigid winds gnaw at cheeks and noses, and fingers and toes grow brittle-stiff at the mere mention of a snow shovel, we are content to curl warmly fireside and let it all go on without us.

But sometimes come rare, sunny afternoons—with "partridge" written all over them. Then we ought to bestir ourselves and take advantage of the situation. Most of the birds will be in the thick cover of pines, cedar swamps, and pothole bogs.

If there's little snow, they'll be feeding on clover and strawberry leaves, but if the snow's piled high, it'll be the buds and catkins of popple, birch, hazel, and sumac. Especially in the last hour or two of sunlight.

Now partridge tend to congregate in the better wintering areas, and we just might kick up more in an hour than we did in a whole weekend a month or two ago.

We won't overdo it though; we want plenty of them around come next spring. We'll flex our muscles, breathe some fresh air, take a bird or two, and head back to the cold, hard seats of the pickup.

Wandering tribes of grosbeaks continue to flock to feeders, when they're good and ready. Mine today, yours tomorrow. For most of us, big game hunting (hardly begun) is nearly over for now. As small game hunters, though, we have much to do. Ice fishing shacks and shanties sprout, with the magic quickness of springtime dandelions, atop crispy-hard lakes, lush with fish below.

Notes

December

Cardinals, Christmas-tree bright, visit feeders. Snowshoe hares have turned the color of snowbanks. Chickadees feed hurriedly before bully blue jays crowd them out. Bullheads lie nearly buried in bottom mud and muck. Chimney swifts have migrated to the upper Amazon. Red-headed woodpeckers hunt for bugs they stuffed, when the living was easy, into cracks and crevices of fence posts, telephone poles, and old buildings.

3 I don't think there's a doubt about it. Squirrels and squirrel hunting made us into the people we are today. Hunting squirrels took us out into early morning woods and taught us to drink the beauty of it. It taught impatient kids the thrill and joy of anticipating a sunrise. It gave us lessons in the importance of responsible gun handling.

It showed us the difference between the cute popcorn-beggars of city parks and the cautious, clever game animals who beat us at our own game nine times out of ten. Or nineteen out of twenty.

It taught us humility. It taught us to appreciate a wild animal—one that was most active just after daybreak and then again towards evening—one that when leaves fall, wisely moves from leafy nests to hollow trees. Which made darn fools of kids who shot into those leafy nests, mostly because it was unsportsmanlike, but partly because it was a waste of ammo.

Squirrel hunting made us feel good about being trusted with a gun and grown-up proud to have supplied the main ingredients for supper stew. And it got us out of a whole pile of chores.

Notes

4 Snowshoeing is one of the finest, most free-spirited, straightforward good times to be had.

True, snowshoeing may not be as gracefully elegant as cross-country skiing, but for many folks, there's no shoes like snowshoes for traveling afoot over the white stuff.

Snowshoes need no waxing and no daily preparation. They do the job on all kinds of snow and they go any- and everywhere. They offer stability to snow walkers and allow the carrying of heavy packs with relative ease.

And other than getting used to the increased length and width of some oversized footwear, showshoes require no particular training.

Many snowshoers use single ski poles in their travels to aid in climbing hills, maneuvering in tricky terrain, or maintaining balance.

Snowshoeing, step-gliding on snow above the ground, is like a kiss that sends a fluttering charge down the spine and out the toes.

It's like catching a thermal and riding on swells of air. It's . . . well, I could go on, but I wouldn't want to overdo it.

Starlings, for the most part, have gone to Mexico. Those that stay wear dull winter coats and black beaks. Downy woodpeckers come to suet feeders. Snowshoe hares feed on buds and twigs, leaving characteristic slanted cuts on the cut-off ends of branches. Their jackrabbit cousins, also hares, have also turned white to match the snowy flatlands they call home. The ice age is upon us and December's sun casts long, long shadows.

Notes

December

Ruffed grouse lie hidden and warm within down-fluffy snowbanks and, with explosive departures, scare the dickens out of unwary passersby. So cracking cold is it tonight (if not tonight, then some other night soon) that trees groan in lonesome desperation—without fireplaces or woodstoves in the house, where do families congregate? In one-to-nothing votes we decide that it's much too early to scout for Christmas gifts.

5 There's not much ballyhooing to it. It commences slowly, hesitantly, at first, and like a silent epidemic, it spreads. One or two men usually start the whole thing (though under all those clothes it's hard to tell, and it doesn't make any difference, anyway).

Pulling sleds of gear, they tippytoe upon the newly thinly frozen surface. Satisfied, they pound a foot hard upon it. It's okay.

They jump up and down on it. It's still okay. So they punch a hole and get to business.

Others espy them there and quietly join them—a comfortable, respectful, couple of arm lengths away. Others come and yet more.

Some must drive many miles. A lucky few merely step out their back doors. Some stay the winter. Some must sneak in an hour or two as they can.

Whole families of all persuasions answer the call of the ice and the promise of what's beneath it.

Villages spring up on icy foundations. Villagers employ mousies, waxies, wigglers, jigs, augers, tip-ups, and tee-pees. They joke, they kid, they share. They're ice fishermen and women.

Notes

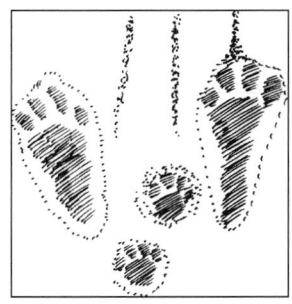

6 Camping is an affair of the heart, a concern of the soul—a call to adventure, to solitude without loneliness, to splendid exertion.

To limit tent sleeping and fire making to calendar say-so days is to waste half a lifetime.

And except that it requires more planning and caution, and that not a live mosquito buzzes within a hundred miles, camping in the snow isn't all that different.

Snow campers do take along a little bit more of everything—just in case. And they slow down. Moving too fast now allows for too many mistakes, when nature tolerates none. This is not a time to drop matches, spill fuel, or work up a sweat that will freeze as soon as activity stops.

Snow campers make camp early, too, allowing them to choose a good spot, clear snow, gather firewood, take care of personal needs, and fuss over supper before the short day drops so winter-quickly into darkness.

And tell me what vocabulary can cope with a sun diving into a snowbank on one horizon and a moon scaling an opposite one, to the strains of a hoot owl symphony.

So much outside sleeps, or has passed on to centrally-heated climates, and yet so many tracks in the snow cue us in on the dramatic lives of our four- and two-legged skinned and furred and feathered neighbors, and mailbox-bruising snowplowers and skiers and snowmobilers. Winter-sleeping tree squirrels wrap bushy tails about themselves for feather-tick comfort. And cross-country skiers stride out to where the sky begins.

Notes

December

7 We usually grow a pretty good garden, and we owe it to Martha, down the road. When she plants, we plant; when she hoes, we hoe; when she waters . . . well, you get the idea.

And it's the same with ice fishing. Only what success we have at this we owe to Gladys, another neighbor. About this time of year we watch Gladys like a kid watches the last piece of pizza. Gladys is one of the lucky ones; she can go ice fishing whenever she wants to, and she does. But she'd gladly trade the rest of the fishing year for the first week of safe ice cover. She knows when the ice is safe, examining it carefully, punching first a hole near shore, then all the way out. It's got to be three inches thick before she'll walk on it—four if I'm following too close.

We'll go fishing dozens of times on the ice this season, but never again under these unique conditions—about the most productive we could ask for. There's still plenty of greenery, plenty of oxygen under that fresh, black ice, and fish are still active—actively hungry, actively feeding, actively hunting for bait at the end of a line, under a hole chipped in new ice.

Oops, there goes Gladys, now.

Notes

8 Unlike downhill skiing, the cross-country kind is not for just the athletic few; it is not expensive; it requires little or no hard practice; it can be executed without crowds and long waiting lines; and best of all, it can take outdoor-lovers of any age as far and as deep into the great white wonderlands of winter as they wish to go.

Ski trails (though cross-country skiing doesn't require trails), thoughtfully planned and carefully groomed, criss-cross city and rural and wilderness alike—wherever snow falls, giving skiers access to so much warmth and color, so many fresh sights and sounds.

Skiing is a clean, natural response to the long-distance calls of nature—often toll-free.

Cross-country skiing is a fine conditioning sport, yet a skier need not be in the best of condition to ski. All it takes is a willingness to come out of hibernation, to glide smoothly (or not) and gracefully (or not so) over the snow. Indeed, agelessly, grandmas and grandpas drift right along with whooping-it-up grandkids. And there are no better sounds. They're together. They're having a grand time, and they're doing it on cross-country skis.

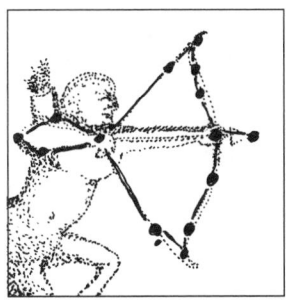

Sagittarius, the archer in the night skies, marks the fall of winter upon us. In a few days, the sun, the earth, and Sagittarius will line up like ducks in a row to signal, calendarily, the beginning of winter. There are no great stars in Sagittarius; much of the archer is lost in the Milky Way, but many watch for it: bowhunters, winter-waiting star watchers, and those born under the sign of the wise old centaur with its bow ever-drawn—a recurve, I think.

Notes

December

9 When the world's bound all around by a horizon of white and the top of the lake is a mass of condensed ice and snow, old Gladys figures she's waited in the wings long enough, and it's time to get ice fishing. Gladys knows, of course she knows, that the key to catching fish in the winter, as it is in the summer, is understanding their habits and work ethics. Especially walleyes.

She says that these big-eyed, bug-eyed beauties are light-shy. So their prime activity periods come just after dawn, before dark, or during dim, cloudy times when there is enough light for them to snag a meal, but not enough to be bothersome.

In the winter, when forage is limited, walleyes depend on minnows, or better yet, perch. So, when Gladys comes across a school of perch in the daytime, she goes back to that spot at dusk with a bucket of two- or three-inch shiners or fatheads for some pretty good walleye fishing. Sometimes she substitutes marabou jigs or Swedish pimples, starting a foot off the bottom, raising them slightly and letting them flutter down like a hurt minnow.

As always, I do what Gladys does. If you'd like some walleyes, you should, too.

Notes

10 Buying fishing tackle, gift-wise or otherwise, is something else again. No Christmas-decorated tree nor garlanded store window has as much glitz and glitter appeal as the gleaming, flickering stuff lining the counters of tackle shops.

What's to buy? What's hot, what's not? What's in? What's out? What will give us run-of-the-mill folks as much fun as the fishermen on TV? Bearish or bullish, when tackle boxes sport barren bins and Christmas stockings hang hollow, decisions must be made, conclusions reached.

The Rubicon must be crossed.

Muskie anglers always need another Marathon Muskie Hawk, a Suick, a Burmeck. Spinning gear trout fishermen never have enough Roostertails or #0 French spinners. For going after bass, it's Hula Poppers; for northern, it's Daredevils; for walleye, it's Rapalas, June Bug spinners, and Lazy Ikes.

All tackle boxes always need night crawler harnesses, Johnson Silver Minnows, Lindy Rigs, Little Cleos, Ugly Bugs, Mister Twisters, some of those purplish things and orange whatchamacallits, and hot pink . . .

To conserve water, pine trees in the snow go into cold storage, their idea of hibernation, though it's a quasi-hibernation, much like that of raccoons and skunks and bears. And to conserve energy, beavers exchange usual days of twelve hours on and twelve off for as much as twice that on and more than twice that off—cutting winter's days in half, I suppose, and what's the difference anyway, in the constant dim and darkness of the lodge.

Notes

December

Pine martens plow lightly through snowy, piney woods hunting for red squirrels. Ice storms leave a glittering but tricky-treacherous world in their wake. Blue-winged teals winter in Central America and parts of South America, peregrine falcons in Latin America, and northern orioles in the tropics, where their winter habitat is being chopped out from under them. Juncos feed on weed seeds shaken loose by December's rattling winds.

11 Of all the images of winter's fragile, rugged beauty, none is more rugged, none more fragile, than the sheets of diamond-ice that gather translucent as smoky glass atop dead-still lakes in the heart of winter. And of all the images of winter, no other is as deceptive.

Frozen lakes are fun, designed specifically for skiing on, for snowmobiling across, for fishing under, for skate gliding and shortcut taking.

None of us trust river ice, but lake ice looks, seems, appears so solid, so safe. And it is, at times. And it isn't at other times. It's hard to tell.

Traveling on ice too early in the season, or too late, means becoming an accident looking for a place to happen.

But even at midseason, we, as drivers on ice, must be ready to leave the vehicle in a hurry, with seat belts undone, windows open, and a plan of action in place—which is to get out right now, get to the edge of the ice we went in on and try to kick-swim up atop it.

You and I will never go through the ice. But just in case. Just in case.

Notes

12 On an early autumn afternoon, a flock of mallards set their wings over a dozen lookalikes anchored to the oozy bottom of a midwest marsh. These ducks have come a long way to this place, and it's taken them a long time to get here. From early October to the middle of November they migrate to southern states and Mexico.

Through November and December they settle in on winter waters, grow fast, carry on courtship rites, and couple up. In January, hens, securely mated, begin a nearly three-month molt into breeding plumage. As early as February and well into March, pairs already begin long pilgrimages back to northern breeding grounds, where hens select nesting sites. In April and May pairs put nests together; then hens lay eggs, set on them for twenty-eight days, and ignore males. Males leave.

By June, eggs hatch and hens and chicks take to the water. Then, as June becomes July, males molt; by August they have new feathers, and hens molt. And by September everybody's grown fat and feathered, and a few remember a midwest marsh somewhere to the south—a stopping-off place on the way to wherever.

To conserve energy, coyotes, when and where they can, hunt windswept, hard-packed snow cover, achieving top speeds of up to forty miles an hour. Rabbits, just ahead of them, can get up to thirty-five, for a little while. Black-capped chickadees depend upon our goodwill feeders for much of their food, though they continue to find insects just under the bark of trees, and seeds they or some other birds have stashed.

Notes

December

Frozen legacies of mosquito larvae or rafts of mosquito eggs lie surrounded by, buried in, crystalline masses of ice—waiting, patiently waiting. Meadow mice travel intertwining pathways beneath blankets of snow, where they feed on seeds and bark and stuff. Efts hibernate under leaves and logs. Tree sparrows feed in feeders and they're welcome to do so, as payment for the many, many weed seeds they ate last summer and fall.

13 Old Gladys, my ice fishing neighbor, has tricks in her parka pocket and up her long-underweared, thick-shirted, heavy-sweatered, parka-coated sleeves.

And she's always thinking.

For instance, on bright, sunshiny days, she chops her holes in the deepest snow she can find on the lake (over suitable cover, of course). She figures fish congregate under these snowy, shady areas just as they collect under logs and brush in the dazzling days of summer.

And she knows when a fish is monkeying around with her bait, because immediately under the smallest bobber she can stand she clips just enough split-shot to barely float it. Then even the slightest munch will jiggle that bobber, and Gladys rolls up all her sleeves, ready for action.

And sometimes, when she wants to see what's happening down below, she drops a bunch of beans down the hole, or some egg shells, and then hunches over it, her precious parka draped over her head and the hole, shutting off all light. Any fish are outlined against the white.

"Better'n television," she says. And we agree.

Notes

14 Of all the great sport to be had in the wintertime, about the sportiest is snow camping. Of course this is not sleeping-under-the-stars camping, nor is it plopping-a-tent-anywhere-anytime camping either. No.

Snow campers find campsites early.

They want a site away from overhanging rocks and trees that tend to let loose their loads around midnight on unsuspecting sleepers. They want one not at the foot of steep slopes, nor on lee slopes, nor in lee valleys, which catch and hold drifting snows.

Winter campers pitch their tents on the protected sides of natural windbreaks of trees or even snowbanks, and facing east, so the rising sun can warm things up.

Before pitching tents, campers dig down to the ground or tamp a solid, even square larger than the tent's floor.

They try to angle the tent opening away from the prevailing winds, but not directly away, so drifts do not block the entrance, causing uncomfortable delays for those whose very first order of business in the morning is to answer nature's call.

And a quick, cold call it is, too.

Expanding ice crystals on the nose, ears, hands, feet, and knees shut off the flow of nutrients to those areas. They become numb, white, waxy, and firm to the touch. It's frostbite. Frostbitten areas are not rubbed or salved or bandaged. Hands are tucked into armpits, crotch areas, or warm (not hot) water. Face areas are covered with dry, gloved hands; toes and feet are soaked in warm water. A shot of booze, in this instance, makes a bad situation worse.

Notes

December

Grublike larvae cause galls to form on goldenrod stems. Inside each is a choice bit of ice fishing bait, unless woodpeckers beat the angler to it. Tiny midges cause pretty, pinecone-looking galls to grow at the tips of willow branches—a dead giveaway, of course, since willows don't grow pinecones, or any cones. Raccoons lie dormant for days at a time in bad weather, living off layers of fat.

15 To each his own, of course, but in the world of sporting dogs, no other breed quite fills as many roles quite as well for quite as many folks as does the Labrador retriever. Labs are quite at home with duck hunters—be it in marshes full of Canada geese, in duck boats of waterlogged hunters, in blinds, or on stools in flooded timber.

And Labs are quite at home with upland game hunters—be it flushing and retrieving pheasants in the midwest or doves in the south.

And Labs are quite at home in bench shows, in every type of retriever field trial or working test in this country and in Great Britain.

And Labs are quite at home at home—be it playing with the kids, watching Saturday morning cartoons, snoozing calmly before the fireplace, or joining the family for Sunday dinner.

It is important, of course, when hunters hunt or hint for such an addition to the family that they be absolutely, one hundred percent certain that the pup comes from stock that has been used successfully and extensively for hunting. Right around Christmastime, in case Santa's interested, it's nice to know.

Notes

16 Now might be a good time to get junior hunting partners a first bow—when we can blame it on Santa Claus.

It's not a decision to be made lightly, nor one to be unnecessarily debated.

It ought to be a compound. They look important, like something a big, responsible person might use—lending credibility to the business at hand. They don't require as much of the youngster as recurves.

With compounds kids can concentrate on form, on hitting the target, on feeling good—not merely on struggling to pull the string back.

Compounds can be fitted specifically to each kid, can be adjusted periodically to grow with the child—increasing draw weights and lengths as skills improve and muscles grow.

First bows need not be rigged with every bell and whistle, but accessories can be added, one by one, in a merit-badge sort of way. Such bows can be investments in child-parent relationships, providing opportunities and excuses to be together, making the old man and Santa Claus look like a pair of pretty smart cookies.

The sun is now, or will be in a few days, over the Tropic of Capricorn—south of the equator. Stand there at noon and the sun is directly overhead. Stand there at noon and cast no shadow. Try that at home today. Capricorn is a democratic constellation—with no great stars there, all having been created equal. Pictured as half goat and half fish, Capricorn is the tenth sign of the zodiac, under which some of the very finest people have been born.

Notes

December

Out for a stroll, partridge patrol on padded, built-in snowshoes over newly fallen snow—snow that insulates sensitive plant tissues from cutting winds. Out for a frolic, otters denning in old muskrat houses, beaver lodges, or bank-side cavities dive and tunnel and slide in snow put there for their private play stuff. Hawks and owls hunt, one by day and one by night, mice and birds and rabbits.

17 What happens now, after the easy-living summer? After the making-fat and making-baby autumn? After the hunt? What happens now to the deer who up to now have been too clever, too fast, too lucky for hunters' fangs or hunters' bullets. What happens now during the barren harshness of winter?

It depends. It depends on how much food there's been—energy-rich foods of acorns, apples, corn, soybeans, winter wheat. Deer heading into winter without layers of stored fat have little chance of survival. And it depends on how much food there'll be.

It depends on the weather—long, snowless autumns allow late-season fawns to grow and fatten, allow bucks to regain fat lost during the rut, allow does, stressed from lactating, to attain maximum fat levels—allowing them all to head into winter with a head start. And it depends on early, relatively blizzard-free springs, allowing the animals early meals of succulent spring growth.

It depends on the cover. It depends on luck. It depends on being at the right place at the right time. In this oh-so-chancy business of survival, it all depends.

Notes

18 When the world crowds around, uncomfortably close, we need not necessarily go to places crawling with signs of deer or pheasants or rabbits or quail, need not necessarily go to where fish dwell below ceilings of ice.

In the heat of surviving in a modern world, when there's more tick than tock in the clock, we need not, if we cannot, make long pilgrimages to find what we need. For close by half a dozen trees grow and a couple of dozen blades of grass blow in the wind or poke through the snow.

In a helter-skelter world of hustle and hype, we can go to where there are no closed seasons, to places where the earth is needle-soft and thick, or where we can stand in patches of green or frozen white quite alone.

Or pass through cathedrals of pines, or listen to symphonies of oak leaves struggling in the wind.

Or where half-frozen brooks tumble over themselves.

In such places we can find, when we most need it, a piece of ourselves, and not just a little bit of our own heart and soul.

Snowbound deer switch from diets of snow-covered grasses to handy buds of small trees. Woodchucks' body temperatures drop from a normal of 100° F to as low as 37°. Their respiration of 235 breaths a minute dwindles to but 4 to 6, and their heartbeats sink from summertime highs of 80 beats a minute to 5. Red-winged blackbirds have moved to swamps and marshes just far enough south to escape the worst of this weather.

Notes

December

Redpolls, called winter finches by some of us, chatter from up above somewhere, eyeball the situation, and then dive quickly to the feeder or to bare birch branches for buds, and as quickly scoot away again. Temporarily. We now have, each day, six hours less of sunlight than we did six months ago, as these shortest days of the year settle down upon us.

19 Perhaps you, like me, graduated from hunting imaginary bears and buffalos with unlimited ammo in make-believe guns to a rusty single-shot .22 and a half dozen father-doled shorts to hunt the wily rabbit. And perhaps you, like me, eventually moved on to bigger game, bigger guns, and better ammo.

But, I'll wager, comes a wintery Sunday afternoon (just between the two of us), we wouldn't mind too much going back (just for the afternoon, mind you) to those easier, simpler, younger days when our whole world was a big backyard, an orchard, a shelterbelt; and high adventure was stalking big game rabbits.

It can still be so for us (for an afternoon). Somewhere close by there's a snow-covered big backyard of some kind, an old orchard, a grown-up shelterbelt with a rabbit or so waiting for a grown boy (who might allow himself more shells than his father did—and longs to boot).

It doesn't take much to hide a rabbit, and it doesn't take much to make a man's boy-heart light (for a Sunday afternoon). Monday mornings come so soon. And so often.

Notes

20 Let us say that in the middle of town, or perhaps at the edge, lies a nice chunk of land—brushy, trees at one end, tall grasses, potholes.

And in this oasis sing songbirds, nest ducks, rest geese. Here wild animals give birth and raise their young. Frogs croak. Bees make honey. Wildflowers grow. Quite undisturbed.

Along comes mega company. Pushing mega bucks and mega talk and mega plans. They say, "We need that wasteland. We'll pave it into progress. We'll put people to work. We'll pay big-time taxes. In the name of progress we'll fill in and neonize that swamp, that eyesore."

They remind the citizens that to be progressive they must rezone, remap, reconsider, rethink their priorities. And they'll live happily ever after—ignoring all the while falling-down sections of slum town begging to be rebuilt.

"Let the birds take their nests and songs elsewhere. Let the ducks find other homes and the animals move to the country and the bees be gone and the flowers die for progress."

And we stand silently and watch, or at most, let fall a watery crocodile tear into our beer.

As Cygnus, the swan, stretches its wings in full flight along the lower reaches of the Milky Way, not far above the horizon in the northwest, bobcats hunt for nearly invisible snowshoe rabbits. Some call the constellation the Northern Cross. Either way it's nice. Brilliant Deneb, near the top, is ten thousand times brighter than the sun. Icicles grow. Flying squirrels wait till the porch light goes out and the TV set is turned off and the head hits the pillow before coming out to play.

Notes

December

To the delight of the anglers, northern pike stay active under the ice, not so active, maybe, as they were last summer and fall, but on the go nonetheless. They are busiest, perhaps, down in the deeper, warmer waters of the lakes and ponds. With a heartbeat of seven hundred pumps a minute, chickadees need to eat the equivalent of their own weight, every day—on cold days.

21 Old Gladys never really knows what she's going to fish for until she gets to fishing. When she hits a day when northern or walleye won't bite, she rather gladly jigs for perch.

For winter perch, Gladys uses a regular stubby jig stick, loaded with braided line to which she has attached a length of four- or six-pound monofilament. During this early part of the season, she jigs, a foot or two (though she's willing to experiment) off the bottom, tipping tiny ice jigs (usually fluorescent orange for now) with wax worms or mousies.

Like most of us, Gladys has her best perch-luck earlier in the morning or later in the afternoon (though she claims that with these so-short days, it doesn't matter too much). Since perch like to take a bait that has some action, Gladys uses a slight rocking motion—slow and gentle—keeping any slack out of the line so she can stay in control at all times. She knows that perch don't really strike in the winter, but rather inhale the bait ever so softly. So she watches. When the baby bobber twitches or moves to the side of the hole, a snap of the wrist gets her what she came for.

Notes

22 Don't bother me with the smell of pines, the call of loons, with hungry fish or babbling brooks, until that first little fire of the morning is started, and the coffee is safely aboil.

Camp coffee. It better be fast. It better be good. Or I'm going home.

When the water's maybe not real safe to drink, the best way to get perfect, heart-starting java in camp is to first boil the water in the pot for ten minutes or so.

Then drop a barely rounded spoonful of coffee per cup into the bubbling water, stir it up and set it away from the fire. Don't boil it anymore.

If you've got enough character to leave the stuff alone for five minutes, do so, then stir it again and let it settle. Two minutes, 120 long seconds later it'll be clear. It'll be ready—hot, black, wonderful.

Reheated coffee tastes terrible, so if you've packed a thermos, pour it in there to keep it good.

Now bring on the pines, the loons, the babbling brooks. Now bait the hook—coffee's ready and all's right with the world.

Though it seems anti-climatic, winter's officially here, and we don't mind it a bit, for no winter has lasted forever. Get out in it and tweak its nose. Make a snowman. Throw a snowball. In the winter darkness, holiday lights shine with the stars, and against the white of day, red-ribboned bows glow. Gray squirrels invade bird feeders. Each squirrel needs around forty pounds of acorns a winter, though ours never seem satisfied with that.

Notes

December

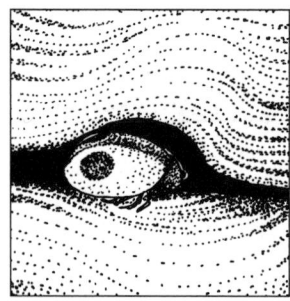

Ladybugs lie snugly dormant beneath layers of leaves and tiers of snow. Jupiter does fine as a morning star, working overtime. Deck the halls. Perfectly poetical trees are decorated. Late Christmas shoppers, in votes of one to everything, use sheer imagination, ingenuity, willpower, and strength to get the job done in record time. Lake ice, expanding as it warms, contracting as it cools, cracks and booms and groans.

23 To folks who love the out-of-doors and hope to instill such a devotion in their kids, these are the times to give gifts that will become gifts of a lifetime.

Now's the time to give the kids cameras to take pictures of bugs and flowers and spiders spinning webs. To give them books that open windows to the mysteries of the natural world, and those that tell of hunters and the hunted, of fishermen and the fished. To give them microscopes and binoculars.

And tents and sleeping bags and packs and pots and pans and the stuff to fill tackle boxes.

What the heck, it's Christmas and Hanukkah. Get them canoes and rods and reels and waders and fly-tying, tackle-making kits and snowshoes.

My goodness, the list is endless. Get them memberships in Ducks Unlimited and Whitetails Unlimited and Grouse Unlimited and Pheasants Forever.

Then, who knows, maybe when others are worried sick about what the kids are doing, you and yours might be sitting around a campfire or in front of a fireplace, telling tales and swapping stories.

It's possible, you know.

Notes

24 All I really want for Christmas is what any outdoorsman wants for Christmas: long Septembers; a cure for buck fever; a duck call I can use; self-igniting, automatic coffee-cooking campfires; long sunsets; anchors that do; more wetlands; a better shooting eye; ten acres in the middle of the Mississippi flyway.

Short portages; more rain; a remedy for cabin fever; a job that requires attendance based on the solunar tables; more ducks; a fishing cabin in Canada; a boat that doesn't leak; a canoe that doesn't leak; a tent that doesn't leak; waders that don't leak; less rain.

Longer Octobers; a new duck blind in real duck waters; every opening day declared a legal holiday; tracking snow; more pheasant habitat; just the right tackle box; acid-rain-free skies; more sharptail habitat.

Novembers where the first three weeks are three times as long and the last one isn't there; more lakes and rivers and streams; more prairies and woods and mountains; more rainbows and more time to enjoy them; the Santa Claus of my youth; and a heart that's grateful for what I've got.

And God, I love that kid of mine.

'Tis the season. For real. "Dear Daddy," goes the handmade Christmas card in the clumsy scrawl of a little girl who spent her Christmas coins on other things. "This year I will clean ten fish for you. Little ones. Pick two ducks if you get that many and four grouse and help you wash the pickup one time. And carry wood next deer season when you're hunting. I will make us good lunches for ice fishing. Love, Katie Santa Claus. P.S. Merry Christmas, Dad."

Notes

December

Chickadees "fee bee" as the sun warms the morning. Red squirrel and mouse tracks crisscross new snowbanks. Fresh deer tracks lead to and from the house. We take a Christmas walk, sing a Christmas carol, listen to the Nutcracker, go to Grandma's house. We see snow buntings, like so many snowflakes, and Bohemian waxwings. We light the Yule log in the fireplace and share its light, its warmth, and its hope with those we love.

Notes

25 It's turkey, of course, for Thanksgiving, but for Christmas, it ought to be goose—a good old goose you got all by yourself.

So first we get the goose. Then we dry-pluck it. We soak the bird in slightly salted water in the refrigerator a couple days. Then we rinse it off, pat it dry, rub a quartered lemon all in and over it, and salt and pepper it, inside and out.

We make a dressing of six cups of chestnuts or pecans, one and one-half cups melted butter, one teaspoon salt, one-half teaspoon pepper, one teaspoon dried sage, three-fourths cup cream, three cups bread (or johnnycake) crumbs, four tablespoons chopped parsley, one and one-half cups chopped celery, two tablespoons grated onion, and two pints raw, drained, halved oysters.

Fill the bird and close it up. Put it on a rack in a roaster, add one-half cup gin and a handful of juniper berries. Coat now and every fifteen minutes with a glaze of one-half cup orange preserves, three tablespoons ginger preserves, two tablespoons each of soy sauce, brandy, and honey. Roast it at 375 degrees for fifteen minutes per pound.

If you can't find juniper berries, sneak in a handful of cranberries and let the gin handle the difference.

26 So, my friend, you say your loved ones never understood the relationship between you and your hat. That they called your hat an awful, smelly, ugly old thing capable of moving under its own power, and they buried it in an unmarked place of interment. And then you say they made you a present of a brand spanking new hat—a total stranger with no character or personality. And you don't know what to do. How to cope.

Well, buck up, old sport. Mourn. Shed the necessary tears. Then make friends with the new chapeau and break it in to the ways of the great outdoors. Place it on the floor and stomp on it many times. Rub it against a dead fish (the deader the better). Sprinkle it with blood. Hang it in a working smokehouse. Float it in the bathtub. Tie it to the pickup and drag it fifty miles over country roads. Whack it against a tree. Let the pups play with it. Stick trout flies all over it and thrust pheasant tail feathers into its band.

Then graciously bid gracias to your family for the fine new sombrero; put it onto your head. And into the gathering twilight, into the morning mist, walk with pride.

In-action pine siskins feast on birch seeds. They flock with redpolls, but have yellow on their wings and no red anywhere. No matter the outside below-zero stuff, or how frozen over the pond, beavers relax in fifty-five to sixty degree comfort in the security of their lodges. The sun creeps southward no more, but edges, each sunset, a little more to the north. We take comfort in that.

Notes

December

27 As long as old Gladys can be out fishing through the ice she's as happy as a high school girl headed for the prom, and though she fishes for anything with fins and gills, she probably favors fishing for crappies. She finds the best fishing for these larger members of the panfish family on lakes with wide open waters and depth and firm bottoms.

Since crappies are open-water fish that spend many daylight hours suspended, and therefore are not always so easy to locate, Gladys likes to go after them in the low-light periods of dusk or dawn, or even better, at night.

Crappies like to feed on small minnows, and small minnows feed on plankton, so when the sun goes down, Gladys sets her lantern right next to the hole. The light attracts the plankton, the plankton attracts the minnows, the minnows attract the crappies, the crappies attract Gladys, and Gladys attracts me (because where ice fishing is concerned, I watch her like a pitcher watches a runner on third), and everybody's happy.

Well, everybody but maybe the big crappies we catch and the ice fishermen who get skunked because they don't have a fishing buddy like good old Gladys.

Notes

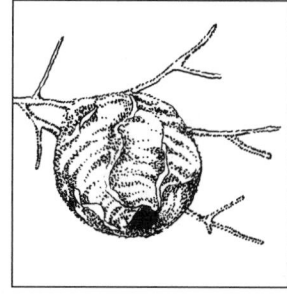

28 What many of us enjoy about the out-of-doors is the aloneness of it, the sometimes delicious loneliness.

What we next enjoy about it is the sharing of it—a walleye, a buck, a sunset—with someone who appreciates such things as we do. Lacking nearby relatives to serve as hunting, fishing, or camping buddies, some of us have to search out such suitable partners from the limited supply of unattached outdoor-lovers not already bound to kindred souls.

It's not easy, for if it's true that we must be a friend to have one, it goes double that to have a buddy with whom to share the outdoors, we must first be one. So, we should try not to be too brilliant on every subject, even if we are, and try to be a bit shy about showing off our skills. We should try not to position ourselves for the best shot or best casts, always pay our fair share and carry more than our mere load.

We must be willing to look the other way when our buddy misses a shot or loses a fish, and when luck smiles on us, take it for what it is. By the way, pal, what are you doing a week from Saturday?

With only the queens surviving, hibernating under bark and whatever, wasp nests hang empty, unraveling, harmless. For those who count, we've had, altogether, around 290 hours of potential daylight at our disposal this month, and right now, we're blessed with about nine hours of daylight and fifteen of the other star-spangled stuff.

Notes

December

Bright-eyed walleyes, even under the dark ice, nibble lightly at minnow-tipped jigs and fill the kitchen with the good smells of their supper-frying. Since there are no hoot owls, it's barred owls or, once in a while, great horned ones that break the stillness of December nights and make the dog whine to come in from the cold kennel to the fireside. Welcome company.

29 Around about this time of year, most barbecue grills have migrated from summer ranges of patios, back porches, and terraces to hibernate in dens lined with rakes and lawn chairs in protected lee corners of garages.

The move was premature. Deer hunters with a few venison chops in the freezer ought to drag the old grill out again. Fire it up, temporarily, for some of the finest eating of any kind, at any time, at any place.

You need a minimum of two chops per person, and must, at that, defensively arm yourself with a stout stick to keep from being mugged for your meat, and to keep things fair and square. Set a good charcoal fire and let it burn down to hot white ashes. Station the grill high enough over the coals so nothing happens too fast. Brush both sides of each chop with melted butter. Don't be stingy with the butter. Lay the meat on the grill—not overcooking it—about eight minutes on side one and six on side two.

Then take it off the grill, salt and pepper it, put it on a warm platter, and, prepared to defend the treasure, race to the table.

Notes

30

Acknowledging that we've all got to put more back into the out-of-doors than ever we take from it, let's make one of the things we put back be a kid (yours, mine, anybody's, nobody's, boy kid, girl kid).

Let's start here at the holidays and make it a gift. Let's take this kid for a long, ageless hike from this horizon to that one.

Along the way we can show him how to swing a paddle, how to tie a fly, to catch a fish, to skip a stone across the water.

We can show her how those who hunt and fish and camp and canoe together always do more than a fair share.

We can help that kid to become self-reliant, to never be afraid of learning new skills, to understand that every bush and bird and bee has its place and that humans themselves must eventually answer the same natural laws as the lowest chipmunk.

We can show him the wonders of a single morning glory. We can help her, if she is to become a hunter, to become a very fine hunter. In all ways. The only cost to the kid will be to someday do the same with some kid, any kid, with the only cost to that kid being to . . .

To bring Christmas back to life, dying Christmas trees are redecorated with seeds and suet balls, peanut butter cups and popcorn, bread and fruit cakes. Released from restrictive buckets and squatty tri-pods, these trees get set out in the backyards and front, on balconies and terraces, as paybacks (for bird songs in winter's stillness, colors against the snow, lively life when nothing else moves but the wind) and just for the heck of it.

Notes

December

There's plenty of snow now for skiers to shed heavy boots and uptown shoes and glide weightlessly toward a new year filled with hope, and for those with snowshoes to stride out and feel the freedom and challenge of marking fresh trails on unmarked seas of white. And it's time for all of us to look over our shoulders at the old year with the knowledge that we did okay and that we're ready, willing, and mostly able to try it all over again.

31 As the year closes, hunters push again oily rags through the barrels of their guns, anglers sort through their tackle boxes. They didn't get out as often as they had hoped; their freezers aren't as full as they might be. They had a good year though, because when they did get out they went glad-hearted and persevered in crunchy leaves, in sleet, in rain, in brush, in wind and sun, without complaining too much. They went with dogged determination and often lasted an hour or two longer than they thought they might. They shot true and cast well some of the time, and when they didn't they didn't dwell on the misses or the snags, and they didn't exactly blame the gun or the rod.

When they went, their footsteps fell softly and they left none of their signs behind them. They saw and heard much of what there was to see and hear, and it looked and sounded good to them.

They went with good people, yet they allowed themselves the splendid solitude of the lone hunter, the lone angler. And they caught a few fish and bagged a bird or two and a deer, picked a berry and smelled a rose, though what that has to do with love, they don't know.

Notes